THE BARE BONES OF ABA

SSG LEARNING THEORY

CARLOS A ALFONSO CENDA

Copyright © 2025 by Carlos Alfonso Cenda

All rights reserved.

No part of this book may be reproduced in any form or by any electronic or mechanical means, including information storage and retrieval systems, without written permission from the author, except for the use of brief quotations in a book review.

This book presents original research, theory, and application of the SSG (Scientific, Simplified, and Graphically Visualized) learning framework developed by the author. The ideas, models, diagrams, and experimental findings contained herein are the intellectual property of Carlos Alfonso Cenda.

The contents of this work are provided for educational and informational purposes only. The author makes no representations or warranties with respect to the accuracy, applicability, or completeness of the contents and specifically disclaims any implied warranties of fitness for a particular purpose. Readers are encouraged to apply the ideas and strategies in professional or educational contexts with appropriate discretion.

The SSG framework and all related figures, diagrams, and terminology are © Carlos Alfonso Cenda and may not be reproduced or adapted for publication, distribution, or instruction without permission.

All rights of translation, adaptation, and reproduction are reserved by the author.

First Edition

ISBN: 979-8-9938202-0-0

Cover Design: Carlos Alfonso Cenda

Printed in the United States of America

For permissions, inquiries, or educational use requests, contact:

alfonsopublishing@gmail.com

To my wife, Amalia Bello, MA, BCBA

This book would not exist without you. Your strength, intellect, and unwavering belief in me have been the driving force behind every page written and every idea realized. You have been more than a source of encouragement, you have been the foundation, the reason, and the quiet persistence that carried this project from concept to completion.

Your own dedication to science, education, and compassion has not only inspired my work but shaped the very essence of SSG itself. In every model, every diagram, and every word that seeks to make the complex simple, I see your influence , your patience, your discipline, and your heart.

You are, and will always be, the greatest support system any man could ask for, and the truest reminder that behind every pursuit of knowledge stands love, understanding, and partnership.

CONTENTS

Authors Note	vii
How to Read This Book	ix
Phase I	xiii

1. SSG Learning Theory — 1
   Repetition Learning
2. Beginning's — 15
   The Development of Behavioral Science
3. ABA to the Bone — 45
   Principles of ABA
4. Welcome to Casino World — 69
   Schedules of Reinforcement
5. Why did I do That? — 119
   Antecedent Conditions
6. Talk to Me!! — 157
   Verbal Behavior
7. Psychology, Meet Science! — 181
   Experimental Design

Phase II — 207

8. One + One is Two In ABA — 209
   The SSG Experiment
9. Who said Video Games Were Lame? — 229
   The Behavioral Future of Gaming
10. Education Sirca Year 1700 — 239
    The Behavioral Crisis in Education
11. The Happy Patient — 249
    The Behavioral Bridge: SSG and Medical Interactions
12. "Your Controls, My Controls" — 261
    SSG in the Sky: Behavioral Precision in Aviation Training

Final Words — 279

Bibliography — 281
Acknowledgments — 285

AUTHORS NOTE

This book began with a question I could never quite let go of: Why do some people understand while others memorize?

As a behavior analyst and lifelong student of learning, I've spent years watching people struggle, not because they lacked curiosity or discipline, but because they were taught in ways that made understanding harder than it needed to be. Across classrooms, clinics, and even in-flight training, I saw a common thread: knowledge without clarity doesn't stay.

SSG or in simple terms, Scientific, Simplified, and Graphically Visualized, was born from that realization. It wasn't created in a single moment of inspiration, but through countless hours of observation, frustration, and experimentation. It developed in the quiet hours after sessions, in the margins of behavior plans, in research notes, and in late nights surrounded by graphs, books, and data.

I wanted to build something that connected the precision of science with the accessibility of clear teaching, a way to make learning measurable, visual, and, most importantly, human.

AUTHORS NOTE

The idea behind SSG is simple yet transformative: that understanding comes when we see behavior, not just describe it. Through years of studying cognitive psychology, retention learning, and behavioral education, I found that visual structure dramatically increases comprehension. When people can see how ideas connect, through flow, feedback, and consequence, they no longer memorize concepts; they internalize them.

From there, SSG evolved into both a teaching tool and a theory of learning, a bridge between data and meaning. I applied it first in during my training in behavior analysis, where it reshaped how I learned foundational ABA concepts. But as I continued to refine it, I realized its reach went far beyond clinical education. The same system could apply to medicine, aviation, and any field where clarity under pressure determines success.

This book is the result of that journey. It is part research, part reflection, and part instruction, built on the belief that science should never be locked behind jargon or complexity.

Each phase of this book mirrors the development of SSG itself:

- Phase 1 teaches through SSG, simplifying the science of behavior.
- Phase 2 applies SSG to the real world, showing how the same learning principles can transform performance, safety, and understanding across professions.

I wrote this book because I believe knowledge should not intimidate. It should illuminate. And if, through these pages, even one reader discovers a clearer way to teach, to learn, or to understand, then SSG has already done its job.

HOW TO READ THIS BOOK

This book was written for those who seek to understand behavior, not only through words and definitions, but through clarity, visualization, and application. It introduces and demonstrates SSG: the Scientific, Simplified, and Graphically Visualized learning theory, a method designed to make complex concepts in Applied Behavior Analysis (ABA) understandable, memorable, and practical. Because readers approach this field with different goals, this book is structured in two distinct phases, each serving a unique purpose and audience. How you choose to read it depends on what you want to gain, theory, practice, or both.

Strategy 1: For the Theorist and the Practitioner

If your primary goal is to explore the SSG learning theory itself, how it works, why it was developed, and how it can be applied across different fields, you can read this book in a selective sequence. Start with Chapter One, which introduces the foundation of the SSG theory, explaining its structure and purpose:

HOW TO READ THIS BOOK

- *Scientific*: how learning remains evidence-based and measurable.
- *Simplified*: how complex behavior concepts can be translated into clear, functional understanding.
- *Graphically Visualized*: how visual representation bridges the gap between information and comprehension.

Once you've built that understanding, skip ahead to Chapter 8, where the book transitions into the real-world applications of SSG. Here, you'll find how SSG influences learning and communication in:

- Education: simplifying instruction and improving retention.
- Medicine and healthcare: enhancing patient understanding and compliance.
- Aviation: increasing precision and safety through behavioral fluency and structured visualization.

This reading path is ideal for professionals, educators, clinicians, or anyone looking to apply SSG rather than study behavior analysis in depth.

Strategy 2: The Recommended Learning Path

If you are new to behavior analysis or wish to see how SSG transforms the way behavioral science can be taught, this is the path for you. Start at the beginning.

Read the book in full sequence, moving from Phase 1 to Phase 2. In Phase 1, you will:

- Learn the history and foundation of ABA.

- Understand core behavioral principles such as reinforcement, punishment, measurement, and experimental design.
- Experience how SSG simplifies traditional teaching methods, turning dense academic theory into visual and interactive understanding.

This phase provides the foundation and vocabulary necessary to fully grasp the chapters that follow. Then, in Phase 2, you'll see how these same principles extend beyond textbooks and into practice, in the classroom, in clinical settings, and even in the cockpit. Here, SSG becomes more than a way of teaching; it becomes a way of thinking, analyzing, and communicating behaviorally.

Choosing Your Path

Whether you're a student of behavior, a practicing analyst, or a professional from another discipline seeking new tools for understanding and teaching, this book adapts to you. If you want to grasp the power of the SSG theory quickly, follow Strategy 1. If you want to learn behavior analysis through SSG, to see how this framework redefines education itself, follow Strategy 2.

Whichever path you choose, remember that the purpose of SSG is not only to teach knowledge but to build comprehension, transforming information into understanding, and understanding into skill.

PHASE I

Every science begins with a question, but in behavior analysis, the most important question has always been "How do we teach what we know?"

Phase 1 of this book is where the SSG model, Scientific, Simplified, and Graphically Visualized, first comes to life. It is here that I lay the groundwork for understanding how SSG transforms the way we learn and teach the principles of Applied Behavior Analysis (ABA). The research behind SSG can be found in Phase II of the book. In this phase, we return to the roots of behavioral science, exploring how the field developed, how its pioneers thought about learning, and how their discoveries can be made accessible through SSG. Concepts such as reinforcement, punishment, stimulus control, shaping, and generalization are often introduced through dense academic texts that leave students struggling to translate theory into practice. Through SSG, these same concepts are rebuilt, visually, behaviorally, and step by step, to create comprehension instead of memorization.

PHASE I

Phase 1 serves two major purposes:

1. To demonstrate how SSG simplifies the teaching of behavioral science without sacrificing precision.
2. To show how even complex research methods, such as single-subject experimental designs, can be understood behaviorally, through patterns, sequences, and visual representation rather than abstract terminology.

Throughout this phase, I guide the reader through the fundamental structure of ABA, connecting historical foundations to modern teaching techniques. SSG becomes the lens through which these ideas are reframed:

- Scientific: Grounded in evidence-based methodology and measurable outcomes.
- Simplified: Translated into understandable, stepwise learning sequences.
- Graphically Visualized: Represented through diagrams, models, and figures that make learning visible.

This phase is not just about learning what ABA is, it's about learning how to learn it. Each chapter uses the SSG framework as both the content and the method, creating an experience where the reader not only absorbs information but sees how understanding is built. As we progress through Phase 1, the reader will experience SSG as a teacher, a guide, and a system, one capable of bringing clarity to a field often misunderstood as complex or inaccessible. The goal is to make behavior analysis not easier, but clearer, and in doing so, to prepare for the next stage, where the same principles will step outside the classroom and into the world itself.

ONE
SSG LEARNING THEORY
REPETITION LEARNING

" We now accept the fact that learning is a lifelong process of keeping abreast of change. And the most pressing task is to teach people how to learn."

PETER DRUCKER

HOW DO WE LEARN?

The process of learning is a complex and dynamic journey that involves acquiring knowledge, skills, or behaviors through various cognitive, behavioral, and social processes. Learning begins with exposure to new information or experiences and culminates in the assimilation and integration of that information into one's existing knowledge and abilities.

The process of learning typically begins with an encounter with new information or stimuli. This initial exposure can occur through sensory perception, direct experience, or the presentation of information through various educational mediums. For example, a student may learn about photosynthesis in a biology class by listening to a lecture, reading a textbook, or conducting a hands-on experiment in a laboratory. The process of learning is often initiated by paying attention to the relevant information, as selective attention helps filter and prioritize what is worth learning.

Secondly, the information or experiences encountered during the learning process are processed and encoded by the learner. This encoding involves mental processes such as comprehension, organization, and storage. Learners strive to understand the material, break it down into manageable components, and connect it to their existing knowledge base. Effective encoding often involves active engagement with the material, whether it's taking notes, asking questions, or engaging in discussions. The quality of encoding plays a significant role in how well the information is retained over time.

Lastly, the final stage of the learning process involves the retrieval and application of the newly acquired knowledge or skills. Learners must be able to recall and utilize what they have learned when needed. This application phase is critical, as it demonstrates the mastery of the material and its practical relevance. Successful learning often requires practice, reinforcement, and real-world application to ensure that the newly acquired knowledge or skills are retained and can be effectively utilized in various contexts. Overall, the process of learning is a dynamic and multifaceted endeavor that encompasses exposure, encoding, and application, and individual differences, motivation, and the learning environment influence it.

Simplification of Concepts

One of the key components of SSG Learning theory is simplification. Complex concepts can often be daunting due to their sheer volume of information or intricate details. To simplify them, we can start by breaking the concept down into smaller, more manageable components. Identify the key ideas, principles, or steps that constitute the concept. Then, present these components in a logical and sequential order, ensuring that each part is understood before moving on to the next. This step-by-step approach allows learners to grasp one aspect at a time, gradually building a comprehensive understanding of the whole concept.

Another great tool which is in the framework of SSG is tying the concepts to analogies, metaphors, and examples. Analogies and metaphors are powerful tools for simplifying complex ideas by relating them to familiar concepts. Find everyday examples or analogies that closely resemble the complex concept you are trying to explain. Analogies create a bridge between the known and the unknown, making it easier for learners to connect and transfer their existing knowledge to the new concept. Metaphors, on the other hand, can provide a vivid mental image that simplifies understanding. For instance, explaining a computer's central processing unit (CPU) as the "brain" of the computer simplifies the abstract concept of its function.

The last way to simplify a concept is actually a crucial step of SSG learning theory and without it, teaching these concepts would be practically impossible. Visual aids, diagrams, and illustrations are invaluable for simplifying complex concepts, as they provide a visual representation of the information. In this book, I create clear and concise diagrams or infographics that depict the relationships, processes, or hierarchies within the concept. Visuals help learners visualize abstract ideas, identify patterns, and see the big picture. They can also serve as memory aids, reinforcing understanding through visual cues. Consider using charts, graphs, flowcharts, or concept maps to simplify and enhance comprehension when presenting complex data or information.

The Discovery of SSG

In my years spent learning as a student, it's fair to say I have struggled to find ways to memorize concepts. It took a lot of trial and error to develop my own learning model, which would target all aspects of cognitive learning through the process of repetition. During graduate school, I realized that the most complex concepts had the most straightforward explanations. This taught me the process of simplifying every scientific concept into everyday language. Ironically, this process would also be one of the characteristics of behavior analysis known as "technological," which we will discuss in the next chapter.

Once I graduated college, I spent some time educating others about the concepts of behavior analysis. During my experience as a professor, I realized that some of the students needed help comprehending the material, even when using my method of simplification. This sparked another question: how can I expand the currently developed learning method? Then, a class survey was completed to understand each student's learning method. Around 65% of the students noted that they were visual learners. That's when graphical visualization was added to the method, adding an extra layer of explanation for the same scientific concept. After implementing this process, more than 90% of the students reported feeling confident about their knowledge of the content, and this is how the SSG Learning Theory was born.

SSG Learning Theory hasn't been released and requires

rigorous testing before it can become a form of teaching. However, through my implementation, results have been impressive with students who have used this method and others who have been taught increasingly challenging concepts, reporting a successful understanding of the principles on their first reading. More significantly, SSG engages a process known as "repetition learning." The psychologist Irvin Rock published a paper in 1958 studying "Repetition and Learning," showing that humans form mental associations to the things they learn instantly. Rock then explains that the role of "repetition" is to help retain the information that was just learned. Unfortunately, humans tend to forget 50% of what they learn within just one hour and can only hold information in short-term memory for about 10 minutes (Sousa, 2001). The theory behind SSG uses the fundamental principles of repetition learning, using three different forms of the same principle.

The first step is learning the scientific concept, the second is understanding the simplified concept, and the third is visualizing the concept, as shown below in **FIGURE 1.1**. SSG engages repetition learning in multiple ways as not only is a singular scientific concept explained in three different ways, associating the idea and transferring the information to long-term memory through repetition, it allocates to different learning styles. SSG will be this book's primary teaching method, as many behavior analysis concepts can be challenging.

[continued on next page]

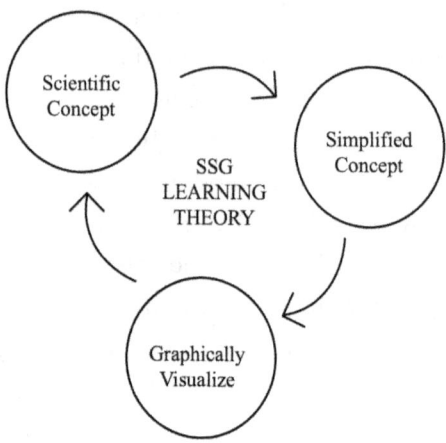

FIGURE 1.1 The SSG cycle.

The most significant finding during the SSG initial testing was that since the process allocates to different learning styles, it was possible to start anywhere in the chain.

- Example: Before learning the scientific concept, you want to learn the simplified version or the graphical version; you can start by looking there first and then moving through the chain until you learn every form of the concept. Once the SSG chain is finished, whichever way you look at the principle, your brain will automatically deduct the definition and process of implementation.

How SSG Learning Theory Will be Implemented in this Book

SSG Learning Theory is takes a new approach to learning and educating, effortlessly being implemented through this book for the reader's benefit. As the book progresses, each concept will be split as follows:

1. Scientific Concept
Define and explain the material scientifically and as intended by the original authors.
2. Simplified Concept
Define and explain in a normative way, expanding the knowledge of an average reader.
3. Graphically Visualize
For visual learners to comprehend the concept using timelines, diagrams, illustrations, and more.

Visual Learning

Since the last part of the SSG theory is included to aid visual learners and those who conceptualize the principle in their head through imagery, we need to understand why visual learning plays an integral part in the human cognitive learning system. Visual learning is a cognitive style in which individuals primarily acquire and process information through visual stimuli, such as images, charts, graphs, diagrams, and videos (Walter, 2009). This learning approach relies on the visual sense as a primary means of comprehension and retention. Visual learners excel when presented with visual aids to help them grasp complex concepts more effectively. For these individuals, seeing a concept or idea represented visually can make it easier to understand, remember, and apply. This learning style is especially prevalent in educational settings, where teachers and instructors often use visual aids to enhance the learning experience. Visual learners tend to benefit from techniques such as mind mapping, concept mapping, and the use of color-coded notes, all of which leverage their strong visual processing abilities to facilitate learning and recall.

One notable advantage of visual learning is its versatility and adaptability across various domains and subjects. Whether it's studying anatomy through detailed diagrams, comprehending mathematical equations through visual representations, or understanding historical events through timelines and charts, visual learning can be applied across a wide range of disciplines. Additionally, in an increasingly digital age, the proliferation of multimedia resources and e-learning platforms has made visual learning more accessible and engaging than ever before, accommodating the preferences of many visual learners. However, it's important to recognize that not all individuals exclusively adhere to one learning style, and many benefit from a combination of visual, auditory, and kinesthetic approaches. Effective educators often incorporate a variety of teaching methods to cater to the diverse learning styles within their classrooms

We must keep in mind, however, that even though many of us can visualize something thought, this doesn't necessarily mean that there is a functional relation to teaching with visual learning techniques. There is no evidence that teaching with this model has any correlation to learning or that it is guaranteed to improve learning, but it also doesn't disprove the method; it just means there isn't enough information or studies to dismiss the idea altogether. Through my own testing and experience, visual learning is still one of the most widely used techniques that provide excellent results not only academically but in everyday life. If an example is needed, think of when you are going to build an IKEA furniture and how the instructions are created. The instructions are a visual representation of what you need to do. This is the basis of visual representation and learning.

The book is structured seamlessly through the SSG Theory, starting with the origins of behavioral science to today's branch of Applied Behavior Analysis. In **FIGURE 1.2**, an example of how the structure takes place demonstrates the ease of reading the book and the smooth and coherent feel it has to it. Another ease SSG brings to this book is the ability to jump to any desired chapter and understand any concept just using the SSG included with each principle discussed throughout the chapter.

Example: Behavioral Contrast

Scientific Concept

The term behavioral contrast was introduced by Reynolds (1961) to refer to a phenomenon in which one component of multiple schedules increases or decreases the rate of behavior that not only counteracts the effects of direct training but also increases the probability that on future occasions, the individual may respond to interpersonal thwarting in an inattentive manner (Cooper et al., 2020, p. 338)

Simplified Concept

In simple words, behavior contrast is the change in one component in a reinforcing schedule, affecting the response in a different component. If a child is eating cookies and is punished by the grandfather for eating too many cookies, the child will lower cookie intake in the presence of the grandfather and increase intake once the grandfather leaves. This is depicted in the graphically visualized section of **FIGURE 1.2**. Another great example is a policy stated in a college about smoking. Anyone who gets caught smoking on campus will receive a monetary fine (punishment); thus, the behavior of smoking decreases on campus. However, although nothing has changed in the home environment, smoking has increased due to the policy. This phenomenon is what we call behavior contrast.

Graphically Visualize

FIGURE 1.2 Example of Behavioral Contrast using SSG Learning Theory.

This process will help associate the term and definition with visual illustrations and simple definitions. The example above shows how a complex term such as behavioral contrast can be easily deduced into understandable bites. SSG Learning Theory has another advantage, which allows the theory to be adapted to any field. SSG in its current form, has the first "S" which stands for Scientific concept; however, it can be changed to fit any other field. For example, if you are teaching concepts in engineering the "S" can become an "E" making it ESG Learning Theory, with the E standing for engineering concept.

This can be done with Music, Math, and any field that comes to mind. Even though SSG theory does not guarantee that you will learn the concept, it will make it easier to understand; however, as the reader, putting in the work is required to fully comprehend these concepts. While reading this book, it is encouraged to create your own examples and investigate further into the principles discussed through the chapters. Most of the topics are evidence-based, with over 100 years of research. In fact, one of the key components of the ICAP Framework hypothesis, which includes active learning, is note taking, concept mapping, and self-engagement, according to Michelene T. H. Chi and Ruth Wylie, professor at Arizona State University.

SSG Learning Theory also tackles one of the six attitudes of science (covered in chapter two), and that is parsimony. This is because SSG holds to a human nature of learning in the most simplistic way possible. In other words, why complicate a concept when it is not necessary? The theory does not complicate the concept further; it does quite the opposite: it extends it and simplifies it in the best way possible.

Hands-on Learning

Even though this learning theory will facilitate the concepts for you and help you learn them faster, it is recommended that you gather experience in the field. Hands-on experience based on the concepts discussed in this book will not only help you remember them, again through repetition learning, but it will further the field as new research and interventions are always needed. Hands-on learning, also known as experiential learning, is an educational approach that emphasizes active participation and engagement with materials, objects, or real-world experiences, by encouraging students to interact with and manipulate the subject matter directly. Hands-on learning offers several distinct advantages for learners.

Firstly, hands-on learning promotes active engagement and deepens understanding. When students physically handle materials or engage in activities, they activate multiple sensory channels, including tactile, visual, and sometimes auditory or olfactory senses. This multisensory experience enhances their comprehension and retention of the subject matter. For example, in a science class, students might conduct experiments to observe chemical reactions firsthand, providing a more profound understanding of the scientific principles involved.

Secondly, hands-on learning fosters critical thinking and problem-solving skills. Through hands-on activities, students are encouraged to explore, experiment, and make decisions based on their observations and experiences. This process empowers them to ask questions, test hypotheses, and develop analytical skills. It also encourages creativity and adaptability, as students often encounter unexpected challenges or outcomes during hands-on tasks and must adjust their approach accordingly.

Lastly, hands-on learning connects theory to practice and prepares learners for real-world applications. By actively engaging with materials and experiences, students gain practical skills that can be directly applied to various situations, professions, or disciplines. This type of learning bridges the gap between abstract knowledge and practical application, making it particularly valuable for vocational training, scientific research, and skill development across a wide range of fields. Whether it involves building a model, conducting a lab experiment, or participating in a simulation, hands-on learning offers a tangible and impactful way for learners to acquire and internalize knowledge and skills.

The Purpose of Reading a Book

My goal in translating this information into a simple, understandable way is to enrich the knowledge of those in the field. Always remember that reading a book is a rich and multifaceted experience that offers numerous benefits to individuals. It is a journey of the mind, a voyage of exploration, and a means of expanding one's knowledge and imagination. When you immerse yourself in a book, you open the door to a world of stories, ideas, and perspectives that can transport you to different times, places, and cultures. Reading allows you to escape the confines of your immediate surroundings and embark on adventures, whether they are fictional, historical, or educational. Moreover, reading is an exercise for the mind. It challenges your cognitive abilities, enhances your vocabulary, and sharpens your comprehension skills. As you engage with the text, your brain processes the words, interprets the meaning, and makes connections with your existing knowledge. This mental workout strengthens your analytical thinking, critical reasoning, and problem-solving abilities. It also stimulates creativity by exposing you to various writing styles, narrative structures, and literary techniques.

Beyond the intellectual benefits, reading a book can be a source of profound emotional and psychological enrichment. It can evoke empathy by allowing you to step into the shoes of the characters and understand their feelings, motivations, and struggles. Reading can also be a form of solace, providing comfort and companionship during challenging times. Whether you seek inspiration, relaxation, or the thrill of a gripping story, the act of reading can fulfill a diverse range of emotional and intellectual needs. In essence, reading a book is not just an activity; it is a transformative experience that has the power to inform, enlighten, and nourish the mind.

TWO
BEGINNING'S
THE DEVELOPMENT OF BEHAVIORAL SCIENCE

"Since I was a child, I always found my biggest reinforcer was something called understanding".

DONALD M. BAER IN HEWARD & WOOD (2003, P. 302)

THE LAW OF EFFECT

Behavior analysis has been revolutionized by the likes of big names such as B.F. Skinner, Ivan Pavlov, and John Watson. But all of them developed their research on the basis of Edward Thorndike's finding of the law of effect. The law of effect is the predecessor of operant conditioning and behaviorism, which were developed in the early 1900s. The law of effect states that the probability that a particular stimulus will repeatedly elicit a particular learned response depends on the perceived consequences of the response (Rafferty, 2023). This means that a response which delivers a reward will likely be repeated again, also called the positive Law of Effect by Thorndike. On the other hand, if the response delivers some punishment, it is less likely to be repeated, called negative Law of Effect by Thorndike. Thorndike developed multiple experiments which involved a cat inside a box. The box had a lever to open the door, allowing the cat to escape and recover food outside the box. The cat created an association between the lever and the box opening to receive food. Thorndike's Law of Effect set the groundwork for Skinner to write his first book, "Behavior of an Organism." In **FIGURE 2.1**, Thorndike's fundamental Law of Effect is demonstrated.

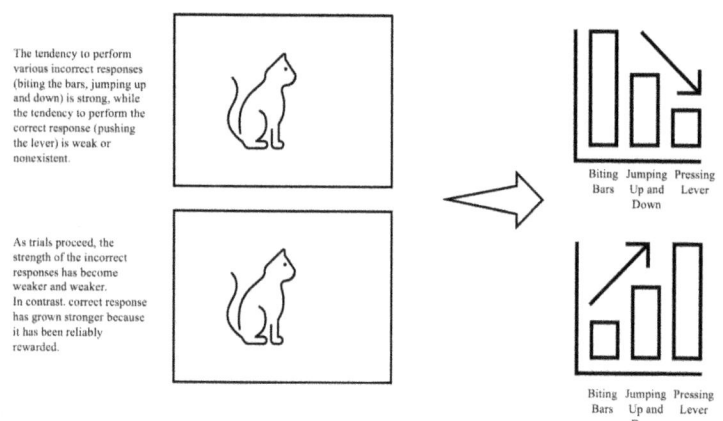

FIGURE 2.1 Thorndike's visualization of the Law of Effect with cat experiment.

Behaviorism

After Thorndike set the groundwork for operant conditioning, John B. Watson began researching behaviorism. Behaviorism was first introduced in 1913 when Watson published an article called " Psychology as the Behaviorist Views It." In this Manifesto, Watson writes his notion of behaviorism; Watson puts the emphasis on the external behavior of people and their reactions to given situations rather than the internal mental state of those people. In his opinion, the analysis of behaviors and reactions was the only objective method to get insight into human actions (Rafferty, 2023). In Watsons point of view, behavior can only be objective, and not internal states such as emotions or feelings could influence this behavior. It wasn't until the 1930s that B.F Skinner dismissed this by introducing radical behaviorism (discussed later in the chapter), involving cognition and emotional states, stating that these cover behaviors are under the same variables as observable behaviors.

Methodological behaviorism is the normative theory about the scientific conduct of psychology. It claims that psychology should concern itself with the behavior of organisms (human and nonhuman animals). Psychology should not concern itself with mental states or events or with constructing internal information processing accounts of behavior. According to methodological behaviorism, reference to mental states, such as animal's beliefs or desires, adds nothing to what psychology can and should understand about the sources of behavior. Mental states are private entities which, given the necessary publicity of science, do not form proper objects of empirical study. (Graham, 2010). Watson considered himself a methodological behaviorist and refused Skinner's implementation of radical behaviorism.

Many of the early research, especially by Watson and Pavlov, focused on how neutral stimuli could elicit a response, which was later coined as respondent conditioning. Respondent conditioning focused on the stimulus-response, in which case the response was usually a reflex. B.F Skinner pioneered the stimulus-response-stimulus concept or the three-term contingency. The concept will later be called operant conditioning (discussed in chapter three) or behavior modification by consequence. In the field of Applied Behavior Analysis, Watson still holds a strong view as many analysts deny holding cognition and emotional states as part of their practice. These analysts hold the concept that behavior can only be measurable and observable and that emotional states, such as feeling, can be measured through environmental variables.

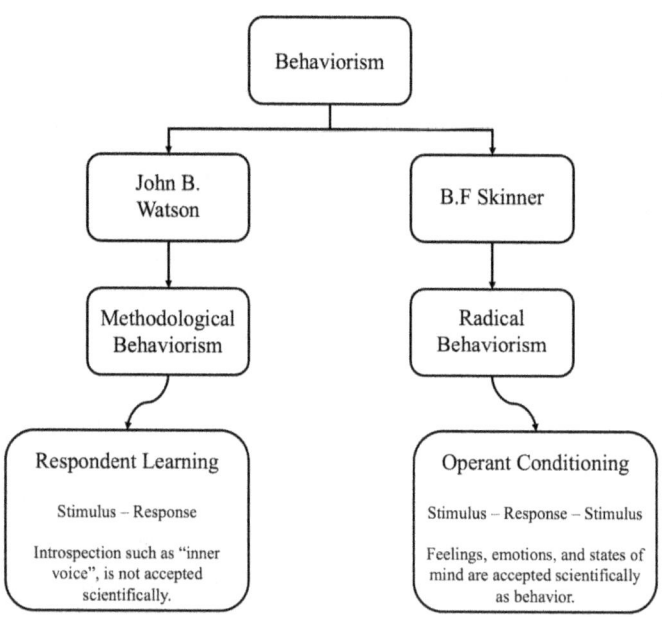

FIGURE 2.2 John B. Watsons vs. B.F Skinner's Behaviorism

Watson's work became very controversial as he tried to use behavioral modification principles to instill fear of white rats in an 11-month-old orphaned baby. This is one of the field's most controversial studies to date and discredits Watson's ability as a psychologist.

Ivan Pavlov

FIGURE 2.3 Ivan Pavlov, most well-known for his research in classical conditioning (*Photograph by Deschiens*)

Ivan Pavlov was one of the greatest influencers in the field of behavior analysis. His work in the late 1890s created classical conditioning through his experimentation with dogs. This led Pavlov to win the Nobel prize in 1904 for his remarkable research. Before the discovery of classical conditioning, it was only possible to view human and animal behavior as subjective. His work on "conditioned reflex" (classical conditioning) showed the effects of stimulus-stimulus paring when his dogs began salivating at the presence of his assistance rather than the food itself. Pavlov's curiosity lightened, focusing on the effects of paring food with a buzzer or metronome. This led to the dogs salivating at the sound of the buzzer alone without the presence of food. This research was another fundamental step for Skinner's first book, mentioning conditioned and unconditioned stimuli. In a further chapter, Ivan Pavlov's work will be discussed, where classical conditioning becomes essential to understanding behavior analysis.

B.F Skinner

FIGURE 2.4 B.F Skinner, the father of today's Applied Behavior Analysis

If B.F Skinner is an unfamiliar name, this book will ensure it is never forgotten. Regarded as the father of behavior analysis and the creator of Radical Behaviorism, Skinner was undoubtedly the most prominent figure in the field. In 1938, with the release of his first book titled, "The Behavior of Organisms," he initiated the branch known today as experimental analysis of behavior. Over his lifetime, Skinner advanced the field of behavioral science more than anyone up to date, researching respondent and operant conditioning, reinforcement and punishment contingencies, token economy, schedules of reinforcement, and verbal behavior. Skinner developed a new approach to verbal behavior and would later go on to write a book about its complexity. Skinner broke verbal behavior into smaller pieces based on the concept of operant conditioning. Through his studies, he stated that an emission of a response was based on consequence. We will discuss verbal behavior and verbal operants in chapter six.

Radical Behaviorism

B.F Skinner created radical behaviorism and expressed it as a "thoroughgoing form of behaviorism that attempts to understand all human behavior, including private events such as thoughts and feelings, terms of controlling variables in the history of the person (ontogeny) and the species (phylogeny)" (Cooper et al., 2007). Ontogeny is what the organism has learned through its lifetime, while phylogeny is unlearned, such as reflexes and the desire for food to survive. When Skinner describes radical, he means that it takes into account the totality of the human experience, including inner states such as emotions and feelings. Radical behaviorists learn to train their mindset to ask questions and gather empirical data to understand human behavior. Radical behaviorism approach does not consider the mind and soul, as it is a natural science rooted in evolutionary science, making it a natural science.

Unlike Skinner, Watson took a methodological behaviorism stand, stating that if behavior cannot be publicly observed, it is not a science. Now we understand that Skinner argued that inner states that come from an evolutionary standpoint, also shape how a human behaves. There are many more forms of behaviorism; however, the one used mainly today, especially in the practice of Applied Behavior Analysis, is Radical Behaviorism. It is widely believed that Skinner was a methodological behaviorist, when in reality, he never was, that's why he created radical behaviorism, which takes the methodological approach and adds thinking, feeling, and emoting and called it behavior.

His argument for this was that just because other people can't observe the behavior, it doesn't make it less valuable; it just makes it hard to confirm that other people see it too, but it is still behavior. In a nutshell, radical behaviorism is the study of understanding the environment's relation with behavior and the effects of evolutionary history.

Teleological Behaviorism

This form of behaviorism is mostly unused, and very few people other than the term's creator, call themselves teleological behaviorists. Teleological Behaviorism says, "an organism's mental life resides in its overt (visible) behavior, in its temporal and social context." Teleological behaviorism has a heavy emphasis on mental life and mental states. It focuses on mental life and states that the mind plays a central role in the science of behavior (Rachlin, 2013). It is also worth noting that Teleological behaviorism does not fall into mentalism, as mentalism is a different approach to the study of behavior. Mentalism will be covered later in this chapter. Simply said, teleological behaviorism considers emotions and thoughts just like radical behaviorism; however, it does not view them as causes of behavior; instead, it treats them as behaviors themselves.

Theoretical Behaviorism

Out of all the forms of behaviorism, theoretical behaviorism is the youngest, developed in the early 1960s by J.E.R Staddon, building on B.F Skinner's concept of radical behaviorism. Staddon stated in his research paper that "theoretical behaviorism can deal with mentalistic problems such as consciousness without ignoring them, obscuring the distinction between what is inside and what is outside the organism (like radical behaviorism), or confusing what is felt with what can be measured. Theoretical behaviorism promises to provide theoretical links between behavior and the brain that rest on a real understanding of the behavior rather than on mentalistic presumptions about how brain–behavior relations must be arranged" (Staddon, 1999). This form of behaviorism is also rarely used, since most behavior scientists prefer to stick to radical behaviorism. Deterring away from behaviorism and the early beginnings of behavioral science, we begin to understand how behavioral construct detaches from mentalistic constructs.

Molecular vs. Molar Behaviorist

Behaviorists have two different ways of looking at behavior one being molar behaviorism and the other being molecular behaviorism. In the most recent years, there has been a shift toward molar behaviorism, but before we continue, let's define both. Molecular behaviorism consists of momentary or discrete responses that constitute instances of classes. Variation in response rate reflects variation in the strength or probability of the response class (Baum, 2002). This basically means that behavior is described in small responses rather than large responses, which, in turn, when the small responses are added together like a chain, make up a more complex behavior. However, according to Baum, molecular behaviorism is victim to hypothetical constructs. On the newer front and the most followed, we have molar behaviorism, which sees behavior as composed of activities that take up varying amounts of time (Baum, 2002). Citing directly from one of Baum's published papers, he states the following:

"The molar view of behavior contrasts with the older, molecular view. The difference is paradigmatic, not theoretical. No experiment can decide between them, because they interpret all the same phenomena, but in different terms. The molecular view relies on the concepts of discrete, momentary events and contiguity between them, whereas the molar view relies on the concepts of temporally extended patterns of activity and correlations. When dealing with phenomena such as avoidance, rule-governed behavior, and choice, the molar view has the advantage that it requires no appeal to hypothetical constructs. The molecular view always appeals to hypothetical constructs to provide immediate reinforcers and stimuli when none are apparent. As a result, the explanations offered by the molar view are straightforward and concrete, whereas those offered by the molecular view are awkward and implausible. The usefulness of the molar view for applied behavior analysis lies in the flexibility and conceptual power it provides for talking about behavior and contingencies over time." (Baum, 2003).

Mentalism

Mentalism is a common approach to many psychological models that differ significantly from Skinner's behavioral work. Mentalism is defined as "an approach to the study of behavior which assumes that a mental or inner dimension exists that differs from a behavioral dimension. This dimension is ordinarily referred to in terms of its neural, psychic, spiritual, subjective, conceptual, or hypothetical properties. Mentalism also assumes that this dimension directly causes some forms of behavior, if not all. Mentalism also shows that an explanation of behavior must appeal directly to the efficacy of this mental phenomenon (Moore, 2003, pp. 181 – 182). Mentalism is never and will never be used in behavioral analysis as it uses a mental construct to control the physical world. What is meant by this is that the "mind" or internal dimension is acting upon the organism to create an action in the physical dimension. Mentalism defies the entire study of behavior and should never be taken as an approach to behavior analysis.

Hypothetical constructs build on mentalism as hypothetical constructs are presumed but un-observed entities that could not be manipulated in an experiment (Cooper et al., 2020 pp. 10). Hypothetical construct also goes hand in hand with explanatory fiction or a fictitious variable that is often simply another name for the observed behavior that contributes nothing to understanding the variable responsible for developing or maintaining the behavior (Cooper et al., 2020, pp. 12). This roughly translates to using or creating something hypothetical and using this newly created hypothetical construct as a cause for behavior. An example of a hypothetical construct is intelligence.

Pragmatism

Pragmatism in behavior analysis is an approach that prioritizes practicality and effectiveness in designing and implementing behavioral interventions (Kesherim, 2023). It emphasizes the importance of selecting interventions and strategies that produce meaningful and positive outcomes for individuals based on empirical evidence and real-world applicability. The role pragmatism has in applied behavior analysis (ABA) is to bring about meaningful and positive changes in the lives of individuals. It encourages practitioners to choose and adapt interventions that are most likely to achieve these outcomes in a practical and ethical manner.

In behavior analysis, pragmatism is highly debated in radical behaviorism, but this is the concept we follow in today's ABA. Pragmatism has the following characteristics which make them highly attractive to any practicing practitioner:

Evidence-Based Practice: Pragmatic behavior analysts use empirical research to guide their interventions. They seek evidence demonstrating the effectiveness of specific behavioral strategies in achieving desired outcomes.

Individualization: Pragmatism recognizes that there is no one-size-fits-all approach to behavior analysis. Interventions are tailored to the individual's unique needs, preferences, and circumstances.

Monitoring and Evaluation: Continuous data collection and ongoing assessment are critical components of pragmatic behavior analysis. Practitioners regularly monitor the progress of interventions and make adjustments as needed to ensure their effectiveness.

Real-World Application: Pragmatic behavior analysts aim to translate behavioral principles and research findings into interventions that can be implemented effectively in real-life settings, such as homes, schools, and community environments.

Attitudes of Science

B.F Skinner has many famous quotes, but one that sticks with every scientist is "Science first of all a set of attitudes," but what exactly are these attitudes?

These attitudes of science-determinism, empiricism, experimentation, replication, parsimony, and philosophic doubt--constitute a set of overriding assumptions and values that guide the work of all scientists (Whaley & Surratt, 1968). These are the attitudes that every scientist guides themselves by; without them, no proper definition of science can exist. Each attitude describes a set of rules a scientist must abide by. We will now go into detail about each attitude and decipher the meaning of what makes a scientist.

Determinism

All scientists presume that the universe is a lawful and orderly place in which all phenomena occur as the result of other events. In other words, events do not just happen willy-nilly; they are related systematically to other factors, which are physical phenomena amenable to scientific investigation (Cooper et al., 2020, pp. 4).

How does this translate into the study of human behavior, you might be asking? B.F Skinner has the answer.

If we are to use the methods of science in the field of human affairs, we must assume behavior is lawful and determined. We must expect to discover what a man does is the result of specifiable conditions and that once these conditions have been discovered, we can anticipate and, to some extent, determine his actions. (Skinner, 1953, p. 6)

Example: Imagine a scenario where a person is considering whether to have water or tea in the morning. According to the deterministic view, this decision is not truly a matter of free will but is determined by various factors. These include biological, environmental, social and cultural, personal history, and psychological factors. This concept challenges the notion of complete free will, asserting that our choices are influenced, if not entirely determined, by preceding factors.

Empiricism

The practice of objective observation and measurement of the phenomena of interest. Objectivity, in this sense, means "independent of the scientist's individual prejudices, tastes, and private opinions. Results of empirical methods are objective in that they are open to anyone's observation and do not depend on the subjective belief of the individual scientist" (Zuriff, 1985, p. 9 as cited in Cooper et al., 2020, p.5).

Every effort to understand, predict, and improve behavior hinges on the behavior analyst's ability to completely define, systematically observe, and accurately and reliably measure occurrences and non-occurrences of the behavior of interest (Cooper et al., 2020, p. 5).

Behavior analysts live by empiricism; it's their bread and butter. Accurately and objectively defining, measuring, and reliably observing, ensuring accurate results is a must in the field of Applied Behavior Analysis.

Empiricism underpins the entire scientific process. It emphasizes the importance of systematically gathering and analyzing empirical evidence to draw conclusions and advance our understanding of the natural world, which is a fundamental principle of the scientific method, and empiricism as a philosophical perspective.

Experimentation

Experimenting to find a functional relation between variables is the strategy used in most sciences. Dinsmoor (2003) explained experimentation as follows: The experimental method isolates the relevant variables within a pattern of events. When the experimental method is employed, it is possible to change one factor at a time (independent variable) while leaving all other aspects of the situation the same, and then to observe what effect this change has on the target behavior (dependent variable). Ideally, a functional relation may be obtained. Formal experimental control techniques are designed to ensure that the conditions being compared are otherwise the same. Use of the experimental method serves as a necessary condition (sine qua non) to distinguish the experimental analysis of behavior from other methods of investigation.

Replication

It goes without saying that replication provides validity through the process of recreating the proposed concept in an experiment. Upon recreating the same results, the concept or principle starts to develop merit and reliability through publications of peer-reviewed articles. Without replicating a proposed concept, no matter how well the experiment is designed and how controlled the variables are created, it will have no base in any scientific field.

Replication is the primary method with which scientists determine the reliability and usefulness of their findings and discover their mistakes (Johnston & Pennypacker, 1980; l993a; Sidman, 1960 as cited in Cooper et al., 2020).

Parsimony

Parsimony states that all simple, logical explanations for the phenomenon under investigation be ruled out, experimentally or conceptually, before more complex or abstract explanations are considered. Parsimonious interpretations help scientists assess and fit new findings within the field's existing knowledge base (Cooper et al., 2020, p. 6). Parsimony suggests that scientific theories, models, or explanations should avoid unnecessary complexity. When multiple explanations are possible, the one that requires the fewest assumptions or entities (e.g., variables, components) is often favored. In other words, keeping it simple is key; why complicate things without necessity?

Philosophic Doubt

This attitude should apply to everything in life, not just science. The most simplified definition of philosophic doubt is to question everything, no matter how factual.

"Science is a willingness to accept facts even when they are opposed to wishes" (Skinner, 1953, p. 12). Humans have a tendency to be biased, which is instilled in our evolutionary history. However, in science, bias is the enemy of success.

Good scientists maintain a healthy level of skepticism. Although being skeptical of others' research may be easy, a more difficult but critical characteristic of scientists is that they remain open to the possibility and look for evidence that their own findings or interpretations are wrong (Cooper et al., 2020).

Practitioners should be as skeptical as researchers. The skeptical practitioner not only requires scientific evidence before implementing a new practice but also continually evaluates its effectiveness once the practice has been implemented. Practitioners must be particularly skeptical of extraordinary claims made for the effectiveness of new theories, therapies, or treatments (Foxx & Mulick, 2016; Maurice, 2017)

What is Applied Behavior Analysis?

Finally, after engaging in the 100-year history of behaviorism, we have reached the branch of applied behavior analysis. Cooper et al., 2020 defined ABA as the following: "Applied behavior analysis is the science in which tactics derived from the principles of behavior are applied systematically to improve socially significant behavior and experimentation is used to identify the variables responsible for behavior change." However, there is a definition that most of the readers reading this book will understand, and it is as follows: Applied Behavior Analysis, or as most of us know it, "ABA," is a systematic and evidence-based approach to understanding and modifying human behavior. It is rooted in the principles of behaviorism and is widely recognized for its effectiveness in addressing a wide range of behavioral challenges and improving the lives of individuals with various needs. ABA is characterized by its focus on observable and measurable behavior, data-driven decision-making, and the application of behavioral principles to create meaningful and positive changes in behavior.

Cooper et al., 2020 wrote that the definition of ABA includes six essential components. First, applied behavior analysis is a science, which means ABA researchers and practitioners are guided by the attitudes and methods of scientific inquiry, which we cover in the previous subtopic. Second, all behavior change procedures are described and implemented systematically and technologically. Third, no means of changing behavior qualifies as applied behavior analysis: The field circumscribes only those tactics conceptually derived from the basic principles of behavior. Fourth, the focus of applied behavior analysis is socially significant behavior. The fifth and sixth parts of the definition specify the twin goals of applied behavior analysis: improvement and understanding. Applied behavior analysis seeks to make meaningful improvements in necessary behavior and analyze the factors responsible for that improvement.

Here is where a philosophical conundrum always takes place especially between methodological and radical behaviorist. One of the six components mentions the words "socially significant." Furman and Lepper (2018) take issue with the definition of applied behavior analysis because it "employs a subjective criterion, again the words "socially significant" taking it out of the realm of an objective science" (p. 103) and suggest that ABA be defined as "the scientific study of behavior change, using the principles of behavior, to evoke or elicit a targeted behavioral change" (p. 104). What is being argued here is that science can't be restrained by the boundaries of the human notion.

Simply when we mention the words "socially significant" we are opening the door to certain ethical and mentalistic constructs. The reason for this debate is because if this simple question: what constitutes as socially significant? When we discovered that hydrogen was an element of the periodic table, this wasn't a construct created by the human psyche but rather a fact and an element of the physical world that we discovered but not created. However, on the other hand, we decide what constitutes as socially significant in the physical dimension. This has led to issues in recent years as what classifies as socially significant can be argued to a rather large extent. Let me explain: if I want to say that sticking my middle finger out in public is a "socially significant" behavior and needs to be reduced, why is it really socially significant? I could argue that in my culture, another mentalistic construct that can't be explained by the scientific principle, sticking the middle finger out is appropriate. Then, this would bring issues of ethics and discrimination against a different background.

This is why the words "socially significant" aren't a one-size-fits-all. In this last example, I have exercised my point of view on why ABA is still a science that holds a fragile line between objectivity and subjectivity. This is another reason we have methodological and radical behaviorist in the field today, with some looking only at what they can measure and observe and others taking into account how "inner states" affect behavior and their interaction with the environment.

First Implementation of Behavior Modification on a Human Subject

Even though the experimental study of behavior analysis had existed for well over a decade after B.F Skinner published his book "The Behavior of Organisms" and started today's behaviorism, all the experiments up to now were done on animal subjects. It wasn't until 1949 that Fuller conducted a study on an 18-year-old severely disabled human. Fuller noted in his report, "The subject was an 18-year-old boy with profound developmental disabilities who was described in the language of the time as a "vegetative idiot." He lay on his back, unable to roll over. Fuller filled a syringe with a warm sugar milk solution and injected a small amount of the fluid into the young man's mouth every time he moved his right arm (that arm was chosen because he moved it infrequently). Within four sessions, the boy was moving his arm to a vertical position at a rate of three times per minute (Cooper et al., 2020, pp.14). The early research in the field, even though it was benefiting those being tested on, primarily focused on whether behavioral principles had a functional relation and could be applied to human subjects.

Once again, according to Cooper et al., 2020, Sidney Bijou (1955, 1957, 1958) researched several principles of behavior with typically developing subjects and people with intellectual disabilities; Don Baer (1960, 1961, 1962) examined the effects of punishment, escape, and avoidance contingencies (all discussed throughout the book) on preschool children; and Ogden Lindsley (1956; Lindsley & Skinner, 1954) assessed the effects of operant conditioning on the behavior of adults with schizophrenia. These early researchers clearly established that the principles of behavior are applicable to human behavior, and they set the stage for the later development of applied behavior analysis.

Donald M. Baer

FIGURE 2.5 Donald M. Baer (*Photograph by ABAI*)

It would be a shame to continue talking about the field of ABA without mentioning one of its greatest contributors, Don Baer. Donald M. Baer, commonly known as Don Baer, was a pioneering figure in the field of psychology and applied behavior analysis. He made significant contributions that have had a lasting impact on the understanding and modification of human behavior. Baer's career was characterized by a deep commitment to the practical application of psychological principles to improve the lives of individuals, particularly those with developmental disabilities.

Don Baer, along with B.F. Skinner and Montrose Wolf, are credited as one of the co-founders of applied behavior analysis. His work, particularly the landmark paper "Some Current Dimensions of Applied Behavior Analysis," published in 1968 with Wolf and Risley, laid the foundation for the field's growth and evolution. In this influential paper, Baer and his colleagues outlined the seven dimensions of ABA, which we will go into detail in the next subtopic, emphasizing the importance of assessing and modifying behavior in real-world settings. His research and advocacy for the practical application of behavioral principles continue to shape the field, making ABA a valuable tool for educators, therapists, and behavior analysts dedicated to improving the lives of individuals with a wide range of behavioral challenges and developmental needs.

Don Baer, had a way of explaining advanced behavioral and philosophical concepts in a way that anyone could understand. He was charismatic and had the ability to enlighten the audience on any topic or subject in a way that made you feel confident about your understanding of the matter. His contributions to the field have helped it evolve to where they are today, and it is fair to say that without his contributions, we would still be developing what we know as today's seven dimensions of ABA.

Montrose Madison Wolf

In Todd Risley's paper, he writes in his abstract, "Montrose Madison Wolf, who discovered the reinforcing power of adult attention for children and, based on that discovery, invented and named the nonviolent parenting procedure time-out; who discovered that absent speech and social development could be artificially created with operant conditioning techniques; who first engineered a token economy into a useful motivational system; who invented the good behavior game; who orchestrated the massive research program that developed and refined the Teaching-Family Model as a residential treatment solution for delinquent development; who reinvented field observation, repeated measurement, and single-subject research methods; who introduced and named the concept of social validity; and who led the founding of the discipline of problem-solving real-world research called applied behavior analysis." (Friman, 2005).

Wolf was another collaborator in the creation of the seven dimensions of ABA. Even though time-out has long been faced out in our field of ABA due to its punishment contingency nature, it was still an excellent replacement for violent actions when clients engaged in what we call maladaptive behavior. We will cover why, as behavior analysts, we stay away from punishment procedures, not only because our field is reinforcement-based, but also because of the ethical considerations needed to implement punishment procedures in the next few chapters.

Behavior Analysis Characteristics

The psychologist mentioned above published a paper in 1968, and in 1987 they reviewed it. In the 1968 paper Baer, Wolf, Risley brought to light the seven dimensions of ABA, which were applied, behavioral, analytic, technological, conceptually systematic, effective, and generalized outcomes. Twenty years later, the same group of psychologists re-evaluated these dimensions and concluded that they still are as effective as they were back then. In ABA, we still believe deeply in these dimensions, and we are guided in everything we do by them. Each dimension signifies something different in the field, and we will discuss them individually, starting with Applied.

Applied

The term applied is an adjective that describes something as being put into practical use or applied in a specific context. It signifies that a particular concept, skill, principle, or technique is being used or implemented to address real-world problems, situations, or challenges. This is the definition of applied in the general term. However, in ABA, the first A stands for applied and has a different definition. Cooper et al., 2020, pp.16 definition of applied is as follows: The "applied" in applied behavior analysis signals ABA's commitment to effecting improvements in behaviors that enhance and improve people's lives. To meet this criterion, the researcher or practitioner must select behaviors to change that are socially significant for participants: social, language, academic, daily living, self-care, vocational, and/or recreation and leisure behaviors that improve the day-to-day life experience of the participants and/or affect their significant others (parents, teachers, peers, employers) in such a way that they behave more positively with and toward the participant.

Behavioral

When we say behavioral, you might be wondering, "Well, duh this is BEHAVIOR analysis", but let's think about it for a moment: what exactly is the behavioral aspect of ABA? The behavioral aspect focuses on observable and measurable behaviors. It emphasizes the importance of defining target behaviors in specific and objective terms to ensure clarity and consistency in assessment and intervention. This dimension underscores the need to precisely define target behaviors, describing them in specific and objective terms to ensure that they can be reliably observed, recorded, and analyzed.

By doing so, behavioral scientist can maintain clarity and consistency in their assessments and interventions, allowing for accurate measurement of behavior change over time. The behavioral dimension also emphasizes the scientific rigor of ABA by requiring that interventions and assessments be rooted in empirical observation. ABA practitioners systematically collect data on the target behavior and its surrounding context to determine whether changes in behavior are occurring as a result of the intervention.

Analytic

The analytic dimension of ABA might be the most crucial dimension of all. This is the dimension responsible for establishing functional relations between variables. This dimension requires that practitioners use objective and empirical methods to demonstrate that the intervention directly led to observable and measurable improvements or modifications in the target behavior. We will discuss experimental design and single-subject research in a further chapter, discussing how functional relations are demonstrated through the process of experimentation. In other words, the experimenter must be able to control the occurrence and non-occurrence of the behavior (Cooper et al., 2020).

The main issue with the analytic dimension in the practice of ABA is that some behaviors are too dangerous to experiment with. If we have a behavior such as self-injurious behavior, we can't go back to the baseline phase as it could have some dire consequences. Conducting experiments to establish a functional relationship between interventions and behavior changes sometimes raises ethical concerns as well. For example, withholding a potentially beneficial intervention for the sake of science and to test for a functional relation can be ethically problematic, mainly when dealing with individuals with special needs.

Technological

The technological dimension of ABA focuses on describing the principle in simple terms so that everyone who reads the term or hears the term, whether educated in the field of behavioral science or not, can understand the meaning. However, the definition noted in Cooper et al., 2020 is as follows "A study in applied behavior analysis is technological when all of its operative procedures are identified and described with sufficient detail and clarity "such that a reader has a fair chance of replicating the application with the same results" (Baer, Blount, Detrich, & Stokes, 1987, p. 320). In other words, especially when focusing on research and the experimental behavior of analysis, it is key that the experiment and its procedures sustain as much detail as possible so that those who want to replicate the study can easily do so.

To fulfill the technological dimension, we must provide detailed and comprehensive descriptions of the procedures, including specific steps, materials, and data collection methods. This level of specificity allows other professionals to replicate the interventions accurately and apply them in similar contexts. Moreover, the technological dimension ensures that ABA is not reliant on vague or subjective descriptions (which is incredibly common in the field) but is based on concrete and well-defined techniques, contributing to the field's credibility and effectiveness in addressing behavioral challenges across various domains and populations.

[continued on next page]

Conceptually systematic

Cooper et al., 2020 define conceptually systematic as follows: procedures for changing behavior and any interpretations of how or why they were effective should be described in terms of the relevant principle from which they were derived.

Let us try to understand this dimension with a different approach and simplify the meaning. As behavioral scientists, we must draw upon the extensive body of research and knowledge in behavior analysis, which the internet can provide hundreds of thousands of peer-reviewed articles on, or you can never go wrong with the bible of ABA (Cooper et al., 2020 massive but insightful Applied Behavior Analysis, Third Edition book). The original principles include reinforcement, punishment, shaping, and extinction, which are used to design interventions that effectively address behavioral challenges or promote skill acquisition. This dimension underscores the idea that ABA is not a collection of isolated techniques but a systematic and coherent approach guided by a deep understanding of the underlying principles.

Effective

When the word "effective" comes to mind, what is your ideal definition? Right, when something is effective, it must mean something worked, which means successful in producing a desired or intended result. In ABA, the effective dimension emphasizes that interventions and behavior modification strategies must produce meaningful and significant behavior change. We get the desired "effect" from the intervention, which makes it "effective".

Now, how do we keep track of the effectiveness of an intervention? Behavior Analysts and researchers continually monitor the progress of the individual, making adjustments to the intervention as needed to ensure that it remains effective in achieving the desired outcomes. Throughout the entirety of the services provided to the "client" (we will describe the client in a later chapter) we as practitioners must monitor all behaviors and signal any anomalies in the data. If we see that a behavior or skill is not advancing at the desired pace, we adapt and change the intervention until an effective intervention is found.

Generality

The last dimension falls into what all practitioners aim to achieve at the end of services. A behavior change has generality if it lasts over time, appears in environments other than the one in which the intervention that initially produced it was implemented, and/or spreads to other behaviors not directly treated by the intervention (behavioral cusp, discussed in later chapter). A behavior change that continues after the original treatment procedures are withdrawn has generality (Cooper et al., 2020).

Generalization, a key term in the principles of ABA, will be covered in detail in chapter #, explaining how to acquire generalization and how to inspire behavioral cusp. We need to remember that the way we interact with our environment triggers behavior. When we see a behavior work in one setting, as a functioning subject, we can easily transfer this behavior across different settings. However, when working with clients with developmental disabilities, this isn't the case.

The interventions chosen lead to behavior change that is durable and applicable in various real-world situations, ensuring that the individual can effectively generalize newly acquired skills or improved behaviors to different environments, people, and circumstances.

ABA as a Pseudoscience and Fad

This subtopic was added for clarification to explain the difference between the field of Applied Behavior Analysis as a treatment and the treatments with no empirical data to back up their claims. Pseudoscience refers to beliefs, practices, or claims that are presented as being scientific or having a scientific basis. Still, they lack the rigorous empirical evidence, scientific methodology, and consensus within the scientific community that is typically required to be considered genuine science. Pseudoscientific claims often mimic the language and trappings of science, but a lack of objectivity, testability, and reliance on anecdotal evidence or flawed reasoning characterizes them. In essence, pseudoscience may appear scientific on the surface, but it does not adhere to the principles and standards of the scientific method.

A Fad is a temporary and popular trend, behavior, or interest that becomes widely embraced and followed by a large number of people within a relatively short period of time. Fads often emerge suddenly, gain rapid popularity, and then decline or disappear just as quickly. They are characterized by their transient nature and their tendency to capture the attention and enthusiasm of a specific group or the general public for a limited time (Foxx, 2014). We have all been victims of fads, keeping up with the trends that grow in popularity and die down after a couple of years, sometimes even months. Some examples of fads can be tracked down to only a couple of years, such as the herbal life movement. This fad claimed to make you healthy and skinny, which took rise in popularity remarkably fast. Another trendy fad that is coming back in style is open-bottom pants from the 70s and 80s.

Autism is a hugely debated topic, and with reason. Over the last ten years, the diagnoses of autism have skyrocketed from one in twenty kids to one in five. This is hugely duo to the

THE BARE BONES OF ABA

diagnosis of ADHD being added to the spectrum and many other characteristics of autism being studied. However, with this rise in popularity have come a ton of new pseudoscience treatments with no evidence to show improvement. Here is where autism is currently struggling and companies seeking money are clinging to parents' hope. Autism has no origin, and we don't necessarily know what causes autism. We only know the symptoms associated with autism and develop tests and assessments based on these symptoms to diagnose. Due to the unknown origin of autism and conspiracy theorists using this to their advantage, parents of kids diagnosed, tend to fall for anything that gives them hope. Sometimes, this can be very dangerous and lead to the child becoming ill or sick to the point of neglect.

Two examples come to mind that really stand out and have no evidence whatsoever that they correlate. The first example is that many believe that vaccines cause autism, which, of course, has no merit, let alone evidence. However, when a hopeful parent believes this and doesn't vaccinate his/her child, they are putting the child's life at risk of severe illness and even death. The second example is one that is downright obsolete and should be a crime for child neglect, that treatment being bleach therapy. This treatment is exactly as it sounds, it claims to cure autism through the bathing and ingestion of small amounts of bleach. Now my view as a scientist will be very one-sided and biased, but, we know that bleach causes severe burns and, when ingested in large amounts, death. This treatment is a crime and should have never been tested.

The treatments we have discussed until now have all been characterized as pseudoscience and dubious. This leads us to behavioral science and, more specifically, the branch of applied behavior analysis. ABA employs methods derived from scientifically established principles of behavior (Baer, Wolf, & Risley,

1968). It has been applied successfully to a wide range of populations and areas, including autism, intellectual disabilities, all forms of education, business, mental health, counseling, marriage counseling, and child abuse, to name but a few (Martin & Pear, 2014).

ABA has played a vital role in revolutionizing treatment and education in ASD by freeing individuals from many behavioral, educational, and adaptive challenges and barriers that had kept them dependent, devalued, and isolated. New research findings are continually being incorporated in order to enhance ABA (Smith, 2013, as stated in Foxx, 2015). The only interventions that had been shown to produce comprehensive, lasting results in ASD were those based on the principles of applied behavior analysis. ABA has no place in any discussion of fads or pseudoscientific, dubious, or controversial and politically correct treatments other than to epitomize what constitutes effective and ethical treatment of individuals with ASD (Foxx, 2015).

ABA adheres to the core principles of the scientific method, including empirical observation, systematic data collection, objective measurement, and rigorous experimentation. Its foundations lie in the work of B.F. Skinner (father of ABA) and other leading figures in the field of psychology. ABA's commitment to empiricism means that its interventions and strategies are based on evidence derived from extensive research and controlled experiments, in contrast to pseudoscientific practices that often rely on anecdotal evidence or unfounded claims.

THREE
ABA TO THE BONE
PRINCIPLES OF ABA

" Don't become a mere recorder of facts, but try to penetrate the mystery of its origin"

IVAN PAVLOV

WHAT IS BEHAVIOR?

The time has come to learn the same principles every behavior analyst knows and overcomplicates. The previous chapter focused on the history of behavioral science and the prominent figures who helped build the field to today's standards. The following three chapters will cover an extensive 100 years of knowledge with complicated scientific concepts, but don't worry, remember SSG Learning Theory? Yes, SSG will be used throughout the following three chapters, ensuring your comprehension of the material. By the end, you will understand the basics of human behavior and how our interaction with the environment affects our every move. Let's first get started with the definition of behavior and what it truly is.

Skinner (1938) (his name is all over the book) defined behavior as follows, "the movement of an organism or of its parts in a frame of reference provided by the organism or by various external objects or fields. However, many in the field at the time had issues with this definition. It wasn't until Johnston and Pennypacker revised this definition, created a more sound articulation of behavior. Johnston and Pennypacker stated that the behavior of an organism is the portion of an organism interacting with its environment, detectable by displacement in space (movement) through time of some part of the organism, and that results in a measurable change in at least one aspect of the environment (2009). Behavior is not a property or attribute of the organism. It happens only when there is an interactive condition between an organism and its surroundings, which include its own body (Johnston & Pennypacker, 1993)

Let's simplify this definition to understand what behavior is. When we think of behavior, we think of the movement of the body, our actions, and our interaction with anything in our environment, any observable and measurable action or response of an individual, including what a person does and says. Think about a time when you suddenly had an urge to do something, maybe going for a drive on a hot day and you see an ice cream truck on the corner. Now that you see the ice cream truck, you change your course and drive toward the truck. Multiple factors added to your behavior of changing course to the ice cream truck. But your environment (seeing the ice cream truck) caused you to engage in a behavior (physical change, or movement that is observable and measurable) to get that ice cream (consequence). This behavior was caused by a lot more than the environment however, for the simplicity of explanation, we will recall this example when discussing motivation operations.

Temporal Locus, Temporal Extent, Repeatability

Behavior can be measured in one of the following three dimensions: temporal locus, temporal extent, and repeatability. The concept of temporal locus plays a vital role in understanding the timing and patterns of behavior. Temporal locus refers to the specific timing or occurrence of a behavior in relation to other events or stimuli. In the field, behavior is carefully analyzed as to when it happens, whether it follows a particular event (antecedent) or leads to specific consequences. This dimension allows behavior analysts to gain a comprehensive understanding of the temporal patterns that influence behavior. In other words, the temporal locus is just knowing when the behavior happened, such as if the learner engaged in behavior at 9:00 AM. The purpose of temporal locus is to figure out when the behavior is most likely to occur.

From the temporal locus, we can deduce what temporal extent will mean. Let's think about this: what does extent mean in the form of time? Extent is the amount to which something is or is believed to be the case. This is precisely what temporal extent means: how long the behavior lasted. Let's take an example of temporal extent, if you want to measure the behavior of screaming with temporal extent, grab a timer and time how long the behavior took from the bigging to the end. The last measurement is repeatability, and it is also the easiest, repeatability refers to how a behavior can be counted or how it can occur repeatedly through time. For example, if the behavior being measured is the behavior of throwing objects, repeatability refers to the fact that you can count how many times the individual throws objects throughout the day or the session (Cooper et al., 2020).

Behavior Components

Now that we have officially defined behavior, let's break down the forms of behavior. When discussing behavior, it should be known that behavior compromises a group of responses that share a physical dimension or function (Cooper et al., 2020). Let's analyze this: behavior is not a singular thing, but rather a group of responses that most times correspond to the same function. Keep in mind behavior can only be produced by a living organism; again, it's evident that a rock can't engage in self-throwing, it requires a living organism to throw it. A response, is a single instance of behavior, for example, let's say Fonsi (fake name) engaged in kicking behavior, a response would be a single instance of kicking or only kicking once. When we differentiate behavior against response, it allows us to measure specificity. If we say that Fonsi engaged in kicking behavior, we will know that he engaged in kicking, but how many times? Thus, breaking down the behavior to a singular response lets us measure multiple responses. **FIGURE 3.1** summarizes the difference between behavior and response in a clear an concise way through the use of SSG.

[*continued on next page*]

Behavior vs. Response

Kicking behavior describes the behavior but not the number of times this behavior happens.

One instance of the topographical response can be measured as happening one time.

FIGURE 3.1 Behavior vs. Response

Behavior is the interaction between the organism, animal or human, with its environment. Remember, for it to be behavior, the organism must interact with its environment and be detectable by displacement in space and time, not the environment acting upon the organism. This is because if the organism is rained on and gets wet, receives gifts, etc., it doesn't mean that the organism acted on its environment, it means the environment acted on the organism. Now, if the organism pulls out an umbrella because it is raining, this will be the organism acting due to an interaction with its environment, and we can call it a behavior or, more specifically, a response.

Environment

We have mentioned the word environment multiple times already and haven't defined it means in terms of behavioral science. Johnston and Pennypacker (2009) defined environment in the following terms: Environment refers to the full set of physical circumstances in which the organism exists. The term is comprehensive in that any facets of the physical world may be considered for their contribution to behavior. The term is specific in that for any particular behavior; the focus is usually on only those environmental events that are functionally related to individual responses.

Let us simplify this definition of environment into a more edible bite that we can all understand. The concept of environment encompasses all the external factors and stimuli that surround an individual and influence their behavior. This includes both physical and social elements of the individual's surroundings. Behavioral science recognizes that behavior does not occur in isolation but is shaped and maintained by the environment in which it occurs.

The Term Stimulus

So far, we have talked about the environment and how it interacts with the organism; this has a term for it, the term we use is "stimulus". Cooper et al., 2020, defines stimulus as an energy change that is detectable by the organism. Let's break down this definition as a lot is packed into one sentence. For something to be called a stimulus, it must have been detected by the organism, which in turn acts upon this detectable change. Let's give an everyday example of this term and how it works. Let's say you are driving and are stopped at a red light, when the light turns green (the stimulus), you (the organism) detect this change, evoking the behavior of accelerating your car. However, if the light turns green, and you (the organism) don't detect this change, then we can't call the light turning green a stimulus. Only when the change is detected can it be called a stimulus; this can be demonstrated in **FIGURE 3.2**.

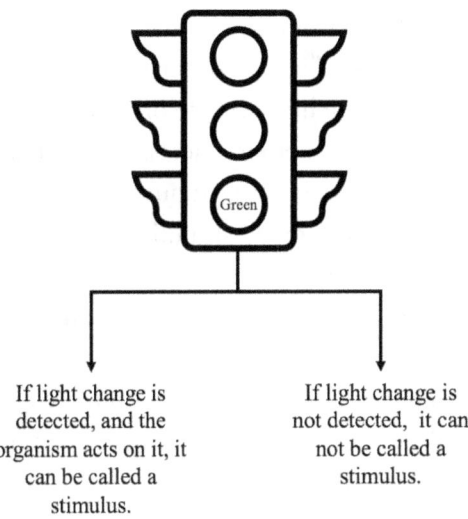

FIGURE 3.2 Stimulus example

The illustration above demonstrates a green light example, but this applies to anything in your surroundings, another example is a car passing by. Let's say you are sitting at a Starbucks, and a car is passing by next to you. You turn your head to see the car pass by. This can be called a stimulus; however, if the car is passing by and you don't notice the car or turn your head, this is not a stimulus as the organism (you) didn't notice this energy change in the environment.

Stimulus Class

Stimulus class is a term that is more complicated to understand, but with SSG, it should be fairly straightforward. Stimulus class is a term used to refer to any group of stimuli sharing a predetermined set of common elements in one or more of these dimensions (Cooper et al., 2020). Stimulus class has three categories, formal, temporal, and functional, which all serve different purposes. The formal category describes a stimulus by its physical features, such as size, color, intensity, weight, and spatial position relative to other objects. The formal dimension helps define the boundaries of a stimulus class by highlighting the physical similarities among stimuli that are likely to evoke the same behavior or response. By identifying and manipulating stimuli with similar formal features, behavior analysts can design interventions that promote generalization, where individuals respond to various stimuli within the class based on shared physical characteristics, enhancing the applicability and adaptability of learned behaviors across different situations and settings.

The temporal dimension of stimulus class refers to the timing or duration of stimuli within that class. It involves examining when stimuli are presented or how long they are presented to elicit a specific behavior or response. The temporal dimension can be a critical consideration when designing interventions, particularly for behaviors that are sensitive to the timing of stimuli. For example, if a child is learning to follow instructions, the temporal dimension may involve varying the time interval between the instruction and the delivery of reinforcement to teach them to respond promptly. By manipulating the temporal dimension of stimuli within a class, we can tailor interventions to address specific timing-related aspects of behavior, contributing to the effectiveness and precision of behavior modification strategies.

The functional dimension of stimulus class refers to the same functionally related class that shares the property of producing a similar behavioral response when presented. For instance, if a child learns to request a favorite toy using verbal language, stimuli within the same functionally related class may include various objects, people, or situations that elicit the same requesting behavior. We use this concept of function to design interventions that teach individuals to respond effectively to stimuli with similar functions, ultimately promoting generalization. This means that the individual is more likely to exhibit the desired behavior not just in the presence of the training stimuli but also in the presence of other stimuli that serve the same function,

Response Class

Response class is much simpler than stimulus class, as it pertains to a group of responses with the same functional effect on the environment. In other words, response class refers to a group or category of behaviors that share similar functions or serve the same purpose within a specific context. For example, if a child exhibits aggressive behavior such as hitting, biting, and kicking when denied access to preferred items, these behaviors may be considered part of the same response class because they all serve the function of gaining access to desired items or escaping aversive situations. A difference between response class and response topography must be made to differentiate the two. When we say topography, we mean the physical shape or form of response, how the response looks described in words. For example, when I mention kicking behavior, we can imagine what kicking looks like, however, in ABA, we can't guide ourselves based on imagination. We need to describe what the behavior of kicking looks like, such as "kicking is referred to any instance Fonsi moves leg back and forth with force making an impact with table, human, or any object. Functions will be discussed in a later chapter, but fo the sake of explanation, we need to understand that the same response topography can be due to different functions while different response topography can be for the same function, in which case it would be called response class.

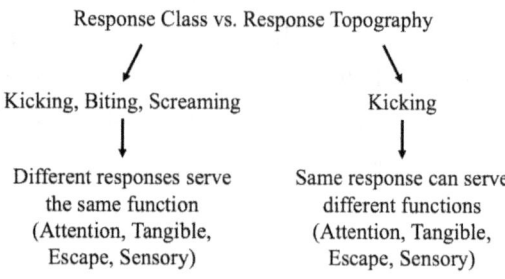

FIGURE 3.3 Difference between Response Class and Response topography

Respondent Conditioning (In-Depth)

We have mentioned respondent conditioning on multiple occasions, especially when discussing Ivan Pavlov's discovery of classical conditioning. Ivan Pavlov walked into his lab one day and noticed that the dogs he had started salivating in the presence of his assistant, even though his assistant didn't have any food in his hands. This got Pavlov's brain cells turning and sparked his curiosity, which he then sought and studied. Pavlov rang a bell every time he brought food to the dogs until the dogs formed an association with the bell. In behavioral science language, we know this as stimulus-stimulus pairing or pairing an unconditioned (unlearned) stimulus with a conditioned (learned) stimulus until the unconditioned stimulus becomes conditioned. Eventually, when Pavlov rang the bell, the dogs began to salivate without food being present. Ivan Pavlov will go on to call this respondent condition or classical conditioning. Before we get started, there are some terms we need to know, and these are:

- Phylogeny: this is the individual's evolutionary history, which they are born with and doesn't require learning.
- Ontogeny: this is the individual's learning history, or what the individual has learned since the day they were born.
- Unconditioned: Unconditioned refers to something unlearned (Phylogeny)
- Conditioned: Conditioned refers to something learned (Ontogeny)

Respondent conditioning can also be explained in a stimulus-response contingency, where a certain conditioned or unconditioned stimulus evokes a response, such as the bell ringing (Stimulus) evoked the dog's salivation (response). In this case, the stimulus is an antecedent; an antecedent is something that occurs right before the behavior. So, putting it all together will look like this: The dog's response of salivation was caused by the antecedent stimulus (the bell) due to the stimulus–stimulus pairing with the food. We need to keep in mind, however, that an unconditioned stimulus (US) cannot, under any circumstance, evoke a conditioned response (CR). This applies in reverse as well, a conditioned stimulus (CS) cannot evoke an unconditioned response (UR). This might seem confusing, but in **FIGURE 3.4,** you can see that an unconditioned stimulus (US) evokes an unconditioned response (UR) and that a conditioned stimulus (CS) evokes a conditioned response (CR). Another critical point to remember is that the word unconditioned stands for unlearned, meaning we have an evolutionary history, so the unconditioned response is also unlearned, and we call this reflexes.

Unconditioned Stimulus (US) ⟶ Removing hand

Unconditioned Response (UR) ⟶ Touching boiling water (Reflex)

Example:

Low Temperature (US) ⟶ Shivering (UR)

High Temperature (US) ⟶ Sweating (UR)

FIGURE 3.4 Example of Unconditioned Stimulus and Response

Now, let us get to the important part of respondent conditioning: how can something unconditioned (unlearned) become conditioned (learned)? Human learning is built through associating tangible and sensory items based on evolutionary history. Our bodies know that food is needed to survive, but it doesn't know what pizza is. Through association, we have developed our knowledge of the environment that impacts our behavior. We now introduce another variable to this already complicated formula: the Neutral Stimulus (NS). The neutral stimulus is precisely as it sounds, it doesn't have any effect on behavior. Let us get deep into respondent conditioning to understand it fully. When we repeatedly pair an unconditioned stimulus (US) with a neutral stimulus (NS), which does not have any effect on behavior, the (NS) will eventually acquire the ability to elicit a response. When this happens, the (NS) becomes a conditioned stimulus (CS), and the response thus evolves into a conditioned response (CR). **FIGURE 3.5** shows this process visually, allowing for full comprehension. This is precisely what Pavlov discovered and tested when he used food (US) and repeatedly paired it with the bell (NS); eventually, the bell became a (CS), evoking the response of salivating and signaling the presence of food or (CR).

FIGURE 3.5 Full Process of Respondent Conditioning

As we can see, respondent conditioning was quite the discovery, and what a beautiful process it embodies to break down how human behavior can be trained to happen under different stimuli. This was the first discovery of conditioning; then, our beloved ABA father, B.F Skinner, extended on this discovery and coined the term operant conditioning, which adds a whole new layer to what we just learned. Operant condition is the standard used in today's practice almost a century later.

[*continued on next page*]

Operant Conditioning

In respondent conditioning, it mentioned that it was shaped by antecedent stimuli eliciting a response or, in other words, stimulus-response relation. However, in B.F Skinner's research, he studied how behavior is shaped by consequence. When we say consequence, we mean the environmental factor that happens immediately after the response. In operant conditioning, behaviors are seen as voluntary actions that can be strengthened or weakened based on the outcomes that follow them. This is a stimulus-response-stimulus relation that can be abbreviated to S-R-S, or many of us know it as the ABC. ABC stands for antecedent, behavior, and consequence, which help us identify problematic behaviors during our field assessments. B.F Skinner's model, the three-term contingency, is based on Pavlov's respondent conditioning but is drastically different. While respondent condition focuses on antecedent stimuli and stimulus-stimulus pairing, operant condition shapes behavior by consequence.

The central premise of operant conditioning is that behaviors that are followed by favorable consequences (reinforcement) are more likely to be repeated in the future, while behaviors followed by negative consequences (punishment) are less likely to recur. Remembering the following sentence will win you debate against other practitioners: Skinner's operant conditioning only shapes FUTURE behavior. By manipulating the consequences that follow a behavior, such as providing rewards for desired behaviors or applying appropriate consequences for undesired behaviors, operant conditioning can be used to shape, strengthen, or modify a wide range of behaviors in humans and animals. It has applications in various fields, including education, parenting, therapy, and animal training, where it is used to promote desired behaviors and reduce problematic ones. **FIGURE 3.6** shows a brief three-term contingency example that helps visualize Skinner's model. It must be noted that if one response is modified by consequence, the whole response class is also affected. For an example of operant conditioning, we can stay with Pavlov's original experiment. Pavlov's ringing the bell function as the antecedent stimuli; the behavior was the dogs salivating for the food, and the consequence was that the dogs received the food (positive reinforcement discussed later in the chapter)

Stimulus ⟶ Response ⟶ Stimulus

Antecedent ⟶ Behavior ⟶ Consequence

Bell ⟶ Salivation ⟶ Food

FIGURE 3.6 Three-term contingency (Operant Conditioning)

Reinforcement Contingency (Simplified)

The term reinforcement is like your name; everyone around you will use your name, and you will never stop hearing it. When we hear someone say "reinforcement," we tend to think of it as a one-time thing; however, reinforcement is a process. Reinforcement is a stimulus change (addition or removal) after a response that increases the future frequency of the behavior. Again, an immensely important word to remember is FUTURE. Reinforcement only increases the frequency in the future, not in the present moment. For this process to work, there must be a reinforcer, which is not reinforcement but it is part of it. A reinforcer is a singular stimulus change used as a consequence of a response.

For example, Fonsi went to the store and asked very nicely for ice cream; the mom said that if he helped her with the groceries, she would buy him ice cream. After Fosni helped with the groceries, the mom bought him the ice cream. Now Fonsi is more likely to help his mom in the future with the groceries. The entire process of rewarding Fonsi was the reinforcement, while the ice cream itself functioned as the reinforcer. Again, it would be inaccurate to say that the ice cream was used as a reinforcement. The appropriate way to make this statement is that ice cream was used as a reinforcer. For an item to be considered a reinforcer, it would have had to increase the future frequency of the behavior. In our example, ice cream did become a reinforcer as it increased Fonsi's behavior of helping his mom do the groceries in the future. Before we move on to the types of reinforcement, there are two things we need to learn: automaticity and immediacy.

- Automaticity states that a consequence is an automatic process that does not require any cognition or mental awareness.
- Immediacy states that the more immediate the consequence, the more effective it is. In other words, the faster we provide the consequence, the more of an effect it will have on the behavior. This is important because if we provide the consequence in a delayed sequence, we risk reinforcing or punishing non-targeted behaviors

We now also need to define the terms "Positive" and "Negative" in the field of behavioral science. Remember, we don't use mentalistic constructs in behavioral science, so the terms positive and negative don't mean good or bad. The term positive is simply the "addition" of stimuli, while the term negative is the "removal" of a stimuli. Reinforcers can take various forms, including tangible items (such as toys or treats), access to preferred activities, social interactions, or even verbal praise. The effectiveness of reinforcement lies in its ability to serve as a consequence that individuals find rewarding or motivating.

Positive reinforcement involves adding a desirable stimulus following a behavior to increase the likelihood of that behavior occurring again. Negative reinforcement involves removing or avoiding an aversive stimulus following a behavior, which also increases the likelihood of the behavior repeating in the future. In **FIGURE 3.7** below, we can see a cheat sheet of reinforcement and punishment contingencies to memorize them.

Negative reinforcement is quite a bit more complicated than positive reinforcement, as it involves the escape contingency and avoidance contingency. Let's remember that negative reinforcement is the removal of a stimulus that will increase the future frequency of the behavior, and this is why the escape contingency fits perfectly. In escape contingency, a response terminates the aversive stimulus, as long as the organism is in contact with the aversive stimulus. For example, if Fonsi is in class and receives classwork from the teacher, Fonsi starts crying very loudly, the teacher then removes this task from Fonsi, and now Fonsi is no longer crying. The removal of this task (negative) will increase Fonsi's crying when he receives work again in the future (reinforcement) thus making this negative reinforcement.

The avoidance contingency is exactly as it sounds: avoiding

something aversive. The definition of the term avoidance is a response that prevents or postpones the aversive stimulus. In avoidance contingency, the organism does not have to be in contact with the aversive stimulus, unlike escape. This makes sense as when you are escaping something, it means you made contact with that stimulus, on the other hand, when you are avoiding something, you haven't made contact and are trying to avoid it. An example of simple avoidance contingency can be again in the school setting. Let us say that Fonsi is sitting in the classroom, and the professor has not arrived. When the professor walks into the room, Fonsi starts to cry very loudly, which causes the professor to leave the room, and Fonsi never receives his task (avoiding task).

Avoidance contingency gets even better as it has two different forms: discriminated avoidance and free-operant avoidance. Discriminated avoidance is the easiest to understand of the two as it simply means that a signal or a trigger is associated with the aversive stimulus which in turn causes a response that prevents the aversive stimulus. A great example everyone can relate to is seeing their boss. When you see your boss (discriminate), you begin doing work (response) to avoid "a talking to from the big guy" (prevent aversive stimulus). Another example is seeing a police officer while driving (discriminate), you reduce your speed (response), which in turn prevents a speeding ticket (prevent aversive stimulus).

The next form is free-operant avoidance, which is most likely from previous consequences as there is no signal, and the response occurs at any time, delaying the aversive stimulus. In free operant avoidance, individuals engage in behaviors that allow them to escape or avoid an unpleasant situation or stimulus independently, without any specific cues or prompts. For example, if a student is given a challenging math assignment and finds it difficult, they may engage in behaviors such as procrastination or asking for help to avoid the discomfort associated with the task. The avoidance behavior occurs freely and is not contingent on a specific external signal or cue.

Reinforcement procedures are extremely extensive and widely used in the field. For more thorough information regarding reinforcement, consult the book Applied Behavior Analysis by Cooper et al., 2020 which has a vast chapter detailing everything about reinforcement.

Punishment Contingency (Simplified)

Punishment is the opposite of reinforcement but is also a process involving a stimulus change after a response. In punishment, the stimulus change will decrease the future frequency of the behavior. The same rules that applied to reinforcement apply to punishment, with a few exceptions covered later in the chapter. A punisher is a component of punishment, and it's a stimulus change such as a reprimand. For something to be called a punisher, it has to decrease the future frequency of behavior if not it cannot be called a punisher. Punishment contingencies are very infrequently used in the field as they are looked down upon. Punishment contingencies also have positive and negative additions. In positive punishment, the addition of a stimulus will decrease the future frequency of the behavior, an example of this is giving Fonsi a time-out. A timeout is the addition of a stimulus, and it will decrease the future frequency of the behavior. On the other hand, negative punishment is the removal of a stimulus that will decrease the future frequency of the behavior. For example, a parent might take away a child's favorite toy if they engage in a disruptive behavior. The absence of the preferred item serves as a consequence that decreases the likelihood of the behavior recurring. An interesting thing about negative reinforcement is that the learner or client who is receiving the punishment must be in contact with the reinforcer or must have had an opportunity to receive the reinforcer. For the punishment procedure to work, motivation for the reinforcer must be in effect; if not, the punishment procedure is rendered obsolete. **FIGURE 3.7** shows the cheat sheet for the contingencies, and it would be worth memorizing.

Punishment contingencies are very complicated and highly debated in the field, as some practitioners agree with the use of punishment procedures while others find it ethically wrong. The use of punishment is generally reserved for severe or dangerous behaviors, and alternative strategies, such as reinforcement-based approaches, are often preferred. Moreover, the intensity and duration of punishment should be carefully managed to ensure that it effectively reduces the targeted behavior without causing unnecessary harm or adverse reactions. The biggest confusion for those learning about ABA is differentiating between negative reinforcement and punishment. Think about it this way: say you are speeding on the streets, and a cop gives you a fine, the behavior here is speeding; remember that punishment affects future behavior. Now, the removal of speeding will in the future decrease the likelihood of a speeding fine. This can then transition to negative reinforcement in the form of avoidance contingency. As a result of receiving a fine now in the future, you keep the speed under the limit, which in turn avoids or prevents a speeding fine, thus negative reinforcement.

Now, as mentioned above, punishment has a lot of drawbacks, and one of these phenomena is known as recovery. When punishment is provided at a low or mild intensity, it can cause the behavior that was punished to return or increase.

This often happens when punishment is discontinued, and that's why, in the field, reinforcement is highly preferred. To avoid this phenomenon, punishment should follow a rigid rule of thumb whenever it is implemented. These rules include immediacy, intensity, schedule, and alternative. When we talk about intensity in punishment procedures, it is necessary to understand that high-intensity implementation is the best way to implement the punishment. Many practitioners believe punishment should start at a low or mild intensity, but, this tends to have an aversive effect on the behavior. It should be mentioned that the principle of using the least restrictive yet effective, level of intensity is still in play as there needs to be a balance and ethical considerations when implementing punishment.

The next rule of immediacy doesn't just apply to punishment procedures; it also applies to reinforcement procedures. When the punishment is delivered right after the behavior occurs, it will have a more robust effect and provide better empirical results. The next rule includes schedules of reinforcement, which will be covered in chapter four. When using schedules of reinforcement or, in this case, punishment, providing punishment in continuous schedules or FR 1 will also be the most effective way to implement punishment. Now, the last rule is absolutely necessary and should be implemented in every behavior plan, and this is finding an alternative behavior to reinforce. When punishing a behavior, an alternative behavior should be reinforced for the organism being punished to learn the appropriate way. This procedure is similar to differential reinforcement, but there is a massive difference, and that is that differential reinforcement does not involve punishment; rather, it implements extinction (discussed in Chapter Four, Schedules of Reinforcement).

	Reinforcement	Punishment
Positive	The **addition** of a stimulus that **increases** the future frequency of the behavior.	The **addition** of a stimulus that **decreases** the future frequency of the behavior.
Negative	The **removal** of a stimulus that **increases** the future frequency of the behavior.	The **removal** of a stimulus that **decreases** the future frequency of the behavior.

FIGURE 3.7 Cheat sheet of Positive/Negative Reinforcement and Punishment

Ethical Considerations for Punishment

Let's explain why punishment is unused in most circumstances, and why it must follow very concrete rules. Ethical considerations play a paramount role in the application of punishment procedures. While punishment may sometimes be a necessary component of behavior modification interventions, it must be implemented with great care and adherence to ethical guidelines to ensure the well-being and dignity of individuals receiving the services.

One of these considerations is always finding the least restrictive alternative to the punishment procedure. A fundamental ethical principle in behavioral science is the concept of the least restrictive alternative. This principle emphasizes that punishment should only be employed when less intrusive interventions, such as reinforcement-based strategies, have proven ineffective or are not feasible. We as practitioners have a responsibility to exhaust all other options before considering punishment, and the decision to use punishment should be made based on a thorough assessment and analysis of the behavior. Another consideration is intensity, as the higher the intensity, the better, however, rules do apply. Practitioners must use the least intrusive level of punishment necessary to achieve the desired behavior change. This means avoiding excessive or harsh forms of punishment that could result in physical or emotional harm, which, of course, goes without saying. Monitoring the individual's well-being and adjusting the intensity of punishment accordingly is essential to ensure ethical practice.

Another ethical conundrum is the continuous measurement and monitoring of the procedure implementation. We must continuously evaluate the effectiveness of the intervention and be prepared to make adjustments or discontinue the use of punishment if it is not achieving the desired outcomes. Regular data collection and analysis are critical to ensure that the individual's progress is closely monitored and that any negative side effects are promptly addressed. When implementing punishment, the data must show the progress and effectiveness of the intervention. If there is no progress, the program must be modified and reinstated after being revised.

The principles of least restrictive alternatives, appropriate intensity, informed consent, and ongoing assessment guide practitioners in making ethical decisions and ensuring that punishment is used judiciously and with the utmost care for the well-being of the individuals receiving services. Ethical practice in the field prioritizes the individual's rights, dignity, and safety while striving to achieve meaningful behavior change.

FOUR
WELCOME TO CASINO WORLD
SCHEDULES OF REINFORCEMENT

"If you are old, don't try to change yourself, change your environment."

B.F SKINNER

INTRODUCTION

We have arrived at the point where we will learn about a crucial element of behavior analysis, and this element is the foundation used by B.F Skinner in his 1938 book, schedules of Reinforcement. Schedules of reinforcement are fundamental principles that govern how and when reinforcement is delivered to shape and maintain behavior. These schedules dictate the timing and criteria for providing rewards or consequences in response to a specific behavior. They have practical applications in a wide range of settings, from education and therapy to animal training and workplace management, where they are used to promote desired behaviors and reduce unwanted ones while considering the frequency and predictability of reinforcement. There is an extensive list of schedules of reinforcement, from the basic schedules to the more complicated compound and progressive schedules. In this chapter, we will discuss the ins and outs of how to use schedules of reinforcement using the SSG learning theory and what they apply to.

Basic Schedules of Reinforcement

Basic schedules of reinforcement are the structure of how we provide reinforcement to the organism to acquire the desired socially significant behavior. The most basic of these schedules is what we call continuous reinforcement. Continuous reinforcement is exactly that: continuously providing the reinforcement after every response. This schedule is mainly used to teach new behavior to the organism as it reinforces every instance of the desired behavior and is shown as FR_1 (fixed ratio 1). For example, let us say you want to teach Fonsi how to write the letter A. When Fonsi writes the letter A or a close approximation, we will reinforce that response. When Fonsi writes the letter A again, we will keep reinforcing until Fonsi writes the letter A continuously. After reinforcing every response, we will change the rate of providing reinforcement and move on to our next basic schedule, intermittent schedules of reinforcement. To understand intermittent schedules, we first need to define fixed and interval contingencies.

- Fixed: the exact amount of responses
- Variable: the average amount of responses.
- Ratio: it simply means a number
- Interval: it simply means time

When we put them together, they make up basic schedules of reinforcement

- Fixed Ratio (FR): in a fixed ratio, a response will be reinforced after a set or fixed amount of responses.
- Fixed Interval (FI): in a fixed interval, a response will be reinforced after a set or fixed amount of time.
- Variable Ratio (VR): in a variable ratio, a response will be reinforced after an average amount of responses.
- Variable Interval (VI): in a variable interval, a response will be reinforced after an average amount of time.

Intermittent schedules don't reinforce every response; instead, they use the above-defined contingencies to reinforce on different occasions. In an intermittent schedule, reinforcement is contingent on the number of responses emitted (ratio schedule), or on both time and response (interval schedule).

We will begin our explanation of these contingencies with fixed ratio and how this schedule works. Fixed ratio, often abbreviated to FR, reinforces a fixed number of responses chosen by the practitioner. For example, let's say that Fonsi finally learned how to write the letter A, and now we want to reinforce Fonsi for every three correct responses for writing the letter A because I am running out of candy. So now, every time Fonsi finishes writing the third letter A, he receives a reinforcement, and we call this fixed ratio three or FR3. Every basic schedule can be depicted in a graph explaining its process, which is precisely what **FIGURE 4.1** depicts for fixed ratio. In a fixed ratio schedule, the organism completes the response requirement without a pause. Once the reinforcement is delivered, the organism takes a pause before it begins to engage in the response again, let us explain with the same Fonsi example. Fonsi knows that he will receive a reward upon completion of the three writing of the letter A, so this will cause Fonsi to work very fast or a high rate of response. Once Fonsi receives his reward, he takes a break (post-reinforcement pause) because he knows when his next reward will be.

After the break, Fonsi again completes three letter A's and gets rewarded. This cycle repeats and is a determining factor of fixed ratio. Another example that we can relate to in the workplace is picking apples. Let us say that Fonsi need to pick 100 apples to receive a reinforcement, or FR100. After Fonsi completes this he receives money, he then takes a break before picking another 100 apples.

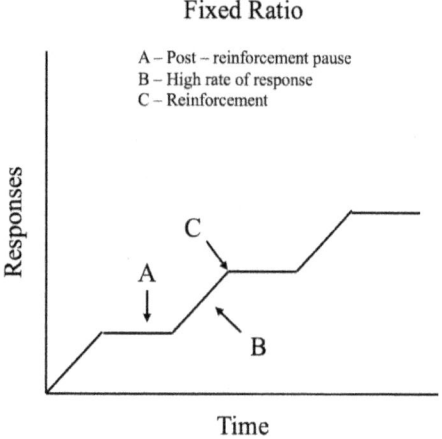

FIGURE 4.1 Fixed ratio depiction in graph form

THE BARE BONES OF ABA

Fixed ratio is less motivational as the organism knows when they will receive the reward so they can choose when to do the behavior and when not to. Another thing to keep in mind is that the longer or larger the requirement is to receive the reward, the longer the post-reinforcement pause will be.

Our next schedule stays in the realm of ratio, but we now have variability, this schedule is variable ratio or VR, or reinforcing a variable or average amount of responses, which in turn produces a reinforcer. This schedule is vastly different than fixed ratio, as the organism will always remain unknown of when they will receive the reward. Let's take Fonsi and his writing of letter A one more time as an example. If we want to reinforce Fonsi on a VR schedule, we need to choose an average number, but for the sake of simplicity, let's stay with the number three. Now we say that we will reward Fonsi for writing the letter A on a VR3 schedule, this will reward an average, (keyword) of three responses. When Fonsi starts writing the letter A, we can reward on the second response; we can then reward on the fourth, and after that, we can reward on the third. When we average this number, we get three, thus making this schedule a VR3.

This schedule is highly effective as it leaves the organism wandering when reinforcement will be delivered, allowing for a continuous rate of response without pause. This schedule does not have a post-reinforcement pause; it keeps you engaged until the next reward arrives. This schedule is exactly what slot machines in casinos use when rewarding a player. Think about a time you have been to the casino and become hooked on a slot machine, this is the result of variable ratio. In the slot machine, you never know when you will be reinforced, so you keep playing until you do. In **FIGURE 4.3,** we show how this schedule doesn't have a pause, achieving a steady, high rate of responding. We can calculate the average of the variable ratio with a simple equation shown in **FIGURE 4.2** using the example above.

$$\frac{\text{Number of Responses}}{\text{Times Rewarded}} = \text{VR} \qquad \frac{2+4+3}{3} = \text{VR}3$$

FIGURE 4.2 Math for Fonsi's example of VR3

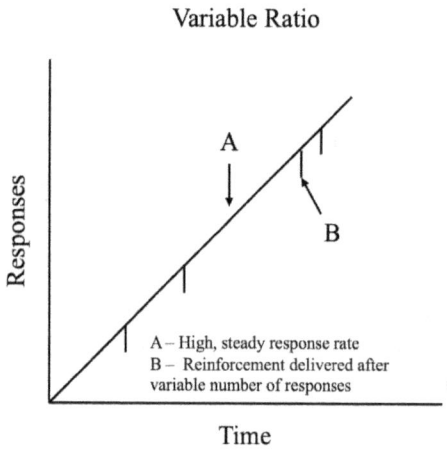

FIGURE 4.3 Variable ratio depicted on a graph

The two schedules we have discussed so far are focused on the number of responses and not time; now, we will discuss the interval schedules starting with fixed intervals. In a fixed interval schedule, we reinforce the first response after a set amount of time has elapsed. Now re-read the last sentence and find the keyword, exactly, the word FIRST. Even though this schedule is based on time, we still need to reinforce a response.

We reinforce the FIRST response after a fixed amount of time has passed. Let's bring Fonsi back and build an example so that we can understand. We will stay with the letter A example so that we can understand all schedules on a different scale. If we want to reinforce Fonsi writing the letter A on a fixed interval three min or FI$_3$ min, this means that we will provide Fonsi with a reward after three minutes have elapsed, and Fonsi writes the letter A. This schedule is actually difficult to use and is seen rarely in real life, but it is essential to understand it.

Just like fixed ratio, this schedule also has a post-reinforcement pause; however, it looks quite different in a graph, as depicted in **FIGURE 4.4**. This difference between the graphs is actually due to the time factor, which is called the fixed interval scallop or FI scallop. Fixed interval tends to have a slow to moderate response rate because it only focuses on the first response rather than the number of responses needed for reinforcement compared to FR. Now, towards the end of the scallop, the response rate increases because the reinforcer starts to become available. Let say that Fonsi is writing the letter A, Fonsi will know that after three minutes, he will receive a reward. If Fonsi starts to write the letter A since the beginning, there will be no reinforcement, so the response rate will slow down. However, towards the end of the interval, the reward is more accessible, and this causes Fonsi rate to increase.

[continued on next page]

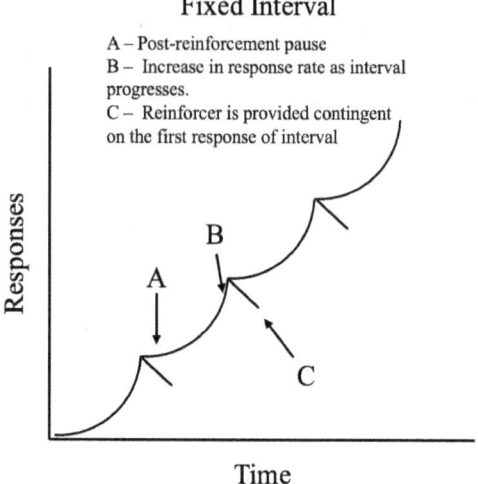

FIGURE 4.4 Demonstration of fixed interval scallop

The last of the four main basic schedules is variable interval, an exciting schedule with great potential. Variable schedule combines variables, the average amount of something, and interval, or time. So, variable interval is the average amount of time elapsed before a reinforcer is provided for the first response. This schedule is very similar to variable ratio in many ways, only thing that changes is from number to time-based. The formula used to calculate the average is the same, with variable interval giving you the average of time. Variable interval, just like variable ratio, doesn't have a post-reinforcement pause, keeping the response rate steady as the reward is unpredictable. Let us use Fonsi one more time to explain this concept with an example using variable interval three or VI3. Fonsi will be rewarded an average of three minutes or VI3 for writing the letter A. So in practice, Fonsi was rewarded after 2 minutes, he was then rewarded after 6 minutes, and he was lastly rewarded after 1 minute. When we use the formula depicted in **FIGURE 4.2**, we get the number three and, in this specific case, three minutes as the average, making this a VI3. The most observable difference between variable ratio and variable interval is the response rate. Even though the response rate is steady in variable intervals, it has a very slow to moderate response rate compared to the variable ratio.

In **FIGURE 4.5** we can see that the graph is very similar to that of variable ratio, and if a description weren't added, no difference would be noticed.

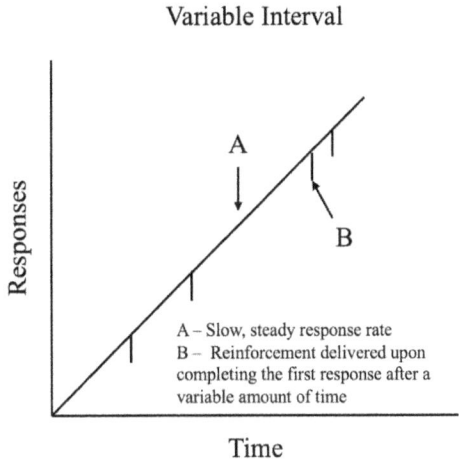

FIGURE 4.5 Depiction of variable interval in a graph from

Overall, variable interval schedules of reinforcement are characterized by unpredictable and varying time intervals between reinforcement deliveries. They promote steady and consistent rates of responding, are resistant to extinction, and are helpful in maintaining behaviors that should occur at consistent rates over time. These schedules have practical applications in various settings, including education, workplace management, and behavior modification programs.

Limited Hold Schedules of Reinforcement

Limited Hold (LH) schedules of reinforcement are a specific variation of reinforcement schedules used in behavioral science. In a limited hold schedule, a reinforcer is available for a specified period after a behavior has been performed. If the behavior occurs within this limited time frame, the reinforcement is delivered; otherwise, it is no longer available. Limited hold schedules have unique characteristics and are applied in specific contexts. One primary function of limited hold schedules is to introduce an element of urgency or temporal constraint into reinforcement. It sets a deadline for the behavior to occur after a specific cue or instruction, encouraging a prompt response.

For example, in a workplace setting, an employee may be told that they have a limited time to complete a task if they want to receive a bonus, which can motivate them to work efficiently and meet deadlines. Limited hold schedules can be particularly effective in time-sensitive situations where immediate or prompt behavior is desired. By specifying a limited window during which the behavior must occur to earn reinforcement, it helps us prioritize and allocate our efforts effectively. These schedules are often used in scenarios where rapid responses are crucial, such as emergency response training, competitive sports, or precision tasks.

Let us continue using Fonsi to teach the example of limited hold using his writing of the letter A. Now that we have learned the basic schedule let take it a step further and add a limited hold to one of those schedules. Let's say that Fonsi will be rewarded on a fixed interval of five minutes or as we know it FI5. Now we add a limited hold of ten seconds to this schedule, showing something like this, FI5 min LH 10 s. Breaking this down we say that after five minutes have elapsed, Fonsi has ten seconds to write the letter A (first response) to receive a reward. If within those ten seconds no response is evoked the reinforcer will no longer be available and Fonsi won't be rewarded.

Schedule Thinning

Schedule thinning focuses on the process of gradually reducing the frequency of reinforcement or making reinforcement less predictable. This process is essential when transitioning from intensive intervention to more naturalistic or less structured environments. Schedule thinning typically begins with a dense schedule of reinforcement, where the target behavior is reinforced frequently. As the individual becomes more proficient at the behavior or when it is generalized to different settings, the schedule is systematically adjusted to become less frequent. This reduction in reinforcement helps individuals maintain the behavior even when reinforcement becomes less consistent in their everyday environment.

The primary goal of schedule thinning is to promote behavior maintenance and generalization. By gradually decreasing reinforcement frequency, individuals learn to rely less on external reinforcement and become more self-reliant in engaging in the desired behavior. This is particularly crucial in the field, where the ultimate objective is to teach individuals functional and adaptive behaviors that can be independently applied across various real-life situations. It's important to note that schedule thinning should be carefully planned and implemented based on the individual's progress and needs. If done too quickly or abruptly, it can lead to a loss of previously acquired behaviors. We must consider factors such as the individual's skill level, the complexity of the behavior, and the specific environment when determining the appropriate schedule for thinning.

Now, how exactly do we implement schedule thinning in the field? Well, the answer is simple: we play around with the newly learned schedules until we have the desired result. There are two main ways to apply schedule thinning to a practical setting: one way is to increase the response ratio or interval, for example, going from FR_1 to FR_2, and so on. The other and less used way is to provide instructions; however, this way needs advanced verbal repertoire organisms. Let's stick with the most used one and grab Fonsi for an example. Let's say we thought Fonsi a new behavior, such as asking for a break. To teach this, we reinforced every instance of the behavior (FR_1 or continuous reinforcement) so that Fonsi could learn it, however, now that Fonsi knows how to ask for a break, there is no need to continue using FR_1. Now, we need to implement schedule thinning, so we reinforce the behavior every three responses now or every four responses. In **FIGURE 4.6**, there is a simple depiction of the process of schedule thinning. There is, however, a limit, and that's why this process must be monitored for ratio strain. Ratio strain is when, all of a sudden, we make a drastic change in the schedule of reinforcement without slowly increasing it. In other words, if Fonsi was on a FR_3 schedule, we can't suddenly go to an FR_{25} as this requirement is insanely large and will cause an abrupt stop of Fonsi's response rate.

FR1 → FR2 → FR3 → FR4

FI1 → FI2 → FI3 → FI4

VR1 → VR2 → VR3 → VR4

VI1 → VI2 → VI3 → VI4

FIGURE 4.6 Example of schedule thinning on all four basic schedules

Time Schedules

Time schedules have nothing special to them, in fact, the definition of it is precisely what it sounds like: a schedule of reinforcement based on time, independent or non-contingent from behavior. In other words, the reinforcement will be provided no matter what behavior the organism is engaging in. This reinforcement is called non-contingent reinforcement or NCR for short, which reinforces the behavior independently from the behavior. e targeted problem behavior occurs or not. This strategy is advantageous when dealing with behaviors that are maintained by attention, access to tangible items, or sensory stimulation. The primary goal of NCR is to eliminate or reduce the individual's motivation for engaging in problem behaviors by ensuring that the reinforcers they seek are readily available without the need to engage in those behaviors. For example, if the organism engages in tantrum behavior to gain attention, an NCR intervention might involve providing a consistent schedule of attention throughout the day, making it unnecessary for the child to tantrum for attention. NCR schedules are carefully designed to match the individual's typical patterns of behavior, ensuring that reinforcers are provided when the problem behavior is most likely to occur. Over time, as the individual realizes that the reinforcers are readily available without engaging in the problem behavior, the motivation for that behavior decreases. This leads to a reduction in the frequency and intensity of the problem behavior.

Non-contingent reinforcement can be separated into two different schedules: fixed time (FT) and variable time (VT). They differ from fixed intervals and variable intervals in that they don't reinforce the first response; instead, they reinforce after the time elapses. In fixed time, the organism is reinforced after a set or fixed amount of time elapses, independent of a response. In other words, the reinforcement will be given non-contingent on the behavior or response of the organism after an exact amount of time. Let's take our hypothetical main character, Fosni, and explain this concept. Fonsi has been engaging in a lot of attention-seeking behavior lately by screaming at his mom, and we want to reduce this. So, Fonsi's mom plans to provide attention to Fonsi every five minutes or FT_5, no matter what behavior he is engaging in. After every five minutes elapses, his mom will give him attention every time. Variable time (VT) is also independent of behavior; however, it does not provide reinforcement in a set amount of time; instead, it provides it in an average amount of time. This schedule is more realistic as it portrays the variability in reinforcement. If we want to reinforce Fonsi on a variable time five or VR_5, we can reinforce him after three minutes, then after seven minutes, and lastly after five minutes. If we implement these numbers into **FIGURE 4.2**, we can calculate it and see that the average is five, hence the VT_5. Overall, time schedules are beneficial for behaviors that aren't hurtful in nature and require consistent availability to diminish the behavior. Now, diminishing behavior leads us to our next subtopic, differential reinforcement.

Differential Reinforcement

Differential reinforcement is a foundational concept in the world of behavioral science. This concept was introduced adequately by Robert L. Burgess and published as "A Differential Association-Reinforcement Theory of Criminal Behavior" (1966), drawing upon earlier work by the American criminologist Edwin Sutherland and the American psychologist B.F. Skinner. However, Skinner did research this theory over 30 years earlier and provided many of the interventions used today. Differential reinforcement involves selectively reinforcing certain behaviors while withholding reinforcement for others (Extinction, covered later in the chapter). The goal of this technique is to increase the occurrence of desired behaviors and reduce or eliminate unwanted or problematic behaviors. There are many types of differential reinforcements, with the most famous and widely used being differential reinforcement of alternative behaviors or DRA.

We will cover a variety of differential reinforcement with examples to understand each one thoroughly. Let's get started with separating each differential reinforcement into categories. There are two categories. the first one being differential reinforcement based on responding rates, such as decreasing or increasing a desired behavior while lowering undesired. The second category is differential reinforcement based on the topography of behavior; this focuses entirely on a different behavior. Differential reinforcement holds two schedules of reinforcement in them, one schedule provides reinforcement, while the other schedule does not. Differential reinforcement places most behavior in extinction, which will be covered in depth, but very simply, it means withholding reinforcement. However, some of the behaviors, as we will see, can be placed under a rate of responding restriction or freedom. In **FIGURE**

4.8, a cheat sheet will be made for ease of remembering these concepts.

Category 1 based on responding rate

Differential reinforcement of high rates or DRH: in differential reinforcement of high rates, the goal is to increase the rate of responding. There are behaviors that we want to increase, and the way to do this is to increase the requirement until it is achieved. For example, we want to increase Fonsi's response rate in reading to 60 words per minute. If Fonsi reads fifty-nine words per minute, he will not get reinforced; however, when he reads sixty words per minute, he will receive reinforcement. This will cause Fonsi to increase his reading response rate in the future to receive reinforcement.

Differential reinforcement of low rates or DRL: in differential reinforcement of low response rate, we want to decrease a behavior without entirely eliminating it. This is helpful for behaviors that tend to be essential but are happening way to often. Let us say that Fonsi is brilliant, and he raises his hand too many times in class. We want to reduce this behavior but not wholly eliminate it, as raising a hand is necessary in school. We will slowly withhold reinforcement every time his hand rising surpasses the necessary amount until we have the desired response rate. Remember, DRL does not eliminate the behavior; instead, it lowers it.

Differential reinforcement of diminishing or DRD: in differential reinforcement of diminishing response rate, we have the same goal as DRL; however, for DRD, we have progressively decreasing criteria that we must meet to reduce the behavior. This differential reinforcement is a goal as we want to reduce the response from a baseline to an appropriate level. Let's say that Fonsi has a baseline tantrum behavior of twenty-one, when we implement DRD, we want to reduce this behavior to a more manageable level, so let's say Fifteen. Now, we slowly diminish the behavior to fifteen and then reset the new desired level.

Differential reinforcement of other behaviors or DRO: differential reinforcement of other behaviors is widely used in this category as it focuses on entirely diminishing and eliminating the behavior. When we implement DRO, we reinforce any other behavior but the target behavior while withholding the reinforcement for the maladaptive. Let us say that Fonsi engages in kicking behavior and is kicking other people nonstop. This is a behavior that we need to eliminate very fast, as it can be dangerous for Fonsi and those around him. When we implement DRO, we will place kicking behavior in extinction and reinforce any other behavior but kicking, even if the other behavior is as bad as kicking. This intervention can have its drawbacks and can be dangerous. Even though we eliminate the problem behavior, we could be reinforcing another problem behavior.

Category 2 based on topography

Differential reinforcement of alternative behaviors or DRA: differential reinforcement of alternative behavior is the single most used intervention in all of behavioral science. Almost every problem behavior an organism engages in is, in one way or another, placed under this intervention. When we have a problem behavior, the best way to eliminate it is to put it in extinction, however, in order for this to be successful, we need to find an alternative behavior to reinforce, this is precisely what DRA does. In the Fonsi example above, we have kicking as the problem behavior, if we wanted to place kicking in extinction, we could replace it with rocking the feet, a more manageable behavior. So, we would reinforce rocking the feet as an alternative and not reinforce kicking behavior.

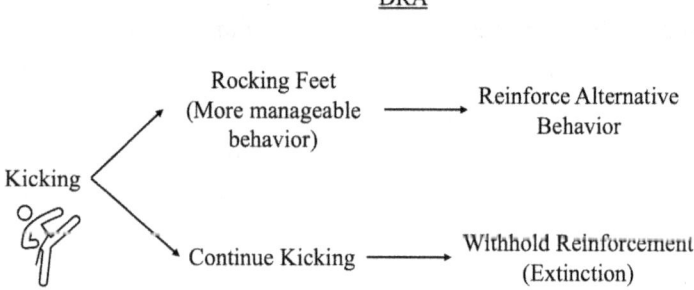

FIGURE 4.7 Example of Graphical DRA

Differential reinforcement of incompatible behavior or DRI: differential reinforcement of incompatible behavior is actually quite interesting, and relatively simple to implement. DRI identifies and reinforces a behavior that cannot be performed simultaneously with the problematic behavior. By reinforcing the incompatible behavior, the individual is less likely to engage in the undesirable behavior because they physically cannot do both actions at the same time. This technique is particularly useful when trying to replace an unwanted behavior with a more socially acceptable one. For example, let's say that Fonsi is in a line and is engaging in pushing other learners from behind. To implement DRI, we could simply disrupt the use of his hands for pushing by giving him books to carry, making the behavior of pushing incompatible with the behavior of carrying books. Another example is Fonsi engaging in hitting behavior towards peers to gain access to a preferred toy. To implement DRI, we can find an alternative behavior that is incompatible with hitting, such as the child handing a toy to a peer when they want to share or engage in play. The practitioner reinforces the child's behavior of handing the toy to their peer with praise, access to a preferred item, or social interaction.

[continued on next page]

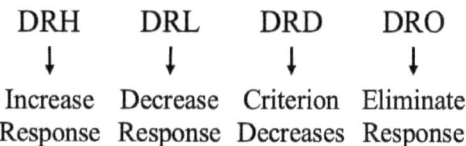

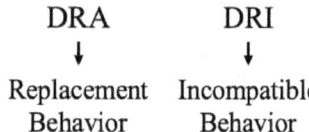

FIGURE 4.8 Differential reinforcement cheat sheet

Overall, differential reinforcement is an excellent tool in behavioral science that provides versatility and effectiveness across various environments. Remember, these are still schedules of reinforcement that have two basic schedules within them. A fantastic feat of differential reinforcement is its adaptability across various populations. Whether applied to children with autism, individuals with developmental disabilities, or students in a classroom, Differential reinforcement can be customized to suit a wide range of behavioral challenges and objectives. It provides a versatile toolkit for anyone in behavioral science to promote skill acquisition, social development, and behavior change effectively.

Progressive Schedules

Progressive schedules of reinforcement are another category in schedules of reinforcement used in behavioral science. These schedules are characterized by systematically changing the criteria for reinforcement independent of the organism's behavior. This is a critical word as progressive schedules resemble non-contingent reinforcement because they reinforce independently of behavior or response. Progressive schedules are designed to promote behavior change and skill acquisition by gradually increasing the requirements for reinforcement, ultimately leading to more independent and complex behaviors. One common type of progressive schedule is the progressive ratio or PR schedule. In a PR schedule, the organism must meet the requirement of increasing the number of responses or tasks to earn each subsequent reinforcement. For example, in a token system used to reinforce Fonsi's academic work, Fonsi may initially earn tokens for completing two math problems, then four, then six, and so on. This progressive increase in the response requirement challenges the individual to engage in more sustained and effortful behavior, promoting skill development and persistence. No matter if the behavior or response is present, the schedule will still progress, making this independent of behavior.

Another form of progressive schedule is the progressive interval (PI) schedule. In a PI schedule, the time interval between opportunities for reinforcement increases gradually. For instance, Fosni might initially earn a reinforcer every 30 seconds for staying on task, but as their behavior improves, the interval may be extended to 60 seconds, then 90 seconds, and so on. This progressive stretching of the time interval encourages the individual to maintain the target behavior for longer durations, leading to improved self-regulation and attention span. Progressive schedules are highly effective for shaping behavior because they provide a systematic way to challenge and expand an individual's skills and capabilities. These schedules are often used when transitioning from more intensive reinforcement schedules, such as continuous reinforcement, to more naturalistic settings where reinforcement occurs less frequently. By gradually increasing the demands for reinforcement, progressive schedules help the organisms become more independent, self-reliant, and capable of performing complex tasks and behaviors in various real-life situations.

Let us dive a little deeper into schedules of reinforcement and visualize PR and PI in **FIGURE 4.9** for a more comprehensive understanding. Progressive ratio and progressive interval have two variants: arithmetic progression and geometric progression. In arithmetic progression, we keep adding to the schedule a fixed number. For example, let's say that we started with PR20 in the arithmetic progression, we would add twenty each time we want to advance so that the following schedule would be PR40, then PR60, and so on until the schedule is entirely eliminated. In geometric progression, we take a different approach and add the schedule on top of each other. We can take the example above and start with PR20, instead of continuously adding twenty every time, we will add the schedule on top of each other. So the following schedule would be PR40, following this, the schedule would be PR80, and so on until we eliminate this schedule.

[continued on next page]

Arithmetic Progression
PR 20 → PR 40 → PR 60 → PR 80

Geometric Progression
PR 20 → PR 40 → PR 80 → PR 160

FIGURE 4.9 PR and PI visualization

Compound Schedules

This subtopic is very lengthy, and I recommend you don't skip this reading as it is another critical aspect of behavioral science. Compound schedules comprise many schedules, each with its own abbreviation. But before we get to the explanations of each, let's be general on what a compound schedule is. Compound schedules combine two or more basic schedules of reinforcement within the same behavioral intervention. These schedules are crucial in shaping behavior, promoting consistency, and addressing complex behaviors. One of the primary reasons compound schedules are essential is their ability to model and analyze real-world scenarios. In everyday life, behaviors are rarely maintained by a single type of reinforcement, if they were this field would be so much simpler. Compound schedules reflect this complexity by incorporating multiple reinforcement contingencies. For example, Fonsi might engage in a behavior because it leads to both attention from a mom, and access to a preferred toy. Compound schedules allow behavioral scientists to study and modify behaviors that involve multiple sources of reinforcement, leading to more effective and ecologically valid interventions.

Another critical aspect of compound schedules is that they

can help address behaviors that are resistant to change. Some behaviors are maintained by multiple reinforcing factors, making them challenging to modify using single-schedule interventions or, as we know them, basic schedules. Compound schedules allow us to design interventions that target the various sources of reinforcement simultaneously. By doing so, these schedules increase the likelihood of behavior change, even when behaviors are profoundly entrenched or complex. Furthermore, compound schedules offer valuable insights into the dynamics of behavior. They help practitioners analyze the relative influence of different reinforcement contingencies on a behavior, allowing for a more accurate assessment of the behavior's function. This enhanced understanding is critical for developing effective behavior intervention plans and tailoring interventions to the specific needs of the organisms. Now that we have an overview of compound schedules let us get very specific with each schedule.

Concurrent Schedule or CONC: concurrent schedules are elementary and determine many daily behaviors we engage in. In a concurrent schedule, an individual is presented with two or more simultaneously available reinforcement options or schedules. Each option is associated with a specific behavior or response, and the individual can choose which behavior to engage in to access the associated reinforcement. Concurrent schedules are handy for studying choice behavior and the allocation of responses between different alternatives. They help behavioral scientists understand how individuals make choices based on the relative rates and magnitudes of reinforcement available, shedding light on decision-making processes and preferences based on the environment acting upon the organism rather than a mental construct. When we simplify this schedule, it just means that we are presenting a simultaneous option independent of each other in which the organism will make a choice based on reinforcement density, this schedule is used in preference assessment, which we will discuss later in the book.

This schedule is prone to the matching law, which simply says that responses are allocated proportionally to reinforcement density. Psychologist Richard Herrnstein first proposed this, suggesting that individuals distribute their behavior among different response options in a way that matches the relative rates. In other words, the matching law suggests that individuals distribute their behavior among different choices in such a way that the rate of responding for each option corresponds to the rate of reinforcement obtained from that option. If the reinforcement is of high value, more responses can be acquired, on the other hand, if the reinforcement is of less value, the fewer responses we will receive.

We will now provide an example of a concurrent schedule with Fonsi and his friend Shawn. Imagine Fonsi and Shawn are in a classroom setting where a teacher is implementing a concurrent schedule for the two of them to promote academic engagement. In this scenario, the teacher provides two options for academic tasks during a designated work period: solving math problems or reading a book. Both students have a choice to make between these two options. For Fonsi, when he chooses to solve math problems (Option A), he earns tokens, which can later be exchanged for his favorite snack. On the other hand, if he selects the reading task (Option B), he earns tokens that can be exchanged for a short break to do whatever he desires. For Shawn, the reinforcement schedule is slightly different. When he chooses to solve math problems (Option A), he earns tokens that can be exchanged for extra computer time, one of his favorite activities. If he opts for reading (Option B), he receives tokens redeemable for a few minutes of playing with a preferred toy.

In this concurrent schedule, both Fonsi and Shawn are presented with two simultaneous options (Option A and Option B). They can choose between math problems and reading, and their choices determine the type of reinforcement they receive. The matching law predicts that each student will allocate their responses to each option in a way that matches the proportion of reinforcement they find most valuable, thus influencing their academic engagement based on their individual preferences. In **FIGURE 4.10,** we have a small illustration of what a concurrent schedule looks like.

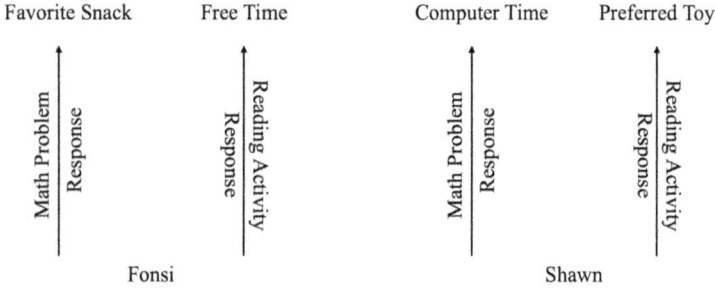

FIGURE 4.10 CONC example of Fonsi and Shawn

Multiple Schedules or MULT: multiple schedules of reinforcement are a little bit more complicated than concurrent schedules. They involve alternating between two or more distinct schedules of reinforcement within a single session, often signaled by specific cues or discriminative stimuli (SD). For example, Fosni might experience reinforcement according to a fixed-ratio (FR) schedule when a red light is on and a fixed-interval (FI) schedule when a green light is on. Multiple schedules allow behavioral scientists to study how different environmental cues influence behavior and the ability to discriminate between reinforcement schedules. They are valuable for understanding how individuals adapt their behavior based on environmental cues and the consequences associated with each schedule. Multiple schedules are prevalent around us and happen across settings throughout the day. Let's expand to another example with Fosni and simplify this concept even further.

Imagine a scenario in a classroom setting where a teacher is using multiple schedules of reinforcement to encourage Fosni's on-task behavior during two different subjects: Math and English. The teacher has set up distinct schedules for each subject, signaled by the color of a visual cue card. When the teacher displays a red card, it signifies the Math subject. During Math time, Fosni is reinforced on a fixed-interval (FI) schedule. He receives a sticker every 5 minutes of sustained on-task behavior, which he can later exchange for extra free time at the end of the day. When the teacher displays a green card, it indicates the English subject. During English time, Fonsi is reinforced on a variable interval (VI) schedule. He receives a sticker at varying, unpredictable intervals of on-task behavior. The stickers can be traded for small classroom privileges, such as choosing a story to be read aloud. In this scenario, the teacher switches between the red and green cards to signal changes in the subject and corresponding reinforcement schedules.

The use of multiple schedules allows the students to discriminate between Math and English lessons and adjust their on-task behavior based on the different reinforcement contingencies. This strategy helps students become more adaptable in their behavior as they learn to respond effectively to varying schedules of reinforcement across different classroom activities. Let us say, however, that Math is being learned in one classroom and English in the other classroom; this can cause Fonsi to behave differently during these two classes, this phenomenon is called behavior contrast. Feel free to return to Chapter 1, SSG Learning Theory, where there is an example of behavior contrast.

Chained Schedule or CHAIN: now we are getting to a fun schedule of reinforcement used almost every day in the field. Chained schedules involve breaking down a complex behavior into a sequence of smaller, linked behaviors, each reinforced individually. The reinforcement for one behavior serves as a cue or motivator for the subsequent behavior in the chain. For example, in teaching our learner, Fonsi, to brush his teeth independently, the first step might be to pick up the toothbrush, followed by applying toothpaste, brushing teeth, and rinsing the mouth. Each of these steps is reinforced as it occurs, and the completion of one step acts as a prompt for the next. Chained schedules are beneficial for teaching multi-step tasks and promoting the development of more complex skills, as they ensure that each component of the behavior is reinforced, reinforcing the entire sequence in the end. Remember this schedule must happen successively and in a specific order, another example of this can be washing hands. Let's say we also want Fonsi to wash his hands; the first step is to break down washing hands into smaller, more attainable steps, this is a process that we call task analysis. After we complete the task analysis, breaking down the task into smaller steps, we begin teaching, making sure that the completion of the first schedule serves as the discriminative stimulus (SD) for the following schedule as it was the last to produce reinforcement. So it would look something like this: turning on the water, water runs out of the tap (SD), which signals the following schedule to put hands under water.

There are three main chained schedules that almost every behavior scientist knows, and these are Forward chaining, Backward chaining, and Total task chaining. Forward chaining is a method of task analysis and skill acquisition where complex behaviors or tasks are broken down into individual steps, and instruction begins with the first step in the sequence. As the learner masters each step, they progress to the next step until they have acquired the entire skill or behavior. Let's go back to Fonsi washing hands, in forward chaining, we teach the first step, which is then followed by Fonsi doing the same step. After Fonsi masters this step, we teach the second step, and now Fonsi has to complete step 1 and step 2. This process repeats itself until the entire skill is mastered and another skill can begin. In Backward chaining, instruction begins with the last step in the sequence. As the learner progresses through the steps, they work backward until they can independently complete the entire skill or behavior. Again, we will use Fonsi's washing hands to explain backward chaining. To teach this, we start by modeling to Fonsi the last step of the chain, and then we let Fonsi do it himself. After it is mastered, we teach the second to last step and allow Fonsi to do the last step and this step combined. This is also done until all the steps are done. The last is total task chaining, in which the learner, in this case Fonsi, is guided through the entire sequence of steps in a single teaching session. In total task chaining, the emphasis is on teaching the entire skill from start to finish during each instructional session.

Mixed Schedule or MIX: mixed schedule of reinforcement is identical to multiple schedule of reinforcement; however, in mixed schedule, we do not have a discriminative stimulus. The main difference between mixed schedules and multiple schedules lies in how reinforcement schedules are presented. Mixed schedules combine different schedules within a single session, creating variability in reinforcement. Multiple schedules present distinct schedules in separate phases or periods, allowing for assessing discrimination skills and observing behavior under different reinforcement conditions. Since mixed schedule has no SD, it possesses the element of surprise, which can translate to a random order of reinforcement, producing a high rate of response. In the example used in multiple schedules of red card and green card, we knew what each card meant, and they serve as the SD. If we now take the red and green cards away, there is no SD; however, there will still be reinforcement, but the organism won't know in what order, making it unpredictable and providing that high response rate.

Tandem Schedule or TAND: tandem schedules are identical to chained schedule; however, they do not have a specific order in which the steps are completed it just focuses on the final goal. Tandem schedules involve the sequential presentation of different reinforcement contingencies within a single behavior, while chained schedules involve breaking down a complex behavior into discrete steps, each associated with its own reinforcement contingency. Tandem schedules are more focused on studying the interaction between contingencies, whereas chained schedules are used for teaching and shaping complex behaviors through a sequence of individual steps. A great example and the easiest way to explain tandem schedules is making soup. When we make soup, we gather ingredients. these ingredients don't change, but they don't have

THE BARE BONES OF ABA

a specific order in which they need to go in. No matter how you put in the ingredients, you will still make the same soup.

Alternative Schedule or ALT: alternative schedule is straightforward and does not complicate itself. This schedule basically states that once the ratio or interval requirement has been fulfilled, the reinforcer will be delivered. In other words, let's say that we want to place Fonsi under an alternative schedule, it can look something like this: ALT FR4 FI 10s. This states that in order for Fonsi to receive reinforcement, he must either complete eight responses or one response after ten seconds have elapsed. In alternative schedule, the organism either completes one or the other but not both.

Conjunctive Schedule or CONJ: in a conjunctive schedule, reinforcement is delivered upon completing both requirements. In alternative schedule, either one or the other had to be completed, in this schedule, both requirements must be met in order to receive reinforcement. Just like in alternative schedule, upon the completion of both ratio and interval, a reinforcer will be delivered. If we place Fonsi under this schedule, it would look like this: CONJ FR 5 FI 10s. So if Fonsi emits five responses and ten seconds have elapsed, he will receive his reinforcement.

Classification of Consequence

Schedules of reinforcement can definitely be a heavy topic to go over, and it might be, at times, daunting, but they are essential to the field of behavioral science. Now we move on to an enjoyable and exciting topic which establishes the classification of consequences. We have established some consequences in previous chapters to be reinforcement and punishment; however, it gets a little more complex than that. These consequences can be classified based on their evolutionary history and their learned or conditioned history. Let's recap on stimulus-stimulus pairing and remember how this is done. The most effective way to pair a stimulus that has no effect on behavior or, as we already know from Chapter Two, a neutral stimulus with a reinforcer is to present the neutral stimulus immediately before presenting the reinforcer and continue until the termination of the reinforcement. Remember, anything in your environment, whether outside or within your skin, interacts with you, upon you acting on this interaction, there will always be a consequence or something reinforcing or punishing that behavior, response or action.

Unconditioned Reinforcement

Let us go back to the definition of unconditioned and understand what unconditioned reinforcers are. Unconditioned means unlearned or born with, when paired with reinforcement, we are talking about things we need since birth. Unconditioned reinforcers are primary reinforcers, these reinforcers are inherently reinforcing, meaning they have a naturally rewarding or satisfying quality without needing prior learning or conditioning. Unconditioned reinforcers are essential because they serve as the foundation upon which many learned behaviors and conditioning processes are built. One typical example of an unconditioned reinforcer is food. Food is an unconditioned reinforcer because it inherently satisfies a basic biological need for nourishment. When an organism is hungry, the consumption of food is naturally reinforcing, leading to feelings of satisfaction and a reduction in hunger.

Similarly, water serves as another unconditioned reinforcer because it quenches thirst, satisfying the body's hydration needs. Unconditioned reinforcers are not limited to physiological needs. Physical comfort, such as warmth on a cold day, can be inherently reinforcing. Additionally, sensory experiences like pleasant smells, soothing sounds, tactile sensations, and sexual stimulation can also serve as unconditioned reinforcers when they produce feelings of pleasure or relief. Unconditioned reinforcement does have a minor drawback: it depends on motivation, more explicitly establishing operations, which we will discuss in Chapter Five. This basically means that the organism must want the reinforcer for it to have a reinforcing effect. If you just ate dinner, and someone offers you another plate of food to get them a water bottle in exchange, you don't need that food; it doesn't have a reinforcing effect. However, if you haven't eaten, this makes the food highly valuable and will cause you to get that water bottle for that plate of food.

Conditioned Reinforcement

Unlike unconditioned reinforcers, which are inherently rewarding, conditioned reinforcers are secondary and learned reinforcers that gain their reinforcing properties through association with other reinforcers over time (Stimulus-Stimulus pairing). These learned reinforcers play a crucial role in shaping and maintaining a wide range of behaviors. One common example of a conditioned reinforcer is money (this is actually a generalized conditioned reinforcer, but it will be discussed later). Money, in itself, has no inherent value or direct utility. However, through learning and social conditioning, individuals come to associate money with the ability to obtain a wide range of primary reinforcers, such as food, clothing, and entertainment. As a result, money becomes a powerful conditioned reinforcer that can motivate various behaviors, such as working, earning an income, and making purchases. Another example of a conditioned reinforcer is praise or verbal approval. For many organisms, animal and human, positive verbal feedback becomes a conditioned reinforcer because it is often associated with the delivery of unconditioned reinforcers, such as attention, affection, or tangible rewards. Over time, organisms learn that engaging in certain behaviors, such as completing a task or demonstrating good behavior, can lead to receiving praise and positive feedback, making these behaviors more likely to occur. Conditioned reinforcers are victims of motivation as well, if the organism doesn't not want it, the reinforcer will have no effect on behavior.

Generalized Conditioned Reinforcement

These reinforcers are unique because they are not tied to specific, immediate, or tangible rewards but instead have broader applicability and can reinforce a wide range of behaviors. Generalized conditioned reinforcers are crucial in shaping complex human behavior and promoting adaptive functioning. One of the most common examples of a generalized conditioned reinforcer is money, as mentioned in the previous subtopic. Money serves as a universal medium of exchange that can be exchanged for a vast array of primary reinforcers, such as food, shelter, entertainment, and more. People learn the value of money through continuous stimulus-stimulus paring over time, making it a powerful generalized conditioned reinforcer. **FIGURE 4.11** has a mini example of what money can acquire as reinforcers. The versatility of money allows it to motivate diverse behaviors, from working and saving to spending and investing. Money provides access to multiple reinforcers and doesn't prioritize any particular reinforcer above any other. Another example of a generalized conditioned reinforcer is praise and social approval. Verbal praise, compliments, and positive feedback are often used as generalized conditioned reinforcers because they can reinforce a wide range of behaviors across various contexts. People seek praise and approval from others because they have learned that these forms of social reinforcement lead to positive outcomes, such as social acceptance, friendship, and cooperation. Token systems are a practical application of generalized conditioned reinforcers. In educational and therapeutic settings, token economies use tokens (conditioned reinforcers) to reinforce appropriate behaviors. Individuals can exchange tokens for various preferred items or activities, making tokens a generalized conditioned reinforcer that bridges the gap between immediate behavior and delayed reinforcement. Generalized Conditioned Reinforcers do not fall victim to motivation as there will always be one reinforcer that works; thus, motivation does not play a role.

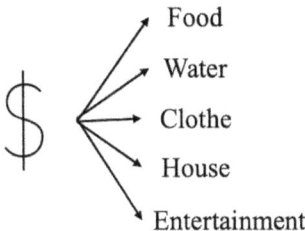

FIGURE 4.11 This shows that money as a GCR can acquire multiple reinforcers.

Unconditioned Punishment

Unconditioned punishers, also known as primary punishers, are stimuli or events that inherently produce aversive or unpleasant consequences without the need for prior learning or conditioning. These punishing stimuli are biologically or inherently aversive to most organisms, and their presentation typically leads to a reduction in the likelihood of the behavior that precedes them. One typical example of an unconditioned punisher is physical pain. Painful stimuli, such as extreme heat, cold, or physical injury, are inherently aversive to humans and animals. Experiencing pain naturally discourages certain behaviors as individuals strive to avoid or escape from painful situations. The avoidance of physical harm is an evolutionary adaptation that enhances survival. Another example of an unconditioned punisher is intense loud noise. Sudden and intense noises, such as a loud explosion or thunderclap, can startle and frighten organisms, as we have seen our dogs hide under the couch every time they hear thunder, leading to a decrease in ongoing behaviors. The startle response is an unconditioned reaction that serves as a protective mechanism against potential threats. Unconditioned punishers can be used for behavior modification when necessary to decrease problematic or dangerous behaviors. For instance, the presentation of loud noises can be used to deter organisms from engaging in unsafe behaviors, such as running into a busy street. By identifying and appropriately applying unconditioned punishers, behavior scientists can help individuals learn to avoid or reduce behaviors that may harm themselves or others. However, we must remember from Chapter Three that when implementing punishment procedures on humans, there are ethical considerations we must look at, and we must avoid punishment procedures unless absolutely necessary.

Conditioned Punishment

Conditioned punishers, also known as secondary or learned punishers, are stimuli or events that acquire their punishing properties through association with other aversive stimuli or experiences. Unlike unconditioned punishers, which inherently produce aversive consequences, conditioned punishers become punishing after they have been paired with an aversive event or have been associated with the reduction or removal of a reinforcer (Stimulus-Stimulus Paring). These learned punishers play a significant role in behavioral science by influencing behavior through learned associations. One common example of a conditioned punisher is a reprimand or verbal scolding (many parents do this on a daily basis). When a person is repeatedly scolded or reprimanded following the occurrence of a specific behavior, the verbal reprimand becomes associated with the aversive experience of criticism or disapproval. As a result, the reprimand itself becomes a conditioned punisher capable of suppressing the behavior it follows. Time-out is another example, which we discussed earlier In the book, of a conditioned punisher. When a child is placed in time-out following disruptive or undesirable behavior, the removal of access to preferred activities and social attention serves as an aversive consequence. Over time, the threat of time-out can become a conditioned punisher, and the mere mention of a time-out can deter the child from engaging in problematic behaviors. The use of conditioned punishers can be effective in reducing behaviors that may pose risks or disrupt social interactions. However, it is essential to apply them appropriately and ethically, ensuring that they are paired with clear, consistent contingencies and that alternative, more desirable behaviors are actively taught and reinforced, as we have discussed, whenever punishment contingencies are implemented, there must be a fade out plan to deter from the punishment.

Generalized Conditioned Punishment

Generalized conditioned punishers are punishers that have been paired with many unconditioned and conditioned punishers. What sets them apart from conditioned punishers is their capacity to suppress a wide range of behaviors, even those unrelated to the original aversive event. One common example of a generalized conditioned punisher is a disapproving facial expression or gesture, such as shaking one's head or frowning. These nonverbal cues become associated with social disapproval and can act as a generalized conditioned punisher. When an organism exhibits behavior that elicits these disapproving signals, the behavior is more likely to decrease, even if it occurs in different situations or with different people. Another example of a generalized conditioned punisher is the loss of privileges or access to preferred activities. When a child experiences the loss of a privilege following problem behavior in one context, they may become more sensitive to potential loss of privileges in other settings as well. This sensitivity can result from the generalization of the conditioned punisher to different environments and behaviors.

Generalized conditioned punishers are especially valuable in behavior management because they can promote consistent behavior change across diverse situations. Behavior scientists can effectively discourage inappropriate behaviors and encourage more adaptive ones by teaching organisms to recognize and respond to these generalized cues or consequences. However, it is crucial to ensure that these aversive stimuli or consequences are applied ethically and in a supportive context, focusing on positive behavior support and teaching alternative, desirable behaviors. Remember, there must be a fade-out plan to deter from the punishment.

Socially Mediated Consequence

Socially mediated consequences, as we can deduct from the subtopic title, are consequences delivered by someone else or produced directly by the behavior. Socially mediated consequences fall in the paradigm of positive and negative reinforcement and positive and negative punishment, however, in this classification, it is delivered by someone else. Let's provide some examples to understand this concept further. Whenever there are two organisms, and one is delivering the consequence to the other, we consider this socially mediated. In **FIGURE 4.12,** we will have a small depiction of the differentiation between Socially mediated and Automatically mediated consequences. These classifications have functions of behavior that fall into them, but we won't cover functions of behavior in this chapter. Some examples of socially mediated consequences include:

- Positive Reinforcement: if Fonsi engages in appropriate behavior in class, the teacher (another organism, not Fonsi) will now deliver a token as reinforcement.
- Negative Reinforcement: If the teacher gives Fonsi work, Fonsi starts to cry, the teacher removes the aversive stimulus, and Fonsi stops crying. The teacher removing stimulus as a consequence is socially mediated.
- Positive Punishment: an example of positive punishment that is socially mediated is actually quite simple, and all of us have experienced it in the past. For this example, we will use Fonsi instead; think of yourself when you were a kid and did something wrong, your mom would come and reprimand you. After she reprimanded you, that

behavior would decrease in the future. However, that consequence wasn't self-provided; instead, it was given by your mother and thus socially mediated.

- Negative Punishment: Using yourself once more as an example, what was another punishment you would receive for doing something wrong? A time-out comes to mind, given by your mom or dad. This is also socially mediated as your caregiver gives you the time out.

Automatic Consequence

Unlike socially mediated consequences, which involve the influence of social interactions, automatic consequences are not dependent on the actions or feedback of others. Instead, they are intrinsic to the behavior itself and can significantly impact an individual's actions. One common example of an automatic mediated consequence is sensory stimulation. Some behaviors inherently produce sensory experiences that individuals find pleasurable or self-reinforcing. For instance, Fonsi engages in repetitive hand-flapping behavior because the sensory feedback of the movement is intrinsically reinforcing, creating a calming or enjoyable effect. Automatic consequences can also include the relief of discomfort or pain. Behaviors that alleviate physical discomfort, such as scratching an itch, can be automatically reinforced because the behavior itself reduces discomfort. Similarly, behaviors like nail-biting or thumb-sucking may persist because they provide self-soothing effects. In automatic consequences, there is no social mediation, and can only be produced by oneself. There is also a difference between self-reinforcement and automatic reinforcement, which we must discuss as these terms cannot be used interchangeably. In automatic reinforcement, the behavior does not require planning as the behavior itself produces the reinforcement, and the organism isn't aware of it. An example of this is again scratching to remove an itch. In self-reinforcement, however, the organism does plan its reinforcer, arranging its own reinforcement contingent on the behavior. This makes the organism aware that they are engaging in the behavior. Automatic punishment is very simple, and it will decrease future behavior for oneself due to the consequences produced by oneself. Some examples of positive punishment that is automatically mediated would be burning your fingers because you touched the stovetop. An example of negative punishment that is automatically mediated would be a cracked phone screen as a result of you dropping it.

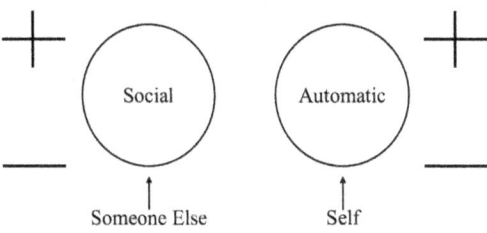

FIGURE 4.12 Social and Automatic Consequence Breakdown

Extinction

This is a concept to get excited about, extinction or EXT has been mentioned since the beginning of the book, and no proper definition and explanation has been provided. Extinction involves the deliberate withholding of reinforcement previously provided for a specific behavior. The goal of extinction is to reduce or eliminate the target behavior by ensuring that it no longer produces the desired outcome. Extinction is based on the principle that behaviors that are not reinforced tend to decrease in frequency over time. We need to be very careful when understanding extinction and not getting it confused with the removal of reinforcement. In extinction, we do not under any circumstances remove reinforcement; we simply withhold (discontinue) this reinforcement. There are two primary types of extinction based on the principles of respondent conditioning and operant conditioning discussed earlier in the book; we call these respondent extinction and operant extinction.

Respondent Extinction: Unlike operant behaviors, which are under the control of their consequences, respondent behaviors are reflexive or involuntary responses to stimuli in the environment. Respondent extinction involves the reduction or elimination of these reflexive behaviors by discontinuing the presentation of the eliciting stimulus; we can also call this unpairing. In order for this to occur, we need to repeatedly present the conditioned stimulus (CS) without the unconditioned stimulus (US) until the conditioned stimulus (CS) can no longer elicit the conditioned response (CR). One common example of respondent extinction is the reduction of the startle response to loud noises. When a loud noise initially occurs, an organism may exhibit a startle response, including physiological changes like increased heart rate and muscle tension, but we remember we don't really get into the psychological aspect. However, with repeated exposure to the same loud noise without any adverse consequences, the startle response tends to diminish or extinguish. In this case, the loud noise serves as the eliciting stimulus and the absence of a negative outcome results in the reduction of the reflexive response. Respondent extinction is not based on consequence, which makes this concept relatively easy to understand.

Operant Extinction: as we mentioned, operant extinction simply refers to the process of reducing or eliminating a previously reinforced behavior by discontinuing the delivery of the reinforcer that maintained it. In operant conditioning, behaviors are influenced by their consequences, and when the consequences for behavior are consistently withheld, that behavior tends to decrease in frequency over time. An example of operant extinction is ignoring attention-seeking behavior in children. If a child engages in tantrums or disruptive behaviors to gain attention from the parents, using operant extinction would involve withholding attention when those behaviors occur. Over time, as the child realizes that their tantrums no longer lead to the desired attention, the behavior is expected to decrease, as it is no longer reinforced. This tends to be the bread and butter of behavioral science and is used in almost every way possible. Operant extinction can be a challenging process, as individuals may initially respond with an extinction burst (discussed further ahead), where the behavior temporarily increases in intensity or frequency in an attempt to obtain the previously effective reinforcer. It's crucial for those involved to remain consistent and not provide reinforcement during this phase, as giving in to the behavior can inadvertently reinforce it and make it more persistent. One key factor to keep in mind is that the behavior that we want to place under extinction must have been reinforced by the reinforcer we will withhold in order for extinction to work. While operant extinction is a valuable tool for reducing unwanted behaviors, it should consistently be implemented ethically and in conjunction with alternative behavior strategies. Behavior scientists conduct functional behavior assessments to understand the function of the target behavior and develop comprehensive intervention plans that may include extinction as one component. The goal is not just to decrease problem behaviors but also to teach and reinforce more appropriate alternatives, ultimately improving an individual's overall functioning and quality of life. However, extinction should not be used with extreme behaviors such as self-injurious behaviors, property destruction, and physical aggression, as during the extinction burst phase, these behaviors escalate and can cause danger to the organism or those around them.

One last thing to mention is the difference between planned ignoring (an intervention in ABA) and extinction. In extinction, we withhold the reinforcement until the behavior is eliminated; however, in planned ignoring, social reinforcers such as verbal exchanges are withdrawn for a brief period of time, contingent on behavior, which makes this intervention negative punishment or removal of a stimulus that decreases the future occurrence of the behavior.

Misconception of Extinction

There are several misconceptions regarding extinction, and as a practicing scientist in the field, I have fallen victim to these misconceptions. Even though extinction is the primary source of behavior reduction, it is not the only intervention that causes behavior reduction. One example of this is the punishment contingencies, which reduce the future frequency of this behavior occurring. Another misconception is that response blocking falls into the realm of extinction, but response block is its own intervention. Response block physically prevents the behavior from occurring, while in extinction, the behavior can still occur, but it will not produce the reinforcement as it is being withheld. The last misconception is that non-contingent reinforcement (NCR) is extinction. In NCR, we create an abolishing operation (part of motivating operations) by delivering the reinforcer on a time-based schedule until the learner is satiated. As we can clearly see, this is incredibly different than extinction, as extinction withholds the reinforcement. Extinction is a helpful intervention, but it is unsuitable for every behavior or situation. It should be used within a comprehensive behavior intervention plan that considers the function of the behavior, alternative behaviors to teach, and ethical considerations. In some cases, other strategies, such as differential reinforcement, may be more appropriate.

Effects of Extinction

We have fully deciphered extinction through most of its nooks and crannies, and we have explained the central concept of extinction and what happens during this process. Let us now take it a step further and graphically (SSG Learning Theory) see how extinction would look in a graph. In **FIGURE 4.13,** we will see how extinction presents itself in the real world and what to expect when implementing extinction.

[continued on next page]

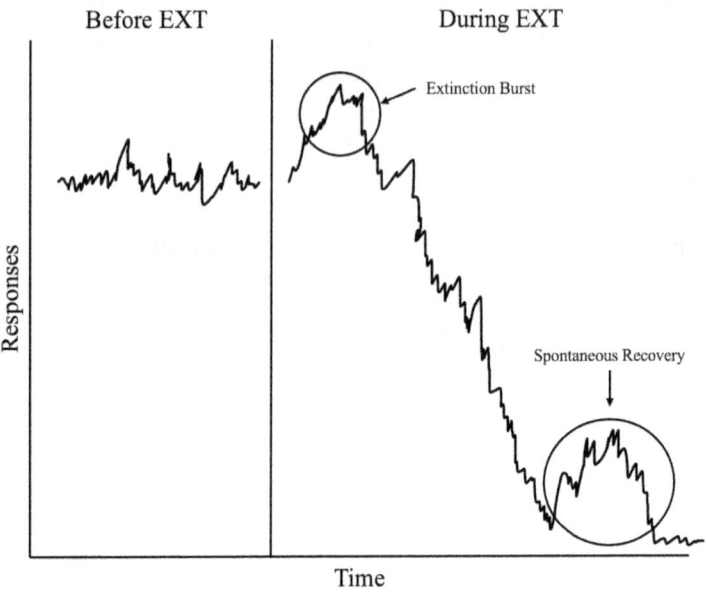

FIGURE 4.13 Basic depiction of extinction in graph form

Looking at this graph, we can see that the behavior in the baseline phase maintains a steady rate of response. Upon the implementation of extinction, we can see an instant increase in the responses as a result of withholding the reinforcement. In behavioral science, we refer to this instant increase as an extinction burst or an increase in frequency of behavior. Let's think about it for a minute: Fonsi is used to getting his way when he tantrums, he is reinforced constantly after he tantrums by getting what he wants, whether it be tangible or attention. If all of a sudden, we withhold or discontinue the reinforcement, Fonsi's tantrum will increase, trying to get the reinforcement back. Upon Fonsi not receiving this reinforcement, no matter how high the extinction burst gets, the behavioral responses will slowly start to decline at a steady rate until they reach zero or a desired level of responses. There is another phenomenon that occurs when extinction reaches zero or almost zero, and we call it spontaneous recovery. Spontaneous recovery is fascinating as the behavior reappears after it is reduced to zero, even though it doesn't produce the desired reinforcement. This phenomenon tends to be very short and limited as it tends to go away in a relatively fast fashion. I like to call spontaneous recovery a more familiar term, "testing the waters," especially since that's precisely what it is. For those of you at home who have children, think of a time when your child engaged in a behavior he/she hadn't engaged in for a long time. In your child's subconscious, he/she is thinking, "hhhhhhhmmmmm, I haven't done this in a while, let's see if it still provides the same reinforcement." Spontaneous recovery serves as a reminder of the importance of maintaining consistency in behavior interventions. Even when a behavior appears to have been successfully reduced through extinction, it is crucial to continue monitoring and managing the behavior to prevent its resurgence. It can be discouraging to think that an undesired behavior has reappeared, next time it happens, just remember spontaneous recovery.

Resistance to Extinction

Resistance to extinction is something all behavior scientists want to avoid, as it can make behavior modification extremely hard. Resistance to extinction refers to the phenomenon where a behavior persists or resists decreasing in frequency when reinforcement is withheld. This resistance occurs because the behavior has been previously reinforced intermittently, meaning that it was not consistently followed by reinforcement.

We have discussed intermittent schedules of reinforcement

and understand how they work, due to this schedule not reinforcing every instance of the behavior like continuous reinforcement, it becomes challenging to place under extinction. Remember, in this schedule, the organism is already used to waiting for the reinforcement, so withholding the reinforcement won't have the desired effect. As a result, individuals may continue to engage in the behavior even when it no longer results in the desired outcome. Resistance to extinction has important implications for behavior modification and understanding why certain behaviors can be challenging to eliminate. One key factor contributing to resistance to extinction is the history of intermittent reinforcement. When behavior has been sporadically reinforced in the past, individuals learn that sometimes it leads to reinforcement, and they are more likely to persist in engaging in the behavior, hoping for a reward. This makes the behavior more resistant to extinction because individuals have learned that persistence can pay off, these are some of the most complex behaviors to place under extinction as they have years of reinforcement history behind them.

Another factor influencing resistance to extinction is the type and schedule of reinforcement. Behaviors that have been reinforced using variable or intermittent schedules, where reinforcement is not delivered every time the behavior occurs, tend to be more resistant to extinction compared to behaviors reinforced on a continuous schedule. This is because individuals have learned that the behavior occasionally results in reinforcement, making them more persistent in trying to obtain it. Resistance to extinction can pose challenges in behavior modification efforts. When trying to reduce unwanted behaviors, it is essential to be aware of this phenomenon and plan interventions accordingly. In **FIGURE 4.14**, we have a little cheat sheet depicting what we mean by what is more complicated to extinct and how we can determine if extinction is the appropriate intervention to use. Two more critical components must be discussed: motivation and response effort. Motivation falls under motivation operation, which we will discuss, but the gist of it for the sake of this subtopic is that if the organism has high motivation or EO, the behavior will resist extinction. The last component is the response effort, which I personally like to call "the lazy rule" because the more energy it takes to elicit a response, the easier it will be to place under extinction. Think about it: If I tell you that you will receive one thousand dollars, but you either have to scream for one hour straight or sit quietly and wait one hour, which one would you choose? I personally would choose to sit for one hour as it requires the least amount of effort, and I receive the same reinforcement. This places screaming under extinction and reduces this behavior instantly, it also used DRA as it provided an alternative behavior.

Higher Resistance to Extinction ↓   Lower Resistance to Extinction ↓

Intermittent Schedules > Continuous Reinforcement

Variable Schedule > Fixed Schedule

Higher Motivation > Lower Motivation

Higher Response Effort > Lower Response Effort

FIGURE 4.14 Cheat sheet to determine resistance to extinction

FIVE
WHY DID I DO THAT?
ANTECEDENT CONDITIONS

"A failure is not always a mistake; it may simply be the best one can do under the circumstances. The real mistake is to stop trying."

B.F SKINNER

STIMULUS CONTROL

A couple of thousand words later, and would you look at that, we are still covering basic behavioral science, but don't worry, this is the last chapter talking about how we look at behavior. This chapter is fundamental and crucial to understanding the highly complex decisions of an organism and how what many of us consider pure psychological components can be deducted into a simple science. We will begin with stimulus control, which refers to the degree to which specific antecedent stimuli or cues influence behavior in the environment. In behavioral science, behaviors are viewed as occurring in response to discriminative stimuli, which are signals or conditions that set the occasion for the behavior to occur. Stimulus control plays a crucial role in understanding, predicting, and modifying behavior. Stimulus control has one goal: to evoke a specific response under particular antecedent conditions reliably and not under any other antecedent conditions. In stimulus control, the presence or absence of an antecedent stimulus alters the present, frequency, latency, duration, or amplitude of behavior. Let us understand this further: when an organism has stimulus control, it will be able to reliably produce the same response or functionally equivalent response under various antecedent stimuli. Two primary forms of antecedent discrimination are highly valuable to understanding behavior: Discriminative Stimulus (SD) and Stimulus Delta (S-Delta).

Discriminative Stimulus (SD)

Discriminative stimulus is, without a doubt, one of the most essential components to understanding the behavior of any organism. So far in the book, we have talked about how the environment interacts with us, evoking a behavior, but we haven't dug deep into why this happens, that is, until now. Simply put, discriminative stimulus signals the availability of reinforcement for a particular behavior. This is kind of like a "green light" in which it signals the go-ahead when driving. We will refer to discriminative stimulus as SD for the rest of the chapter, as that is the abbreviation used in practice. SD is an antecedent stimulus, in the previously discussed model of operant conditioning, stimulus-response-stimulus, SD's falls under the first stimulus. In practice, most of us know it as the ABC (antecedent, behavior, consequence); from this, we can

THE BARE BONES OF ABA

deduct it falls under the antecedent or what happens immediately before the behavior. In **FIGURE 5.1**, we will graphically visualize an example of SD and S-Delta, which can be helpful in understanding these concepts. SD is an immediate antecedent, so for us as behavior scientists to call an evoking stimulus an SD, it must happen right before the behavior happens, a stimulus that happens five seconds before the behavior cannot be called the SD as it wasn't immediate. I personally have a three-second rule where anything in those three seconds can be considered the SD, but in literature, the SD must be immediate. To summarize SD in one sentence, SD is an antecedent stimulus that signals the availability of reinforcement and has complete control over a response. Let's use Fonsi for a quick example and say that Fonsi wants cookies. In this example, Fonsi's grandfather always gives him cookies whenever possible. Over time, Fonsi has associated the grandfather with providing cookies (stimulus-stimulus pairing and operant conditioning). Now, every time Fonsi sees the grandfather (SD), which signals the reinforcement (cookies), Fonsi asks for a cookie, which the grandfather provides without hesitation. Seeing the grandfather evoked the behavior of asking for cookies as the grandfather signals the availability of the cookies, thus becoming the SD.

Stimulus Delta (S-Delta)

Now, for those of you who study the sciences, you know that for every action, there is an equal and opposite reaction, the same applies to the concept of SD and S-Delta. That is a perfect hint as to what S-Delta means, think about it: if SD signals reinforcer, what would be the opposite of this? Exactly stimulus delta, or as we will refer to it, S-Delta, is a cue that signals the absence of reinforcement for a particular behavior. In essence, an S- Delta is a "red light" that communicates to an individual that engaging in a particular behavior is unlikely to result in any desired outcome or reward. Just like SD, this antecedent stimulus has many attributes with some differences, such as not evoking a response and abating (avoiding) the response. As mentioned above in **FIGURE 5.1**, There will be a graphical visualization (SSG Learning Theory) example of these concepts. S-Delta is also an immediate antecedent, meaning that my three-second rule does apply. S-Delta's are very interesting and are seen very often in the field, mainly when an organism has two different ways of being thought. In my years of experience, I have noticed that when a child is being taught, usually the parents are seen either as SD or S-Delta. This is because the child gets reinforced in the presence of one parent and reprimanded in the presence of another. I'll provide another example with Fonsi and his grandmother now, which will help you understand the differences between these concepts. As we saw in the last example, Fonsi asks for the cookie (behavior) in the presence of the grandfather due to association and the grandfather being the SD. Over the years, Fonsi got reprimanded by his grandmother for asking for cookies and never received a cookie in her presence (stimulus-stimulus pairing and operant conditioning), which caused the grandmother to become the S-Delta, signaling the absence of the reinforcer. Now, whenever Fonsi entered the room and saw the grandmother (S-Delta), he didn't ask for a cookie, meaning no response was evoked, as he knew he wasn't going to get the cookie. When we understand the immediate antecedent stimulus, behavior modification becomes reasonably easy, as manipulating these antecedent variables will change and provide desired results.

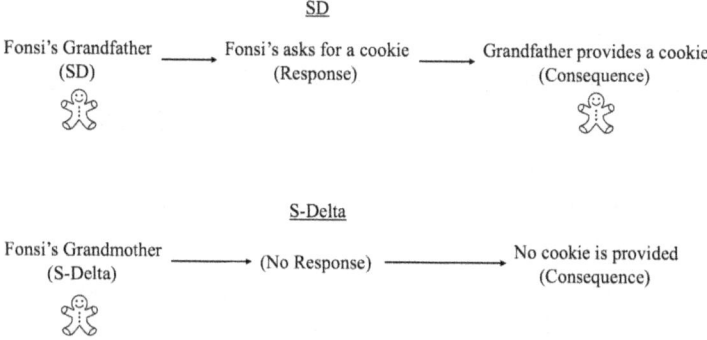

FIGURE 5.1 SD vs. S-Delta example

Now that we have the example let's explain a little to avoid any confusion and combine these terms. Let us say that the grandparents live together, and Fonsi goes to visit every week; we already established who the SD and the S-Delta are in this example. When Fonsi walks around the house and sees the grandfather (SD), he immediately asks for a cookie (response) and receives this cookie. A little bit later, Fonsi is walking around again and sees his grandmother (S-Delta), this time, however, he doesn't ask for the cookie as he knows he won't get one. Fonsi did not evoke the behavior of asking for a cookie as he knew there was no signal for reinforcement and he wouldn't receive one. Before we finish the subtopic, I have been hiding a little surprise to see who, during the understanding of SD and S-Delta, associated S-Delta with an already learned term. If we see in **FIGURE 5.1**, in S-Delta, the consequence is no cookie being provided, which is also another way of saying withholding reinforcement or extinction. This will be important when we distinguish SDP and S-Delta.

Stimulus Equivalence (Quick Glance)

Stimulus equivalence is unique and quite complex to understand but is an essential process of behavior. Often associated with the work of Dr. Murray Sidman. It refers to the phenomenon where individuals demonstrate the ability to respond to one stimulus (the conditional stimulus or CS) as if it were another stimulus (the equivalent stimulus or ES), even though they may not have directly learned the specific association between the two stimuli. This concept is central to understanding how humans acquire language and engage in complex cognitive processes. Let's make it simpler when a response is correctly displayed in the presence of a stimulus that has not been trained or reinforced; this is stimulus equivalence. This means that the organism has made a connection between stimulus and correct response without being trained. In order for stimulus equivalence to fully succeed, three criteria must be met: reflexivity, symmetry, and transitivity, which we will discuss further in the chapter.

CS vs. SD

Even though conditioned stimulus and discriminative stimulus are similar, we must remember that one belongs in respondent conditioning and the other in operant conditioning. A quick recap of a conditioned stimulus(CS) is a previously neutral stimulus that, through repeated pairing with an unconditioned stimulus (US), comes to evoke a conditioned response (CR) similar to the response elicited initially by the US. In classical conditioning, CSs are associated with involuntary or reflexive responses. For example, if a bell (CS) is repeatedly paired with the presentation of food (US) to a dog, the bell alone can eventually elicit salivation (CR) in anticipation of food (Pavlov's original work). CSs are typically associated with the development of conditioned responses through the process of classical conditioning. On the other hand, a discriminative stimulus (SD) is a stimulus in the environment that signals the availability of reinforcement for a specific behavior. In operant conditioning, SDs are associated with voluntary, operant behaviors. When an SD is present, a particular behavior is more likely to occur because the individual has learned that engaging in that behavior under those specific conditions is likely to be reinforced. The key difference between conditioned stimuli (CS) and discriminative stimuli (SD) is their functions and associations. CSs are associated with classical conditioning and evoke conditioned responses based on prior pairings with unconditioned stimuli. SDs, on the other hand, are associated with operant conditioning and signal the availability of reinforcement for specific voluntary behaviors. While both play significant roles in behavior modification, they operate in distinct ways and serve different functions in the learning process. The main point to remember here is that a discriminative stimulus (SD) has the ability to evoke a response because of its association with reinforcement. Remember, in **FIGURE 5.1**, Fonsi was able to determine who was the SD and the S-Delta due to its association with reinforcement.

SDP

We have arrived at a more complex aspect of behavioral science, where we have to discuss some of the more confusing topics. We already know that SD stands for discriminative stimulus, but what does SDP stand for? Well, the P stands for punishment, so when put together, we have a discriminative stimulus for punishment. This has a straightforward definition due to its combined nature, think about it: what does SD do? it signals reinforcement, well, SDP signals the opposite, it signals punishment contingency. SDP is a stimulus condition under which a response has lowered the frequency due to the association between stimulus and punishment for the response in the past. SDPs signal the availability of punishment or the likelihood that a specific behavior will result in aversive consequences. SDPs are instrumental in behavior management when the goal is to reduce or eliminate unwanted behaviors through the application of punishment procedures. Let's explain it with the following example:

Imagine a classroom setting where a teacher has established a rule that students should not talk out of turn during class discussions. The teacher notices that one particular student, Fonsi (of course), frequently interrupts and speaks without raising his hand. In this context, The teacher's disapproving glance and raised eyebrow (visual cues) whenever Fonsi begins speaking without being called on serves as an SDP for punishment. Fonsi has learned that when he interrupts the teacher or her classmates, the teacher's disapproving look signals that he will likely face a consequence, such as being asked to sit quietly for a few minutes or losing a privilege. In this scenario, the teacher's disapproving glance and raised eyebrow function as discriminative stimuli for punishment because they signal to Fonsi that his behavior (speaking out of turn) will likely result in an aversive consequence. Fonsi then has the opportunity to make a choice based on the presence of this SDP. He can choose to continue speaking out of turn, knowing that it may lead to punishment, or he can choose to wait his turn and raise his hand, avoiding the aversive consequence. This use of SDP helps shape Fonsi's behavior by making him more likely to engage in the desired behavior of raising his hand during class discussions. An even simpler example is a teacher who constantly paired herself/himself with a reprimand for a particular response, the teacher will become the SDP for reprimand; thus, in the presence of the teacher, the frequency of response is lowered.

SDP vs. S-Delta

There might be some confusion distinguishing between S-Delta and SDP, especially as they both tend to abate or suppress the behavior. But there is a key difference that separates the two, and to understand it, we must remember the punishment contingencies discussed in Chapter Three and the schedules of reinforcement in Chapter Four. In SDP, we work based on consequence and correlation with the punishment contingency. In other words, through shaping by consequence and association of punishment procedures, the stimulus (anyone, such as the teacher in the above example) acquires the property of the punishment itself. So, it signals that there will be punishment if the behavior is evoked. In S-Delta, we do have associations through consequence but not through punishment procedures, as no punishment contingency is used. Instead, we withhold the reinforcement as a consequence, which will associate a stimulus with the absence of the reinforcement. Rephrasing this, we can quickly tell the difference as punishment procedures shape SDP, and the other is shaped by not providing reinforcement or withholding, which is the S-Delta.

Stimulus Salience

Stimulus Salience refers to how a stimulus stands out or captures an individual's attention within a given context or environment. Salient stimuli are typically those that are most noticeable or conspicuous, often due to their sensory characteristics, novelty, or relevance to the individual's current goals or needs. Understanding stimulus salience is essential in various fields, including cognitive psychology, sensory perception, and behavioral sciences. Salience is closely related to an individual's perception and attention. Salient stimuli tend to draw attention because they are more visually or audibly distinct from their surroundings. For example, in a crowded room, a person wearing a bright red shirt might be more salient than others dressed in neutral colors, making them stand out and capture the observer's attention.

In the field of behavioral sciences, stimulus salience plays a significant role in influencing behavior. When a stimulus is highly salient, it is more likely to prompt a response from an individual. This is because salient stimuli are more noticeable and can elicit quicker reactions. For example, a loud and sudden noise in a quiet room may immediately capture someone's attention and cause them to react. Additionally, stimulus salience is essential in understanding how individuals prioritize information in their environment. Highly salient stimuli often have a more substantial impact on behavior and decision-making. In marketing and advertising, for instance, companies use salient visual elements or slogans to attract consumers' attention and influence their choices. Salient stimuli are more likely to capture attention and influence behavior due to their distinctiveness or relevance. This is essential to us because the more salience we have, the more stimulus control we have. And remember, as behavior scientists, all we can ever hope for is complete stimulus control. An example of this can be teaching a student (organism) to sound letters out loud. Letters are typically isolated and enlarged so that the student will correctly point and sound them out (this is a form of discrimination training). However, if those same letters are in complex words or sentences, it will be more difficult for students to pay attention.

Masking

Again, for every action, there is an equal and opposite reaction, so if there is stimulus salience, which refers to something that captures the individual's attention and evokes a response, there has to be something that does the opposite, in comes masking. Masking is when a more recently established response competes with or inhibits a previously learned behavior. This interference can occur when a new behavior that is similar to an existing behavior is introduced, leading to a reduction in the frequency or strength of the original behavior.

Masking can influence behavior modification efforts and the generalization of new skills. For example, consider a Fonsi, who has been taught to say "please" when asking for a desired item. Later, Fonsi is taught a more direct request, such as "Can I have the toy?" If the new response is taught too closely in time or context to the original response, the more direct request might mask the use of the word "please." In this case, the child may rely more on the new response and use "please" less frequently. Masking can also occur in scenarios involving competing responses. For instance, if an organism is learning to replace an undesirable behavior like hitting with a more appropriate behavior like requesting, the new behavior may initially mask or suppress the occurrence of hitting. However, as the individual becomes more proficient in the new skill, the masking effect may diminish, allowing the previously learned behavior to resurface. Behavior scientists must be aware of masking effects. To mitigate masking, we often implement strategies such as teaching functionally equivalent replacement behaviors, ensuring that the new responses do not entirely suppress the original behaviors. Additionally, monitoring for the potential resurgence of masked behaviors is crucial to maintaining long-term behavior change and ensuring that organisms have a diverse repertoire of responses to adapt to various situations.

Overshadowing

Overshadowing is similar to masking, however, instead of having a competing stimulus, overshadowing interferes acquisition of stimulus control due to a more salient stimulus. In other words, overshowing refers to a situation where one stimulus in a compound stimulus (a combination of multiple stimuli presented together) becomes more salient or attention-grabbing than another, resulting in the overshadowed stimulus having a weaker influence on an organism's behavior.

Overshadowing is particularly relevant in the context of stimulus discrimination and the development of conditioned responses. For example, consider a scenario in which Fonsi is learning to associate a specific sound, such as a bell ringing, and a specific visual cue, like a flashing light, with the delivery of a treat (reinforcement). If both the sound and the light are presented together when the treat is delivered, and the sound is louder or more noticeable than the light, the sound may overshadow the light. In this case, Fonsi may primarily associate the sound with the treat, and the light's role in signaling reinforcement may be diminished. Overshadowing can occur when there is competition for attention or when one stimulus is more intense, salient, or relevant to an individual's goals or needs than another. It can affect the formation of associations between stimuli and responses, leading to imbalances in how different elements of a compound stimulus influence behavior. Another more relatable example is that a student could not focus when practicing his presentation because there would be an English test the next day, which he hadn't studied for. In this example, the English test is more salient; this interfered with his presentation practice.

Motivating Operations (MO) (Critical Material)

This subtopic is very high on the list of crucial information to remember and understand for the complete comprehension of behavioral science. In this subtopic, we will cover Motivating Operations, as well as something I've mentioned in the book for some time now: ABC's and his cousin, which I like to call M-ABC. Motivating Operations or more commonly referred to as Mos, are environmental variables or conditions that alter the effectiveness of reinforcers or punishers and, consequently, the likelihood of a specific behavior occurring. MO's are distant antecedents, instead of immediate, like SD and S-Delta. MO has two main functions: value-altering effect and behavior-altering effect.

They can be classified into two categories: establishing operations (EO) and abolishing operations (AO). Establishing operations (EO) increases the value or effectiveness of a specific reinforcer, making it more desirable. When an EO is in effect, the reinforcing consequence becomes more potent, and the targeted behavior is more likely to occur. For example, if an organism is hungry, the value of food as a reinforcer increases, making the person more motivated to engage in behaviors like requesting or searching for food. Conversely, abolishing operations (AOs) decreases the value or effectiveness of a reinforcer, making it less desirable. When an AO is present, the reinforcer's potency diminishes, reducing the motivation for the targeted behavior. For instance, if an organism has just eaten a large meal, the value of food as a reinforcer decreases, making it less likely to engage in eating-related behaviors. You will also hear the term "satiation" referring to AO, which basically means that the organism has had too much of something and is "satiated," or the reinforcer no longer works. The value-altering effect focuses on the consequence, using the example above, if you are hungry, food increases in value thus receiving food as part of the consequence. However, to acquire the food, a behavior must happen, and this is where the behavior-altering effect takes place. The behavior-altering effect evokes or abates current behavior that has been reinforced or punished. It is behavior-altering because the current frequency of the behavior changes, rather than the future frequency, like that of reinforcement and punishment contingency. In **FIGURE 5.2**, the process of MO's is depicted to visualize and fully grasp this concept. To fully understand the behavior-altering effect, here is an example:

Consider Fonsi, who has a favorite toy, a stuffed animal named Teddy. Fonsi's parents usually keep Teddy in a high cabinet, making it difficult for Fonsi to access. Typically, Teddy is an effective reinforcer for Fonsi's behavior. However, on this particular day, the parents have placed Teddy within easy reach on the living room floor. As a result of the sudden approximation, Teddy becomes more desirable and valuable to Fonsi. The change in the environment has increased the effectiveness of Teddy as a reinforcer. In response to this heightened motivation, Fonsi begins to engage in behaviors like reaching for Teddy, vocalizing his excitement, or playing with the toy. The EO has altered Fonsi's behavior, making him more likely to engage in actions that result in him gaining access to Teddy. This example shows how the behavior-altering effect of an MO can lead to changes in an individual's actions based on the motivation created by altering the value or availability of a reinforcer. In this case, the EO made Teddy more motivating, and Fonsi's behavior shifted to take advantage of this increased motivation to obtain his favorite toy.

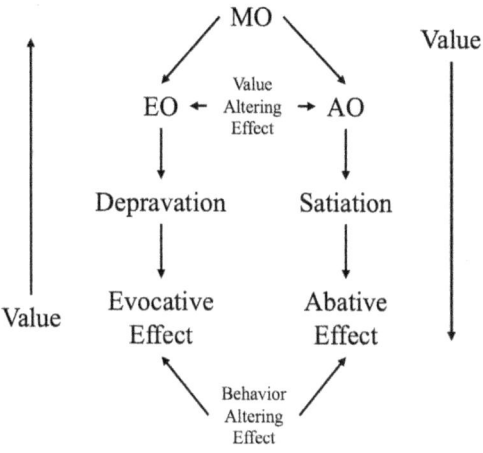

FIGURE 5.2 Diagram of Motivating Operations

Now that we have discussed MO's, and clarified that they are distant antecedents, how do they fit into this whole ABC craziness? Let's remember that ABC stands for antecedent, behavior, and consequence. We have discussed that consequences can be classified into reinforcement and punishment contingencies. We have also discussed behavior and what behavior is, and lastly, we recently discovered that we can classify antecedents into SD's and S-Delta's. The concept of ABC can also be known as the three-term contingency and is widely used in the field to determine functions of behavior. However, we can take ABC and take it a step further and make it a slightly complex four-term contingency I like to call M-ABC, pronounced: "M-Back." Can anyone guess what the M stands for? Exactly what we just went over MO's, since MO's are distant antecedents. The four-term contingency or M-ABC are as follows: motivating operation (EO/AO), antecedent (SD/S-Delta), behavior, and consequence. In **FIGURE 5.3**, we will see the first representation of ABC and M-ABC.

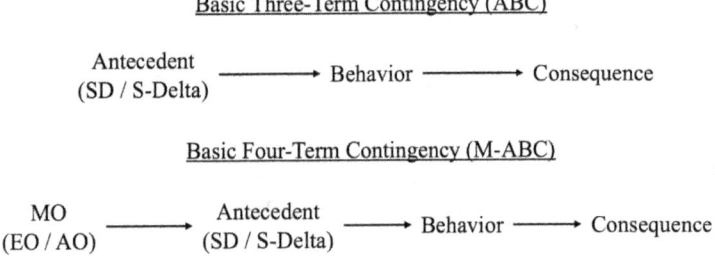

FIGURE 5.3 Graphical visualization of Three and Four-term contingency

Let's combine this entire subtopic and create an example of ABC and M-ABC that everyone reading this book can relate to. Before we continue, it must be stated that an antecedent will always be an SD and never an S-Delta, because an antecedent evokes a response, and S-Delta does not evoke a response. Starting with ABC, we can say that the antecedent or SD sees a pizza sign while driving; the behavior will be taking the exit to get pizza, and the consequence is eating the pizza. This ABC is straightforward, now the same example but with M-ABC.

The MO, which in this case is an EO will be hunger, the antecedent seeing the pizza sign, the behavior will be taking the exit, and the consequence is eating the pizza. Now we can see how this all comes together and depicts every action and behavior we have ever done. Another everyday example of M-ABC would be something like watching TV. In this example, the EO would be wanting to watch TV; the antecedent would be seeing the remote on top of the counter; the behavior would be grabbing the remote and turning the TV on, and the consequence would be watching TV.

Unconditioned Motivating Operations (UMO)

Breaking down this concept into two will be the best way to decipher its meaning, especially when it gets more complex in the subsequent three subtopics. If we remember, Unconditioned means unlearned, relating to phylogenic, so when combined with motivation operation, we are talking about things we get motivated by without having learned what they were and are necessary for sustaining life. There are nine total unconditioned motivating operations or UMOs.

Five of them involve Depravation and Satiation

- Water
- Food
- Oxygen
- Activity
- Sleep

The other four are sensory

- Sexual Stimulation

- Cold Temperature
- Warm Temperature
- Painful Stimulation

UMO's can also be expressed as UEO's and UAO's as they can establish and abolish the effectiveness of the above-mentioned UMO's. For example, let's take sexual stimulation and say that sex deprivation can function as a UEO, thus establishing sex as an effective reinforcement, sexual stimulation, or orgasm, as it is more commonly referred to, can function as the UAO abolishing the effectiveness of sexual reinforcer.

Let us explain it a little further; as mentioned UMO' can be categorized into two main types: unconditioned establishing operations (UEO's) and unconditioned abolishing operations (UAO's). Unconditioned establishing operations (UEO's) increase the value or effectiveness of a reinforcer. Hunger and thirst are classic examples of UEOs. When an organism is hungry, the value of food as a reinforcer increases, making them more motivated to seek and consume food. Similarly, when thirsty, the value of water as a reinforcer is enhanced, prompting the organism to engage in behaviors to access water. These UMO's are biologically based and serve to maintain an individual's basic survival. Unconditioned abolishing operations (UAO's), on the other hand, decrease the value or effectiveness of a reinforcer. For instance, if an organism has recently eaten a large meal, the UAO of satiety is in effect, reducing the effectiveness of food as a reinforcer. In this state, the organism is less motivated to eat. UAO's, like UEOs, are rooted in biological needs and evolved to help maintain homeostasis and prevent overconsumption.

Conditioned Motivating Operation (CMO)

Conditioned motivating operations (CMO's) are a critical concept in behavioral science that have a significant influence on an individual's behavior by altering the value or effectiveness of specific reinforcers and punishers. Unlike unconditioned motivating operations (UMO's), which are biologically or inherently relevant, CMO's acquire their properties through learning and conditioning, often through their association with specific environmental events, which we know as ontogenic history. There are two primary types of CMO's: conditioned establishing operations (CEO's) and conditioned abolishing operations (CAO's). Conditioned establishing operations (CEOs) are stimuli or events that have become associated with an increase in the value or effectiveness of a reinforcer. For example, if Fonsi has repeatedly experienced praise and attention (a reinforcer) contingent on completing his homework, the presence of a teacher's attention or praise may function as a CEO, increasing the value of the reinforcer and making Fonsi more motivated to complete his assignments. Conditioned abolishing operations (CAO's) are stimuli or events that have become associated with a decrease in the value or effectiveness of a reinforcer. If Fonsi has previously experienced a loss of recess time (a punishment) for not completing his homework, the teacher's disapproval or the sight of unfinished homework may serve as a CAO, decreasing the value of the reinforcer of playing during recess, leading Fonsi to be less motivated to complete his work. Now CMO's do gets slightly more complicated as there are precisely three types of CMO's.

- Surrogate (CMO-S)
- Reflexive (CMO-R)
- Transitive (CMO-T)

We will cover each of these topics in detail in different subtopics as there is a lot of information that goes into them, and I would like for everyone reading this to understand the differences and make it easier. I can tell you from experience that learning these specific topics is quite the task, my job as a teacher using SSG learning theory is to prove to you no matter how complicated the topic is, we will learn it. Let us get started with CMO-S the easiest of the three.

Conditioned Motivating Operation: Surrogate (CMO-S)

CMO-S is one of the subtypes of conditioned motivating operations (CMO's), and it refers to stimuli or events that have acquired their value-altering properties by preceding another motivating operation. In simpler terms, a CMO-S is an event or stimulus that becomes a motivator because it is associated with the onset or offset of another motivating operation, usually a UMO. It functions as an indirect influence on behavior. For example, if a teacher consistently praises a student after they complete their math homework (a motivating operation), the student might come to find math homework inherently motivating because the praise is associated with it. In this case, the praise (CMO-S) serves to enhance the value of completing math homework, making it a more potent reinforcer. Another example can be pairing the color blue with cold temperatures, the blue color may acquire both value-altering and behavior-altering effects.

To make this concept even more accessible, here is a more concrete example detailing every step: Imagine a student named Fonsi (of course) who is working on his math assignments in a classroom setting. In this scenario, the teacher introduces a game where Fonsi receives a token after completing each math problem correctly. Accumulating tokens can be exchanged for a preferred item, like a small toy or extra free time, which serves as a reinforcer. Over time, Fonsi associates the tokens with the opportunity to access his favorite items or activities, making the tokens a conditioned motivating operation - surrogate (CMO-S). As a result, the presence of tokens becomes a motivator for Fonsi to engage in math problems. He values the tokens not only for their immediate reinforcing properties but also because they signal the opportunity to obtain his preferred items or activities. In this example, the tokens have become CMO-S because they have acquired their value-altering properties by associating with the reinforcing events (exchange for preferred items or activities). The presence of tokens enhances the motivation for Fonsi to complete math problems, illustrating how CMO-S can indirectly influence an individual's behavior by signaling the availability of reinforcers.

Conditioned Motivating Operation: Reflexive (CMO-R)

Conditioned Motivating Operation - Reflexive (CMO-R) is a highly complex variation of CMO and can be very difficult to understand. But in very simple terms, CMO-R is a situation or stimulus that makes a specific behavior more likely because that behavior relieves discomfort or improves the situation. For example, think about being really thirsty (the CMO-R). When you're very thirsty, you are motivated to engage in a behavior like drinking water. Why? Because drinking water (the behavior) will relieve your thirst and make you feel better. So, the CMO-R (being thirsty) makes the behavior (drinking water) more likely because it helps you feel better. CMO-Rs highlight how our environment and how we feel can influence the actions we take. They show that certain conditions or situations can make specific behaviors more appealing because they help us in some way, like relieving discomfort or meeting our needs. In the field of Behavioral science, understanding CMO-Rs helps professionals design strategies to encourage desirable behaviors and understand why organisms do what they do. Now that the simple definition is out of the way, let's get a little bit more complicated.

CMO-R falls into two categories like many of the other CMO's: CEO-R and CAO-R. These correlate with a worsening (CEO-R) or improving conditions (CAO-R), which, at first sight, you will be confused as this doesn't make much sense. CMO-R signals an aversive event that might be occurring soon; this alters the value of its own removal or continued presence. Knowing this, we can tell the reason that a worsening condition is a CEO-R, is because it gives value to its own removal or negative reinforcement, which evokes a response that terminates that aversive event. This is actually something we call discriminated avoidance contingency, but we won't discuss this topic until later in the chapter. Again CEO-R increases the value of the removal of the worsening condition, in other words, the removal of the aversive condition is reinforcement. CEO-R tends to evoke avoidance behavior, while CAO-R does not. CAO-R decreases the value of the removal of worsening conditions. This means that the removal of the worsening condition no longer serves as reinforcement. I recommend reading this subtopic multiple times to fully understand it and continue to CMO-T, my favorite of the three and the easiest to explain.

Conditioned Motivating Operation: Transitive (CMO-T)

Conditioned Motivating Operation - Transitive (CMO-T) has to be my favorite CMO as it is simple and influential in the field of behavioral science. CMO-T is a situation where something becomes more motivating or valuable because it is connected to something else that we want or need. For example, think about a student in school. They really like getting gold stars as a reward. Over time, they've learned that they usually get a gold star when they do their homework. So, doing homework becomes more motivating because it's connected to the gold star, which is something they want. In this case, the CMO-T is the homework. It's not valuable by itself but becomes more valuable because it's connected to the gold star, which is a reward. CMO-T helps us understand how things become more appealing or motivating when they're linked to something we desire or find valuable.

CMO-T gives value to a needed stimuli for a reinforcer, which in turn provides that reinforcement. In the example above, we used a school setting, but how about a home setting with a child who loves to eat (Fonsi)? Let us say that Fonsi loves to eat and sneaks to the fridge in the middle of the night to get food (reinforcer). After noticing this, Fonsi's parents decide to put a lock on the fridge so that Fonsi can no longer get food in the middle of the night. Now, things get interesting, as a lock protects the food (the reinforcer). CMO-T states that the key that opens the lock for the food now acquires the reinforcing capabilities of the food as it is needed to open the fridge. So Fonsi will now seek the key, which has the same reinforcement value as the food due to CMO-T. This example is clearly demonstrated in **FIGURE 5.4,** showing this exact example step by step.

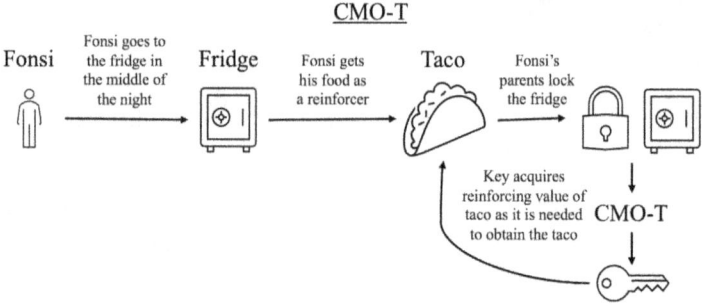

FIGURE 5.4 Locked fridge example

For the sake of complete understanding, we will include another example, this time in the school setting. Imagine you are hungry in school, and you begin looking for your teacher; let's call her teacher A. After finding teacher A, you request for food, which she politely provides. In this example, hunger is the CMO-T as it establishes the reinforcing effectiveness of teacher A (conditioned reinforcer) and evokes the behavior of searching for teacher A. If we continue to break this down, teacher A by herself is not food, but it is a necessary component in this chain for the organism (aka you) to receive the food. Finally, all the UMO's discussed can function as CMO-T for establishing stimuli as conditioned reinforcers. Think about it: hunger establishes the fridge as CMO-T, thirst establishes the water bottle as CMO-T, and oxygen deprivation establishes the oxygen tank as CMO-T.

Simple Discrimination

We discussed stimulus control at the beginning of the chapter, in which an organism behaves differently in the presence of stimuli. However, have you ever wondered how we, as organisms, can differentiate between stimuli? Well, stimulus control has two different forms of discrimination: simple discrimination and conditional discrimination. The latter half, which is simple discrimination, is precisely as it sounds: simple. Simple discrimination involves an organism responding differently to distinct stimuli or cues. It plays a vital role in learning and behavior change by helping organisms differentiate between various environmental stimuli and appropriately respond to each one. In simple discrimination, two or more stimuli are presented, and the organism learns to respond to one while not responding to the others. This can be exemplified in a classroom setting, where a student is taught to raise their hand when the teacher asks a question but refrain from raising their hand when other students ask questions. Here, the teacher's cues act as discriminative stimuli, signaling when the behavior (raising hand) is appropriate. In **FIGURE 5.5**, simple discrimination is easily portrayed in its simplicity and understanding.

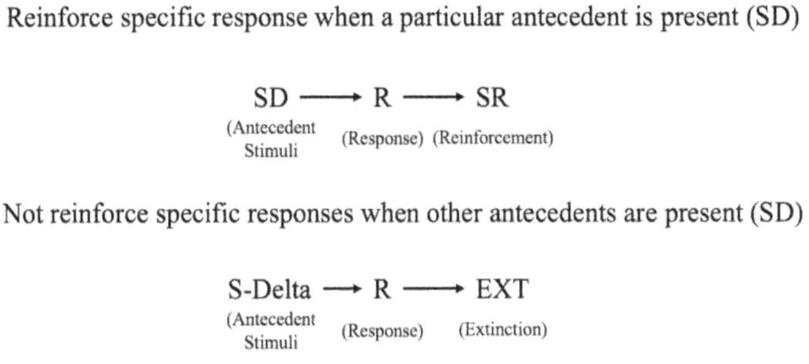

Reinforce specific response when a particular antecedent is present (SD)

SD ⟶ R ⟶ SR
(Antecedent Stimuli) (Response) (Reinforcement)

Not reinforce specific responses when other antecedents are present (SD)

S-Delta ⟶ R ⟶ EXT
(Antecedent Stimuli) (Response) (Extinction)

FIGURE 5.5 Simple Discrimination depicted graphically

As we can see in **FIGURE 5.5**, simple discrimination simply discriminates what response to evoke under a specific stimulus. If the response is elicited under any other stimulus, it will not provide reinforcement, thus placing any other response on extinction. As we can also see, simple discrimination employs the three-term contingency and works only with antecedent stimuli. This helps discriminate when the organism can do something and when it can't or shouldn't. This is as simple as discrimination gets because conditional discrimination takes this concept to a whole new level.

Conditional Discrimination

Conditional discrimination is quite the concept, and it explains how we make choices based on context. Conditional discrimination involves the ability of an organism to respond to various stimuli based on the presence of specific discriminative cues. Unlike simple discrimination, where individuals respond differently to distinct stimuli, conditional discrimination requires the recognition of contextual cues or conditional relations to determine the appropriate response. This skill is essential for understanding and responding to complex and context-dependent situations. In conditional discrimination, organisms learn to make discriminations based on conditional cues, which are cues that indicate which stimulus or response is relevant given the context. For example, in a classroom, students may learn to respond to math problems differently from reading comprehension questions, depending on the teacher's instructions or the type of material presented. Conditional discrimination is at the core of advanced cognitive and problem-solving skills, allowing organisms to adapt their behavior to various situations.

Conditional discrimination employs a four-term contingency that is quite different from the one we already know in motivating operations. In **FIGURE 5.6**, we will showcase an example of conditional discrimination and how it is applied to behavioral decisions. In simplistic terms, we have a conditional stimulus (which can also be called contextual stimulus) followed by the antecedent, response, and consequence. This basically means that the response will reinforce the antecedent under a particular context.

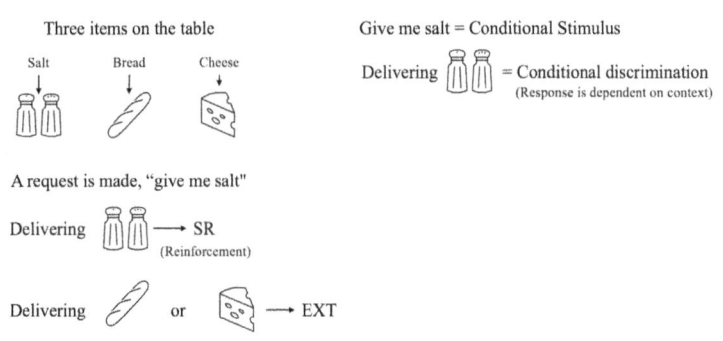

FIGURE 5.6 Detailed example of conditional discrimination depicting the necessity of context in decision-making.

In the example above, we have chosen three random items and placed them on a table. As we can see, the items were salt, bread, and cheese, which are all common household items. Let us use Fonsi as our organism, in which he has to provide the correct response contextually. If I request Fonsi to give me the salt, which is located among the other items, Fonsi will give me the salt. In response to this, Fonsi will receive social reinforcement from me, however, if Fonsi gives me the bread or cheese instead, the reinforcement will be withheld and maybe even punished. In this example, "give me salt" functions as the contextual stimulus; if the request is not made, there is no need to grab the salt. I encourage all of you who read this book to test this experiment out with any family member. Place multiple condiments during dinner time and ask them to grab you a specific one. Upon receiving this condiment, analyze how this response occurred and why the organism employs conditional discrimination on a daily basis.

Another example that every self-driving organism will relate to is running a light. Imagine you are running late for work, and there is a yellow light; you will most likely drive through the yellow light. Now imagine the same scenario, but next to the light, there is a cop, you will probably slow down and wait for the next green light. As we can see in this example, we are discriminating based on the context or condition.

Derived Stimulus Relations

Derived stimulus relations is a beefy concept but rather simple and can be explained very easily. It describes how individuals can acquire new skills and behaviors through the formation of relations between stimuli, often without direct training. This phenomenon reflects the complex ways in which organisms learn and adapt to their environment. Derived stimulus relations encompass a variety of relations, including symmetry, transitivity, and reflexivity. But before we can discuss these three topics, we need to discuss antecedent stimulus class. The antecedent stimulus class evokes responses in the same operant response class or elicits the same respondent behavior. There are two types of antecedent stimulus classes: Feature stimulus class and Arbitrary stimulus class. A feature stimulus class is a concept that plays a significant role in understanding and analyzing behavior. It refers to a group of stimuli that share standard physical features or characteristics, and responding to any stimulus within the class typically results in a similar behavior. Feature stimulus classes are defined by their perceptual similarities rather than their specific functions. For example, different types of dogs, tables, lights, and more all share common characteristics.

On the other hand, we have an arbitrary stimulus class, which is another essential concept in behavioral science that helps explain how organisms respond to stimuli based on their learned or conditioned associations rather than inherent physical properties. In an arbitrary stimulus class, stimuli are related not by shared physical features but by their function or meaning, as established through prior learning. One classic example of an arbitrary stimulus class is language. Words that belong to the same category are part of an arbitrary stimulus class. The words themselves do not share physical features but are related based on their function or meaning, making it possible for individuals to respond appropriately to them. We need to remember that even though arbitrary stimulus classes share no similar factors, it can still evoke the same response. Arbitrary stimulus class helps us develop stimulus equivalence and can be taught using matching to sample procedures.

Stimulus Equivalence (Reflexivity, Symmetry, Transitivity)

Earlier in the chapter, we discussed stimulus equivalence but didn't discuss the three stimulus-stimulus relations within this concept. In **FIGURE 5.7,** we will display all three relations as a cheat sheet for everyone to remember. We will start with reflexivity, which is the ability to recognize a relationship between a stimulus and itself. In simpler terms, it means understanding that a stimulus is the same as itself; thus the organism selects a stimulus matched to itself. Reflexivity is one of the core features of derived stimulus relations, which involve the formation of complex stimulus relations through learning. For example, if an organism learns that the word "cat" (A) represents a furry pet (also A) with whiskers and then realizes that "cat" also means the same furry pet (A=A), they have acquired the concept of reflexivity. This simple understanding is foundational for language development and cognitive skills.

Next, we have symmetry, which involves understanding that if one stimulus relates to another in a certain way, the reverse relationship also holds true. For example, if an organism learns that A is the same as B (A = B), then they have acquired the concept of symmetry, which means they can also infer that B is the same as A (B = A). This bidirectional understanding is essential for language development, reading comprehension, and other complex cognitive skills.

Transitivity takes the last two relations and combines them to form a new relation. Transitivity is the formation of derived stimulus relations, specifically when an organism recognizes and responds to the relationships between stimuli in a chain-like or transitive manner. It is a cognitive ability that allows organisms to make inferences and draw conclusions about stimuli or relationships between stimuli that they may not have been explicitly taught. To illustrate transitivity, let's consider an example. If an organism learns that A is related to B (A = B) and also that B is related to C (B = C), they can infer that A is related to C (A = C) without direct training.

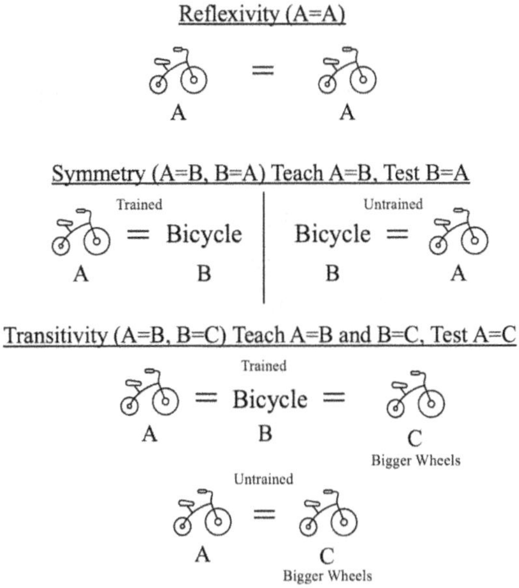

THE BARE BONES OF ABA

Reflexivity (A=A)

🚲 = 🚲
A   A

Symmetry (A=B, B=A) Teach A=B, Test B=A

Trained	Untrained
🚲 = Bicycle	Bicycle = 🚲
A B	B A

Transitivity (A=B, B=C) Teach A=B and B=C, Test A=C

Trained
🚲 = Bicycle = 🚲
A   B   C
Bigger Wheels

Untrained
🚲 = 🚲
A   C
Bigger Wheels

FIGURE 5.7 Cheat sheet for all three derived stimulus relations

Novel Stimulus

This concept is not very well known, but the introduction of it might help determine the necessity in the field. Novel Stimulus refers to stimuli or objects that an organism has not encountered or been exposed to before, making them "novel" or new to them. Understanding and responding to novel stimuli is a critical skill, as it demonstrates an organism's ability to adapt to new situations and generalize their learning. Novel stimulus control is an essential aspect of behavioral science, and it encompasses various aspects of learning and behavior. In behavioral modification, one of the primary goals is to teach organisms to respond appropriately to novel stimuli. This skill is essential for helping organisms adapt to change and navigate unfamiliar environments. For instance, if a child has learned to read and recognize a specific set of words, they may be able to generalize that skill to read new terms they have never seen before. This ability to respond to novel stimuli is crucial for academic, social, and life skills development. Behavior scientists may introduce novel stimuli to assess the organism's ability to transfer learned skills to unfamiliar settings or novel conditions. This information is valuable for tailoring interventions and ensuring that organism can apply their skills in real-world situations.

Stimulus Generalization

Stimulus generalization is essential for an organism to learn with long-term memory. Stimulus generalization is a core concept that refers to the process by which an individual responds to stimuli that are similar to a previously learned stimulus. It is an essential aspect of learning and behavior change and plays a key role in helping organisms apply their acquired skills and knowledge to a broader range of situations. Stimulus generalization is often used to describe how behaviors taught in one context or with one set of stimuli can be generalized to other similar situations. For example, suppose a child learns to say dog in the presence of a dog picture, now, whenever the child sees the picture of a dog, sees a real dog, or furry friend, he will evoke the same response under these different stimuli. The extent of stimulus generalization can vary, and it is influenced by factors such as the similarity between the original stimulus and the novel stimulus, the consistency of reinforcement, and the individual's learning history. Stimulus generalization is not limited to academic or social skills; it also applies to reducing problem behaviors. In behavior modification, interventions are designed to address specific target behaviors, and stimulus generalization helps ensure that the changes in behavior occur not just in the therapy or training environment but also in the individual's daily life.

Setting/Situation Generalization

Setting generalization is precisely as it sounds: generalizing a behavior in a different setting where the behavior hasn't been trained before. Setting generalization is a concept that extends the idea of stimulus generalization by emphasizing the transfer of learned behaviors and skills across different settings or environments. It is a crucial aspect of behavioral science that aims to ensure that organisms can effectively apply their acquired skills and behaviors in various real-life contexts, promoting adaptability and independence. The ultimate goal is to help organisms generalize the skills they have acquired in therapy or controlled settings to their everyday lives. Setting generalization involves teaching organisms how to respond appropriately in a therapy or training environment and how to carry those behaviors to other settings, such as home, school, work, or community situations.

Setting generalizations is vital for those with diverse needs. For example, Fonsi has learned to use social greetings and appropriate communication in a therapeutic setting; he should also be able to apply these skills when interacting with family, peers, or teachers outside of therapy. Likewise, take a functioning adult who has acquired vocational skills in a job training program should be able to perform those skills in a real workplace. Behavior scientists assess and measure the extent to which individuals can independently demonstrate targeted behaviors or skills in their natural environment. We need to remember that a generalized setting is a setting where a response is desired, and it must differ from the instructional setting in some meaningful way.

Response Generalization

Response generalization is a concept that focuses on the transfer of learned behaviors and skills to new and untaught responses that are functionally equivalent to the target behavior. This phenomenon highlights the versatility of acquired skills and behaviors, allowing organisms to apply what they have learned to a broader range of situations and responses. Response generalization is fundamental when teaching complex skills or behaviors. It involves teaching a specific response and ensuring that the organism can use similar, untrained responses when necessary. For instance, Fonsi learns to request a desired item by saying, "May I have the toy, please?" (specific response), response generalization means he can also use other appropriate requests like, "Can I play with the toy?" or "'Toy, please?" (untrained responses).

Response generalization is a key component of functional communication training. In the field, practitioners aim to teach individuals a range of communication responses to meet their needs effectively, allowing them to express their desires, preferences, and needs in various ways. This is particularly important for individuals with communication challenges. Generalization can occur in different ways. Stimulus generalization involves applying the behavior to similar stimuli in various contexts, while response generalization focuses on different but functionally equivalent behaviors. Both types of generalization are critical for ensuring that individuals can adapt their skills to multiple situations.

THE BARE BONES OF ABA

Overgeneralization and Faulty Stimulus Control

Overgeneralization refers to a behavioral phenomenon in which an organism exhibits a learned behavior in situations beyond those in which it was initially taught. It can manifest when a behavior learned in a specific training context is displayed in a broader range of situations or settings than intended. While generalization is a common and often desired outcome, it can sometimes lead to challenges that require further intervention and fine-tuning. Generalization involves teaching behavior in one context or with particular stimuli and then ensuring that the individual can use that behavior effectively in various other contexts or with a wide range of related stimuli. For example, suppose Fonsi is taught to say "dad" every time he sees his dad. In that case, overgeneralization might occur when he starts calling every other man "dad." As we can see, this can be an issue as not everyone is his dad; now, we must teach Fonsi to use a different feature to associate who the real dad is.

Faulty stimulus control is used to describe a situation where behavior is under the control of a stimulus or stimuli inappropriately or inaccurately. This means that the individual's behavior is not appropriately matched to the relevant antecedent stimuli or cues, leading to responses that are out of context, maladaptive, or irrelevant. One typical example of faulty stimulus control is when a child is taught to raise his/her hand in class to ask for help or permission. If the child raises their hand at home or in a social setting to request something, it demonstrates faulty stimulus control. In this case, the behavior (raising the hand) is not appropriately controlled by the relevant stimulus (being in a classroom or educational setting). Another example of faulty stimulus control can be when a student is shown a white table, and learns to name the table, but now the student labels everything white as a table. In this example, the four legs should've acquired the stimulus control; instead, the white color acquired it, making it faulty. Faulty stimulus control can lead to communication challenges and social difficulties for organisms. It can result in misinterpretations and miscommunications because the behavior is not contextually appropriate.

Response Maintenance

The last subtopic sums it all up and shows us how to maintain everything we learned for a long time. In **FIGURE 5.8**, we sum up all the differences for future use and are able to choose the appropriate intervention. Response maintenance is a key concept that pertains to the persistence and continued performance of a learned behavior over time. It focuses on the sustainability of behaviors that have been acquired or changed through behavior modification programs. Understanding response maintenance is crucial for ensuring that positive behavior changes last and continue to benefit individuals in the long term. Response maintenance is a desirable outcome of interventions. It implies that the organism continues to exhibit the target behavior even after the intervention has concluded. This is significant because it demonstrates that the behavior change is not temporary but has become a part of the organism's repertoire, promoting lasting improvements in their daily life. To achieve response maintenance, we tend to use strategies like reinforcement, fading, and generalization. Fading entails gradually reducing the level of reinforcement while maintaining the behavior.

<u>Distinguishing Between Concepts</u>

Stimulus / Setting Generalization
- Same behavior, different stimuli, or setting

Response Generalization
- Different Behavior

Response Maintenance
- Same behavior over time

FIGURE 5.8 Differentiation between the above-learned concepts

SIX
TALK TO ME!!
VERBAL BEHAVIOR

"An important fact about verbal behavior is that the speaker and listener may reside within the same skin."

B.F SKINNER

INTRODUCTION

Welcome to chapter six; we have finally moved on from all the basic principles that behavior analysis employs. This chapter is an extension of the basic principles; however, it is very different as it relates to verbal behavior and its characteristics. This chapter will be concise as it tackles a singular concept. Due to this, I recommend re-reading this chapter multiple times until your understanding of verbal comprehension is at a level where you will feel comfortable explaining it to those around you.

Properties of Language

There are essentially two properties of language that fall under verbal behavior: formal and functional. The formal property of language refers to language's structural or grammatical aspects, including rules and conventions that dictate how words and sentences are organized. Understanding the formal properties of language is crucial for teaching individuals (for this chapter, we will refrain from using the term "organism" as language generally is an aspect of human individuals) with language deficits to communicate effectively and engage in socially meaningful interactions. One aspect of the formal property of language is syntax, which involves the rules governing the order and arrangement of words in sentences. Programs often target syntax by teaching individuals to construct grammatically correct sentences. For example, they may learn to place subject-verb-object in the correct order, use verb tenses appropriately, and apply other grammatical rules. Another critical element of the formal property of language is morphology, which focuses on the structure of words and the formation of word forms. Individuals may be taught morphological rules related to plurals, verb conjugations, possessives, and other aspects of word formation. This helps them produce and understand words and sentences correctly. Phonology, the study of speech sounds and their organization in language, is also part of the formal property of language. Interventions may target phonological skills by teaching individuals to articulate speech sounds accurately, distinguish between sounds, and recognize the phonemic structure of words. Pragmatics, while often considered a separate property of language, is also connected to the formal property. Pragmatics involves the rules for using language in social contexts, including turn-taking in conversations, maintaining eye contact, and understanding the implied meaning in communication.

The functional property is significantly different than that of formal property. The function property of language refers to the purpose or role of language in communication. Understanding the function of language is critical for individuals with language deficits because it helps in comprehending why people use language and how it serves specific purposes in various social contexts. One fundamental aspect of the function property of language is communication. Teaching individuals how to use language to convey their wants, needs, desires, and thoughts effectively. Communication may involve making requests, expressing preferences, seeking information, or sharing experiences by teaching the function of communication. Another critical function of language is social interaction. Language is a powerful tool for building and maintaining relationships, as well as participating in social activities. Interventions often target social functions by teaching individuals how to initiate and maintain conversations, engage in turn-taking during interactions, and understand the importance of nonverbal cues in social communication. Problem-solving and self-regulation are also functions of language that programs may address. Individuals are taught to use language to identify problems, discuss potential solutions, and make decisions. Language helps individuals manage their emotions, cope with challenges, and plan for the future.

B.F Skinner 1957 Book "Verbal Behavior"

B.F. Skinner's 1957 book, "Verbal Behavior," is a seminal work that explores the analysis of language and verbal behavior within the framework of operant conditioning and behaviorism. The book represents a significant contribution to the field of psychology and behavior analysis, as it provides a comprehensive analysis of language, which Skinner views as a set of learned behaviors. Skinner's book introduces the notion that language and verbal behavior can be understood through the principles of operant conditioning. He suggests that just like any other behavior, verbal behavior is shaped, maintained, and influenced by environmental consequences. According to Skinner, language is essentially a set of behaviors learned through reinforcement, shaping, and the principles of operant conditioning. One of the central concepts discussed in "Verbal Behavior" is the distinction between different functions of verbal behavior. Skinner identifies various verbal operants (discussed further in the chapter), which are the different functions of language, including mand (requesting), tact (labeling or naming things), echoic (repeating what is heard), intraverbal (responding to questions or statements with related words), and textual (reading or textual responses). These operants illustrate the diverse ways language is used and how they are shaped through environmental contingencies.

Skinner also discusses the importance of analyzing the antecedents and consequences of verbal behavior. He emphasizes the role of antecedent stimuli (discriminative stimuli) and the consequences (reinforcement or punishment) in shaping language. Skinner's analysis of verbal behavior helps shed light on how individuals acquire language and the conditions under which they acquire new verbal behaviors. Furthermore, "Verbal Behavior" delves into the concept of generative language and the role of grammar in shaping language. Skinner's analysis suggests that complex verbal behavior, including the use of grammar and syntax, can be explained through the principles of operant conditioning and the reinforcement of grammatically correct responses. B.F. Skinner's "Verbal Behavior" is a foundational text offering a behaviorist language and communication perspective. It highlights the idea that language is a set of learned behaviors shaped by environmental contingencies. Skinner's analysis of verbal operants, antecedents, and consequences has had a profound impact on the field of behavior analysis and the understanding of language acquisition and communication. This book remains a significant reference in the study of language and serves as a cornerstone in the field of behaviorism and operant conditioning. I truly recommend everyone reading this book to follow up verbal behavior with Skinner's original work.

Skinner's Functional Definition of Verbal Behavior

We need to remember that language is learned behavior controlled by the same environmental variables and principles as non-verbal behavior. We can say that verbal behavior is behavior that is reinforced only through the mediation of a listener. In contrast with the response that produces reinforcement by acting upon the environment, the effects of verbal behavior on the environment are indirect as another person mediates it. In **FIGURE 6.1**, I will provide an example using three-term contingency to differentiate between non-verbal behavior and verbal behavior.

[continued on next page]

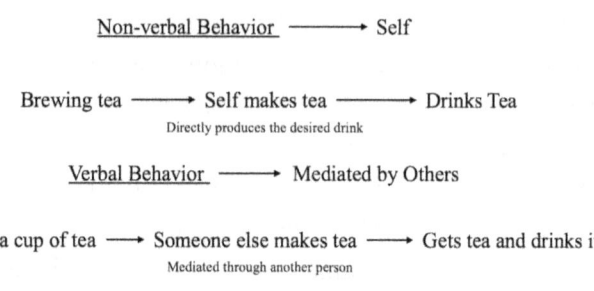

FIGURE 6.1 Non-verbal behavior vs. Verbal behavior

Speaker and Listener

In order for verbal behavior to be called verbal behavior, it requires a speaker and a listener. However, that sentence might be very misleading as it never mentions requiring another individual, thus stating that the speaker and the listener can be within themselves. The behavior of the speaker acquires control of the environment through the response of the listener, such as making a request. Remember, the listener can be the same individual, and to clear confusion, let us provide an example. Have you ever been doing a job or tackling daily chores and given yourself mental instructions on how to approach said instructions? When you are giving yourself mental instructions, you are the speaker and the listener, as the mental instructions evoke a behavior, verbal or non-verbal.

The speaker is the individual who emits verbal behavior to communicate with others. In this role, the focus is on the production of language and expressing thoughts, needs, or desires defined in a behavioral form. The speaker selects appropriate verbal responses based on the current context and the desired outcome. The speaker's goal is to engage in effective communication by conveying meaningful messages to the listener. Conversely, the listener role involves receiving and comprehending the verbal behavior emitted by the speaker. Listeners interpret and understand the messages conveyed by the speaker, allowing them to respond appropriately. Skinner emphasized the importance of this role in understanding language acquisition. Listeners play a critical role in language development as they provide feedback and reinforcement to the speaker. Their ability to respond to speaker behavior reinforces the speaker's communication attempts, contributing to the reinforcement of language.

Molecular vs. Molar Verbal Behavior

Molecular and molar verbal behavior are two contrasting yet complementary perspectives in the analysis of language and communication, as proposed by B.F. Skinner, in his book "Verbal Behavior," which we have mentioned and summarized above. These two viewpoints offer distinct lenses through which to examine the complexities of human language. Molecular verbal behavior focuses on the minutiae of language, breaking it down into its most minor functional units. This perspective hones in on individual words, phonemes, or isolated responses. It is akin to analyzing language at the microlevel, studying the acquisition and functions of these elementary components. For example, in molecular analysis, researchers might explore how a child learns and reinforces the word "cookie." This level of scrutiny delves into the specific behaviors associated with vocalizing or recognizing the word and the corresponding consequences that shape its usage.

Conversely, molar verbal behavior takes a more holistic approach, emphasizing language's broader context and functional aspects. It views language as a social tool used to convey meaning and accomplish various communicative functions. In this framework, language is analyzed at the macro-level, examining entire conversations, narratives, or speech acts. For instance, molar analysis might involve studying a conversation between two individuals, with a focus on the social function it serves, such as requesting, commenting, or narrating a story. This approach is less concerned with the isolated components of language and more interested in understanding how language operates within larger social interactions. Molecular and molar perspectives in verbal behavior analysis are not mutually exclusive; they complement each other. Molecular analysis can inform our understanding of how individual words or responses are learned and reinforced. Meanwhile, molar analysis helps us grasp the overarching communicative purposes and social functions of language. In practice, the choice between these perspectives depends on the specific research or clinical goals. While molecular analysis is valuable for understanding language acquisition and the building blocks of communication, molar analysis provides insights into how language functions as a social tool, conveying meaning and facilitating human interaction. Together, these perspectives offer a comprehensive understanding of the intricacies of verbal behavior in the realm of behavior analysis.

Verbal Operant (6 Elementary Verbal Operant)

We have reached the largest subtopic of the chapter, with the development of the verbal operants and what each of them controls. Before moving on, we need to understand the difference between verbal behavior in behavioral science and verbal behavior in other disciplines. In the field of behavioral science, verbal behavior can be vocal or non-vocal behavior, while in other fields, verbal behavior simply means vocal behavior. In **FIGURE 6.2**, there will be an example of vocal and non-vocal

THE BARE BONES OF ABA

verbal behavior. These examples will depict how non-vocal verbal behavior can elicit the same response from the listener as vocal verbal behavior. In the example, we use sign language to request tea and vocal verbal behavior to request tea. As we can see, the response and the consequence are the same (receiving tea), while the forms of communication are very different. Another form of non-vocal language can be answering questions on an exam or worksheet. This is not vocalized; instead, it is written down on a paper (acting as the speaker) and responded by the listener, which answers the questions. In behavioral science, verbal behavior was broken down into units called verbal operants by B.F Skinner. Verbal operant is a functional relation between the type of responses and the same variable that controls non-verbal behavior such as the previously discussed MO's, SD's, and consequences from operant conditioning.

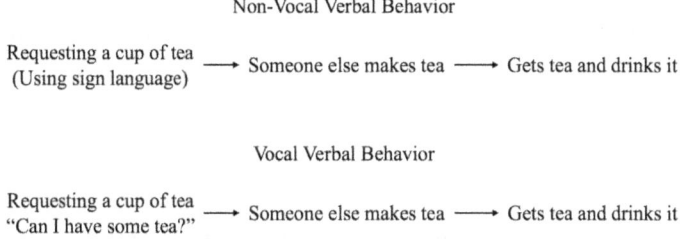

FIGURE 6.2 Example of Vocal and Non-vocal verbal behavior

After understanding this, moving on to verbal operants will become a lot easier to understand, as each operant is highly unique and have different antecedents, whether it be distant or immediate. There are six elementary verbal operants that all behavior scientists should know: Mand, Tact, Echoic, Interverbal, Textual, and Transcription.

Mand

A mand is a verbal behavior that serves the purpose of requesting something. It involves an individual communicating their desires or needs to others, with the expectation that their request will be met. Mands can take various forms, including spoken words, signs, gestures, or other communicative modalities, depending on the individual's communication abilities. A mand is essentially a request for a specific item, action, or event. It is driven by the individual's motivation to fulfill a particular need or desire. For example, Fonsi saying, "I want juice, please," or using a communication device to request a preferred toy is manding. The organism emits the mand with the expectation that it will result in obtaining the desired item or outcome. Manding is crucial for several reasons. It enhances an individual's ability to interact with their environment, express their preferences, and reduce frustration. Teaching mands can lead to improved social interactions, as it enables individuals to initiate and maintain conversations, request assistance, and engage in activities they enjoy. Moreover, manding can be pivotal in reducing challenging behaviors that may emerge due to communication difficulties. When individuals can effectively mand for their needs, they are less likely to engage in problem behavior to communicate their desires.

Now let us dig into the nooks and crannies of mand and the extreme importance of this verbal operant. First and foremost, it has to be stated and remembered that mand cannot and will not ever be emitted unless an MO is present. In other words, in order for an organism to engage in manding, there needs to be an MO present as the distant antecedent, which will cause the mand (request) evoking a response. And if we remember from MO's, EO's are the only antecedent to evoke behavior, so in order for manding to happen, the organism must want the reinforcer. I know this might sound confusing, but in **FIGURE 6.3**, there will be a representation of mand, which can be tied back to this definition.

Another critical point to remember is that mand is the building block of all the other verbal operants, and it is the first verbal operant acquired by human children and infants. Think about a self-example of when you were a non-vocal child and got hungry; you would point at the food or cry for food. In a way, mand is tied and developed by unconditioned reinforcers. Mand is the only verbal operant to fully and directly benefit the speaker. Many of the problem behaviors exhibited by organisms in the field are usually due to a lack of proper manding. For example, let us say that Fonsi (our beloved exemplar) is very hungry; through operant conditioning, he has learned to mand with crying, as every time he cries, he receives food. Now, this behavior is usually an undesired behavior in the field and very socially significant. Practitioners counteract this effect by teaching an alternative mand, such as asking for food when the organism is vocal and pointing at the food when the organism is non-vocal.

[continued on next page]

<u>Mand</u>

EO ⟶ Antecedent ⟶ Behavior ⟶ Consequence

Hunger ⟶ See food ⟶ Mand ⟶ Reinforcer related to the EO

FIGURE 6.3 Simplified and Graphically Visualized Mand Definition

Tact

A tact is essentially the expression of a verbal response when an individual observes or experiences something in their environment. This verbal response typically serves only some immediate tangible purpose, unlike a mand, which seeks to gain access to something specific. For example, when a child says, "Look, a red apple," or "I hear a dog barking," they are emitting tacts by describing what they see and hear. In other words, tact is simply naming things the speaker is in contact with in any sense nodes, which include seeing, hearing, feeling, smelling, and tasting. Tact, unlike mand, is controlled by a nonverbal SD, which is then followed by tact. In **FIGURE 6.4**, this process will be shown graphically once again using SSG. Tact itself is fairly simple, but like any good old book story, nothing is ever as it seems. Tact can be broken down even further into four different extensions: generic extension, metaphorical extension, metonymical extension, and solistic extension.

Generic extension: in a generic extension, a novel stimulus (remember, no effect) shares all of the defining features of the original stimulus. The generic extension of a tact refers to the ability of an individual to extend or generalize their labeling or description of items, events, or experiences beyond the specific instances they have encountered during training. This means that the individual can use their tacting skills to describe novel or similar items or situations that were not part of their training. Generic extension is a critical component of language development and communication. Let us provide an example of the generic extension using dogs. Remember, tact, in simple terms, is naming things, so let's say that Fonsi learned to tact "dog" upon seeing a Boston terrier, in generic extension. Fonsi tacts "dog" upon seeing a novel dog such as a goldendoodle or golden retriever.

Metaphorical extension: in metaphorical extension, unlike generic extension, a novel stimulus shares some of the defining features of the original stimulus. This is exactly as it sounds: "a metaphor" but described in behavioral terms. In generic extension, in order to generalize the stimulus, the novel stimulus has to share all features (in other words, it has to be another dog), while metaphorical only shares some features such as smell. For example, let's say that a flower smells very nice, and Fonsi also smells very nice; in this extension, we would say that "Fonsi smells like a flower".

Metonymical extension: metonymical extension differs heavily from both generic extension and metaphorical extension, as the novel stimulus shares none of the relevant features needed. Remember, tact uses any sense node, including visual, thus allowing for tacting even though the stimulus does not share any of the features. For example, let us say that Fonsi sees a picture of a bed; this causes Fonsi to say "sleeping." Even though the picture only shows a bed and no one sleeping, Fonsi was able to tact through this extension as he visually saw the bed and associated it with its purpose.

Solistic Extension: Solistic extension of tact is a linguistic phenomenon in which an individual applies a label or description to a specific item, event, or experience while excluding or ignoring other similar items or instances. This type of extension of tact can result in overly precise or rigid language use, where the individual fails to generalize a label to all appropriate instances. This tends to occur when an individual uses a label or description for a specific item in a highly restrictive manner. They may apply the term accurately to one item but struggle to extend it to other similar items, even when the label is appropriate. For example, a child (obviously Fonsi) might accurately label their pet dog as "Fido" but fail to recognize other dogs as "dogs" or use the term exclusively for their specific pet. In this case, the child demonstrates solistic extension by narrowly applying the label.

Tact

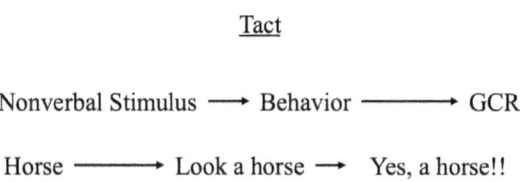

Figure 6.4 Depicting Tact under the Control of a Nonverbal Stimulus

Echoic

Echoic is exactly as it sounds, the listener echoing you or others. In other words, whenever you or another person speaks, the listener will repeat precisely the same. To better define the term, an echoic is a type of verbal behavior where the speaker repeats or echoes what another person has said, maintaining point-to-point correspondence and similarity in sound between the stimulus and the response. This form of verbal operant plays a crucial role in language acquisition and the development of more complex verbal behaviors. For those who skipped the previous sentence, I will reiterate again as it is perhaps the most important aspect of echoic. Echoic is a verbal operant controlled by a verbal SD, producing a verbal response with POINT-TO-POINT correspondence and formal similarity with the verbal SD. Once that criteria has been met it produces once again a Generalized conditioned reinforcer. For instance, lets say the word "apple," and the learner responds with "apple," this is an example of an echoic response. The key characteristics of echoic behavior include point-to-point correspondence, where each part of the verbal stimulus is matched by the corresponding part of the response, and formal similarity, meaning that the echoed words sound similar to the original stimulus. The beginning, middle, and end of the antecedent stimulus and the evoked response must be exactly the same in order for it to be considered echoic. Echoic has two further extensions which are categorized as non-vocal, the imitation of sign language and coping a text.

Imitation of sign language: exactly as it sounds, initiating sign language with point-to-point correspondence and formal similarity between the model and the response.

Copying a text: before defining this one, remember when you used to engage in socially significant behavior in school and your teacher would make you copy down or write down a sentence 20 or 40 times? Yes? now you can see where I'm coming with this, copying a text is the written verbal stimulus that has point-to-point correspondence and shares formal similarity with the product from copying a text. In elementary words, If you see the written word "cookie" and write down "cookie," it's an extension of echoic.

Intraverbal

Intraverbals are defined by their lack of formal similarity between the verbal stimulus and the response. For example, when Fonsi asks, "What do you wear on your feet?" and the response is "shoes," this is an intraverbal response. The stimulus "What do you wear on your feet?" and the response "shoes" are related but not identical in form or sound. Intraverbals play a crucial role in the development of conversational skills and other complex language abilities because they require understanding and producing language that is contextually appropriate rather than simply mimicking the original verbal stimulus (echoic). In other words, Intraverbal is the same as having a conversation, where the antecedent stimulus and the verbal response do not necessarily need to have point-to-point correspondence. Intraverbal although very simple to understand, expands beyond complexity and usage, as it can be used in social settings, where strong intraverbal skills enable individuals to engage in fluid and dynamic conversations, enhancing their social interactions and relationships. In educational contexts, intraverbals support academic achievement by facilitating participation in discussions, comprehension of verbal instructions, and the ability to articulate knowledge. Additionally, intraverbal training can be tailored to specific goals, such as preparing for job interviews or improving public speaking skills. Intraverbal is also controlled by a verbal SD, evoking a different verbal response and producing a generalized conditioned reinforcement.

Textual

Textual verbal operants are distinct from other verbal operants because they specifically involve reading. For example, when Fonsi sees the written word "cookie" and says "cookie" aloud, they are exhibiting textual behavior. The key features of textual operants include the accurate reproduction of the written text in spoken form and the ability to read aloud without necessarily understanding the meaning of the text. This type of behavior is fundamental for literacy and is often a primary focus in early education. Lets break it down even further and explain how textual works. Textual verbal operant is under the control of visual/tactual verbal SD, which evokes a response that shares point-to-point correspondence with the SD but in a different form such as above mention, vocally.

Transcription

Transcription verbal operants involve the accurate and consistent conversion of spoken words into written form. For example, when Fonsi hears the word "Bear" and writes "Bear" on paper, he is engaging in transcription behavior. This operant requires the individual to listen to the spoken word, understand its phonetic components, and reproduce these components accurately in written form. Unlike echoic behavior, which involves repeating spoken words, transcription specifically requires the conversion of auditory information into a different modality writing. The precision and fluency of transcription are critical, especially in contexts where accurate written records are necessary. Simplistically put, transcription is the writing or spelling of spoken words, controlled by a spoken verbal SD, evoking a verbal response that once again shares point to point correspondence with the SD but in the form of writing, producing a GCR.

Special Mention
Even though this subtopic is long and at times daunting it holds a special place in my heart, due to verbal operants being a major part of my thesis. These results can be found online by typing my name (the author) on simple google search.

Convergent and Divergent Multiple Control

Verbal behavior is very complex, and I recommend reading B.F. Skinner's analysis of behavior, as it is truly remarkable. Verbal behavior contains multiple relations among responses and environmental stimuli, which is what we will be discussing in this subtopic of Multiple control. As you can already guess by the title "Multiple Control" we will be talking about how verbal behavior can be controlled by multiple variables, known as convergent multiple control, or how one antecedent variable can affect the strength of multiple responses, known as divergent multiple control.

Convergent Multiple Control: convergent multiple control refers to a situation where a single verbal response is influenced or controlled by multiple antecedent stimuli. This concept is rooted in B.F. Skinner's analysis of verbal behavior and highlights how different types of antecedent stimuli can converge to evoke a specific verbal behavior. In other words, a particular verbal response is shaped and controlled by several factors, such as different discriminative stimuli, motivational operations, and contextual cues, working together to influence the behavior. The following examples are property of Arizona State University and are highly complex if you haven't been reading this subtopic.

Seeing a full garbage can + MO = "Hey! The garbage is full"

- This is an impure tact, it seems as a tact but is also a mand.

Seeing Chocolate + MO = "I want chocolate"

- Impure mand, it is also controlled by a non-verbal SD

Seeing an orange and hearing the question, "What is an orange?" = "fruit"

- Impure tact, since it is also controlled by a verbal SD

As we can see in the example provided above, something that might seem simple will hold some surprises, in our case, being under the control of multiple variables.

Divergent Multiple Control: divergent multiple control refers to a scenario where a single antecedent stimulus influences multiple verbal responses. This concept is also rooted in B.F. Skinner's analysis of verbal behavior highlights how one stimulus can lead to various responses depending on different factors such as the context, the individual's learning history, and current motivational states. Divergent multiple control describes how one stimulus can branch out and control different verbal behaviors. Divergent is simpler than convergent as we only focus on one controlling variable evoking multiple responses.

- Hunger (EO) = "I feel hungry"
- Hunger (EO) = "Pass me the food"

As we can see the same EO (hunger) evokes two different responses in the example above with the first being an impure tact, while the second being a pure mand (requesting the food).

Autoclitics

Autoclitics are a fascinating and complex aspect of B.F. Skinner's analysis of verbal behavior, adding layers of meaning and function to primary verbal operants such as mands, tacts, and intraverbals. The term "autoclitic" refers to verbal behavior that modifies the effects of the speaker's own verbal behavior, essentially providing commentary or clarification on the primary verbal operants. These can be thought of as the "grammar" or "syntax" of verbal behavior, adding nuances that help listeners interpret the speaker's intent more accurately. For example, saying "I think the sky is blue" versus "The sky is blue" introduces an autoclitic element that indicates the speaker's level of certainty. Autoclitics play a crucial role in effective communication by helping to convey the speaker's attitudes, beliefs, and emotional states. They can modify the strength, intensity, or scope of the primary verbal behavior, providing context that can change the meaning of the statement. For instance, the statement "I strongly believe it will rain today" uses the autoclitic "strongly believe" to emphasize the speaker's conviction. This additional layer of meaning can help listeners gauge the reliability of the information being communicated and respond appropriately. Autoclitics can be expanded into two different versions: autoclitic tact and autoclitic mand.

Autoclitic Tact: also known as secondary or descriptive autoclitics, are a specific form of verbal behavior in which an individual comments on or describes the characteristics of an object, event, or situation. Unlike primary tacts, which involve simply labeling or identifying stimuli, autoclitic tacts add layers of information by including descriptors that modify the primary verbal behavior. For example, saying "That's a big dog" adds an autoclitic element "big" to the primary tact "dog", providing additional information about the size of the dog. Since tact works with the senses, we can add "I hear" to inform that we are using auditory SD, "I see" to inform that we are using visual SD, and "I believe it is" to indicate strength or weakness (magnitude) of control source.

Autoclitic Mand: also known as secondary or descriptive mands, are a specific type of verbal behavior in which individuals request or command based on the characteristics of a stimulus or situation. Autoclitic mand tends to be controlled by Mos like its counterpart mand. However, unlike primary mands that request an item or action, autoclitic mands include descriptive elements that modify the primary verbal behavior. For instance, saying "Can I have a cold glass of water?" incorporates an autoclitic element "cold" to the primary mand "glass of water", specifying the desired temperature of the water.

Rule-Governed Behavior

Rule-governed behavior is a fundamental concept that refers to behavior that is controlled by verbal or written instructions, rules, or guidelines. Unlike directly observable contingencies, such as reinforcement or punishment, rule-governed behavior relies on the individual's ability to understand and follow abstract instructions. These rules can be explicit (clearly stated) or implicit (understood without being explicitly stated), and they play a crucial role in guiding human behavior across various contexts One key aspect of rule-governed behavior is that it allows individuals to engage in complex and flexible behavior beyond what can be directly learned through trial and error. For example, when someone follows traffic rules while driving, they are engaging in rule-governed behavior by adhering to instructions learned through education and experience rather than relying solely on immediate consequences like getting a ticket.

Rule-governed behavior often involves the use of verbal behavior, such as instructions, explanations, or warnings, to guide actions. This type of behavior is particularly prevalent in educational settings, where students learn rules and procedures that guide their academic performance. For instance, a teacher might provide instructions on how to solve a math problem or guidelines for completing a science experiment, and students follow these rules to achieve the desired outcomes. Another essential aspect of rule-governed behavior is its role in self-regulation and self-control. Individuals who can follow internalized rules and guidelines can better manage their behavior, emotions (part of radical behaviorism), and impulses (characterized by previously reinforced behavior). A crucial aspect of rule-governed behavior is that behavior may never be in contact with the actual consequences. Even though we have mentioned rule-governed behavior, what exactly are rules?

Rules

Rule refers to a verbal or written statement that guides behavior by providing instructions, guidelines, or expectations. Rules are a form of antecedent control, meaning they influence behavior before it occurs by setting the occasion for specific actions or responses.

Now that we understand rule-governed behavior, how can we tell if a behavior may be rule-governed? Simple, three factors we look at to determine this are as follows:

1. If there is a lack of immediate consequence
2. Response = Consequence delay is greater than 30 seconds.
3. Behavior changes or is maintained without apparent reinforcement

Contingency Shaped Behavior

Contingency-shaped behavior refers to behavior shaped and maintained by direct contingencies between actions and consequences. In other words, the behavior is influenced by the immediate effects that follow it, such as reinforcement or punishment. This type of behavior is contrasted with rule-governed behavior, where behavior is guided by verbal instructions or rules. One key aspect of contingency-shaped behavior is that it is shaped through direct experience and learning. When an individual engages in a behavior and experiences a reinforcement, they are more likely to repeat that behavior in the future. Conversely, if the behavior leads to punishment, they are less likely to engage in that behavior again. This process of reinforcement and punishment shapes the individual's behavior over time.

Contingency-shaped behavior is often observed in everyday life, where actions are influenced by their immediate outcomes. For example, a child learns to say "please" when asking for something because they have learned that using polite language often leads to reinforcement, such as receiving the desired item. This can be simplified even further, let say Fonsi decided to cook and make soup. Fonsi follows the instructions when cooking his soup (rule-governed behavior), but when he taste the soup it taste very salty. Next time Fonsi will put less salt in the soup (contingency-shaped behavior). Why? Because the behavior of putting less salt is CONTINGENT on the soup being slaty, if the soup wasn't salty, the behavior would change, and it would be contingency shaped behavior.

SEVEN
PSYCHOLOGY, MEET SCIENCE!
EXPERIMENTAL DESIGN

"Nothing has such power to broaden the mind as the ability to investigate systematically and truly all that comes under thy observation in life"

MARCUS AURELIUS

INTRODUCTION

Welcome to another incredibly important yet simple-to-understand chapter. In the previous chapters, we have been working under the assumption that behaviorism is a science, but you might have asked yourself, how is this not psychology? In behavior analysis the scientific approach to understanding and modifying behavior is tied to a strict adherence to the principles of scientific methodology, while psychology, as a broader field, includes a variety of approaches and methodologies, some of which may not adhere as strictly to scientific principles. ABA relies heavily on empirical methods to study and modify behavior. It involves systematic observation, measurement, and experimentation to identify functional relationships between behavior and environmental variables. ABA practitioners collect data before, during, and after interventions to evaluate their effectiveness. In contrast, psychology encompasses a wide range of methods, including qualitative research, introspective methods, and case studies, which may not always involve rigorous empirical testing.

In this field, behaviors are defined operationally in precise, observable, and measurable terms. This ensures clarity and consistency in how behaviors are identified and measured, which is essential for scientific research and replication. While many areas of psychology also strive for operational definitions, some psychological concepts (e.g., emotions, cognitions) can be more abstract and harder to measure directly and consistently. Behavior analysis emphasizes experimental control to establish causal relationships between interventions and behavior changes. Techniques like single-subject designs and controlled experiments are commonly used to isolate the effects of specific variables. Although experimental control is also valued in psychology, the field's diversity includes approaches that may not prioritize or achieve the same level of experimental rigor, such as certain forms of psychotherapy or psychoanalysis.

We tend to place a strong emphasis on replication and reliability of findings. Interventions and results are expected to be reproducible across different settings and populations, which reinforces the scientific validity of behavior analysis practices. Psychology, being a broader field, includes subfields where replication and reliability are challenging. The "replication crisis" in psychology (which you can research through multiple studies) has highlighted difficulties in reproducing results from many psychological studies. A core component of behavioral science is functional analysis, which involves identifying the antecedents and consequences that maintain problematic behaviors. This approach is highly systematic and data-driven, focusing on observable interactions between the individual and their environment. While psychology also examines behavior-environment interactions, many psychological theories emphasize internal mental states, unconscious processes, and other factors that are not directly observable or measurable, making them less empirically grounded. As a side note, though radical behaviorism does include private events such as thoughts and feelings, they are still under the control of the environmental variables we follow in behavioral analysis, which, during Skinner's experiments, he didn't really use. Also noticed through this introduction, and from the previous chapter's learning, one of the seven dimensions stands out, that being technological. Writing the procedures, the results, and the full research in clear and concise terms is critical to the replication of the experiments in our field.

Why Experiment?

Common sense and logic dictate that things are a certain way because of experience. However, your life experience, the very one you developed these ideologies under, are entirely different than mine. In other words, your common sense and logic will be drastically different than mine or another individual's. Breaking them down even further, we can state that common sense focuses more on the individual's experience. However, logic is more thorough and concrete, but arguing a point logically does not make this point true; making the logical argument, at most, is a hypothesis that hasn't been proven. That's why we experiment, so we can separate assumptions, theories, "feelings", common sense, logic, and arguments from factual and evidence-based answers (Something politics and journalism need nowadays).

Experimentation is a fundamental aspect of scientific inquiry and serves several crucial purposes across various fields of study, including our own. One primary reason we experiment is to establish causal relationships (this action caused this reaction). Experiments are designed to test hypotheses about cause-and-effect relationships by manipulating one or more independent variables and observing the effects on a dependent variable. This allows researchers to determine whether changes in the independent variable directly cause changes in the dependent variable, helping to understand the underlying mechanisms of behavior and other phenomena. Another key purpose of experimentation is the control of variables. Experiments enable researchers to control extraneous variables that might otherwise confound the results. By creating controlled environments and using random assignment, researchers can isolate the effects of the independent variable, ensuring that the observed changes in the dependent variable are due to the manipulation and not other factors. This precise control is essential for drawing valid conclusions from the data. Experiments also facilitate replication and reliability, which are essential for verifying the reliability and validity of findings. Keep in mind in our current technological advancement, we are incapable of achieving 100% control of variables, especially extraneous variables, which, more often than not, we can't control.

By repeating experiments under similar conditions, researchers can confirm whether the results are consistent and generalizable across different contexts and populations, strengthening the evidence base for scientific theories and interventions. This iterative process of hypothesis testing, data collection, and theory refinement is central to scientific progress, contributing to the advancement of knowledge and theory development. In applied fields like ABA, experiments provide evidence for the effectiveness of interventions and treatments. By rigorously testing different strategies and techniques, practitioners can determine which approaches work best for addressing specific problems, ensuring that interventions are grounded in scientific research and leading to better outcomes for individuals and communities. Engaging in experimental research also fosters critical thinking and problem-solving skills. Researchers must design robust experiments, analyze data, and interpret results critically, developing analytical skills and promoting a deeper understanding of the subject matter. Through carefully designed and executed experiments, researchers can generate reliable evidence that contributes to scientific progress and practical applications.

Single Case Research Design vs. Group Design

Single-case research designs (SCRD) and group designs are two primary approaches to conducting research in fields like psychology, education, and behavior analysis. Each has unique characteristics, advantages, and limitations, making them suitable for different types of research questions and settings.

Single Case Research Design

Single-case research designs focus on the intensive study of a single subject or a small group of subjects. The primary goal is to observe the effects of an intervention or treatment on individual behavior over time. These designs are often used in our beloved Applied Behavior Analysis (ABA) and other fields where detailed observation and analysis of individual behavior are crucial. There are several types of SCRD, including the reversal ABAB design (discussed further on), multiple baseline design, and alternating treatments design. One of SCRD's main advantages is its ability to provide detailed, in-depth information about the effects of an intervention on a single subject. This is particularly valuable in clinical and educational settings where individualized interventions are necessary. SCRD allows for the direct observation of behavior changes, making it easier to establish a functional relationship between the intervention and the observed outcomes. Additionally, SCRD can be highly flexible, allowing researchers to adapt their methods to the specific needs of the subject and the research context. However, SCRD has some limitations. One significant drawback is the difficulty in generalizing findings to larger populations. Because SCRD focuses on a small number of subjects, the results may not be applicable to other individuals or settings. Additionally, SCRD can be time-consuming and labor-intensive, requiring continuous observation and data collection over extended periods.

Group Design

Group designs, on the other hand, involve comparing the behavior or outcomes of two or more groups of subjects. The most common group design is the randomized controlled trial (RCT), where subjects are randomly assigned to either an experimental group (receiving the intervention) or a control group (not receiving the intervention). The primary goal of group design is to evaluate the average effect of an intervention across a large number of subjects, providing a broader perspective on its efficacy. One of the main advantages of group design is its ability to generalize findings to larger populations. By studying a large sample, researchers can make more confident conclusions about the effectiveness of an intervention for a broader audience. Group designs also allow for the use of statistical analysis to determine the significance of the results, providing a more rigorous test of the hypotheses. However, group designs also have limitations. They may not capture the individual variability in responses to an intervention, potentially overlooking essential differences in how subjects respond. Additionally, group designs can be less flexible than SCRD, as they require larger sample sizes and more stringent control over variables, which can be challenging and costly to implement.

Basic Graph

Before we move on to more detailed and complex chapter concepts, let's have a little high school review of the most basic graph that can exist, the line graph. When we think of the line graph we think of the classic X and Y Axis with a line all over the place in the middle. More specifically a line graph, also known as a line chart, is a type of data visualization used to display information as a series of data points called 'markers' connected by straight line segments. This type of graph is particularly useful for showing trends over time, comparing changes in different data sets, and illustrating the relationship between variables (very important in our field). The components of a line graph include axes, data points, line segments, labels, and scale. Each point on the graph represents a data value, and the data points are connected by straight lines to show the progression or trend of the data across the x-axis. Axes should be labeled to indicate what they represent, and a title for the graph helps convey the overall content or purpose of the data visualization.

Line graphs are excellent for identifying trends over time, comparing different data sets, and providing a clear and straightforward way to present data. They allow easy identification of whether the data values are increasing, decreasing, or remaining constant, and when multiple lines are plotted on the same graph, it is easy to compare different data sets, such as sales figures across different years or different products. The simplicity and clarity of line graphs make them easy to understand for a broad audience.

In our field, we tend to use a line graph with a phase line, which transitions from baseline to intervention. This is the most basic line graph in behavior analysis. As we dive deeper into experimental design, we will see countless single-subject research designs ranging from Multi-baseline to alternating treatment designs. In (**Figure 7.1**), we will see an example of a very basic withdrawal design line graph with a phase line.

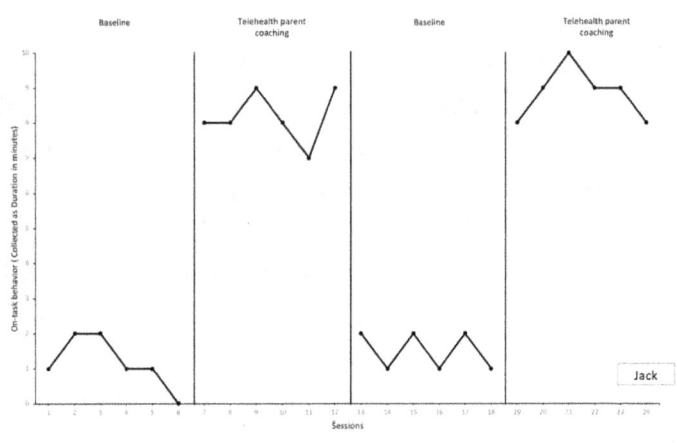

Figure 1 "Will a telehealth parent coaching model improve on-task behavior for children with autism?"

Figure 7.1: Typical Graph used in EAB, withdraw ABAB.

Next we can see a multiple baseline across subjects.

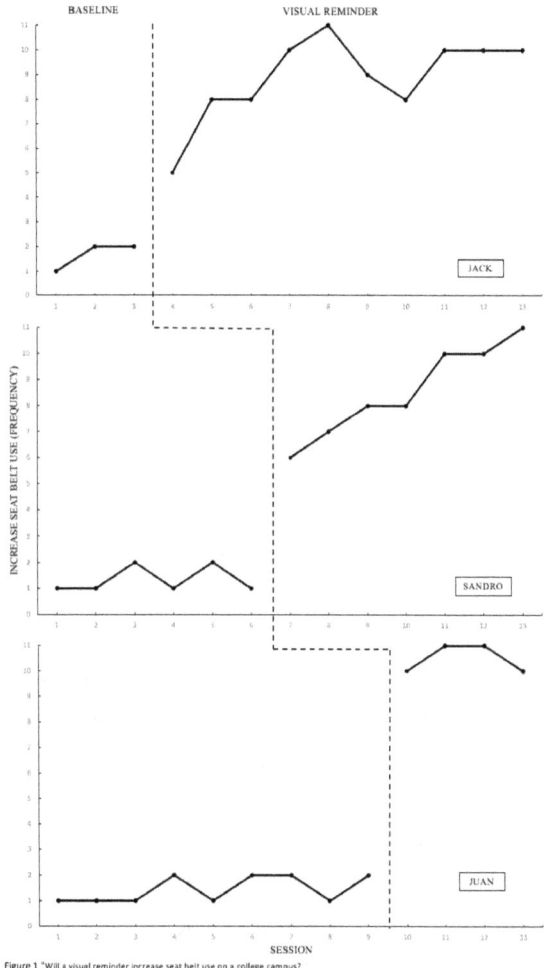

Figure 7.2: Multiple baseline design

And lastly we can see a alternating treatment design.

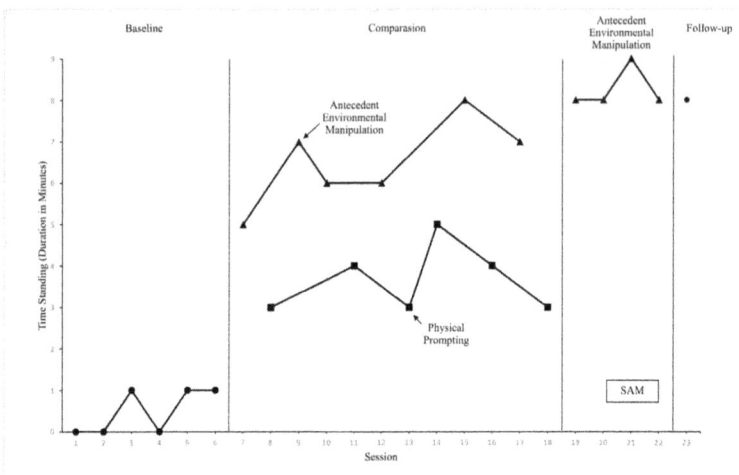

Figure 7.3: Alternating Treatment design

These are some of the graph you can encounter on everyday EAB, however typically a graph with a baseline, and an intervention phase is what is used in the real world.

IV, DV, Confounding Variable, Extraneous Variable

This subtopic will involve a quick summary of four very important components of experimentation. From high school and middle school science, we all should know what IV and DV stand for. If we don't, let's refresh our memory and see what they are not only in natural sciences like biology and chemistry but also how they differ in ABA.

Independent Variable (IV): an independent variable is a key component in research and scientific experiments that refers to the variable that is intentionally manipulated or changed by the researcher to observe its effects on other variables. It is called "independent" because it is not influenced by other variables in the experiment but rather stands alone as the factor that is being tested. The independent variable is typically the presumed cause in a cause-and-effect relationship, and it is expected to have an impact on the dependent variable, which is the outcome being measured.

Dependent Variable (DV): a dependent variable is the variable in an experiment or study that is observed and measured to assess the effect of changes made to the independent variable. It is called "dependent" because its value is thought to depend on or be influenced by the independent variable. In essence, the dependent variable represents the outcome or effect that researchers are interested in understanding or predicting.

Confounding Variable or Extraneous Variable: confounding variables are extraneous variables in a study or experiment that can affect the relationship between the independent and dependent variables, potentially leading to erroneous conclusions. These variables can interfere with the ability to accurately establish a cause-and-effect relationship because they introduce alternative explanations for the observed effects. Confounding variables can obscure the true effect of the independent variable on the dependent variable by creating a false impression of an association or by exaggerating or underestimating the strength of the relationship. When a confounding variable is present, it becomes difficult to determine whether changes in the dependent variable are actually due to the manipulation of the independent variable or due to the influence of the confounding variable. This is one of the biggest risk to research reliability and validity, especially in a field like ABA where the environment carries many factors.

Functional Relation

Functional relation has its own subtopic due to the importance of understanding it for research and understanding. A functional relation refers to a systematic and predictable relationship between two variables, where changes in one variable correspond to changes in another variable consistently and reliably. In other words, a functional relation describes how one variable influences or affects another variable. This concept is fundamental in various fields, including behavior analysis, psychology, economics, physics, and engineering.

In research, a functional relation is often investigated through experimental studies, where researchers manipulate an independent variable (IV) to observe its effect on a dependent variable (DV). By systematically varying the IV and measuring changes in the DV, researchers can establish whether there is a functional relation between the two variables. For example, in a study examining the effect of sleep duration on cognitive performance, sleep duration would be the independent variable, and cognitive performance would be the dependent variable. If increasing sleep duration consistently leads to improved cognitive performance, a functional relation between sleep duration and cognitive performance would be demonstrated (yes a psychology example, but a true research).

Functional relations are crucial for understanding cause-and-effect relationships and making predictions about how changes in one variable will impact another variable. They form the basis of scientific inquiry and allow researchers to draw conclusions about the relationships between variables based on empirical evidence. Establishing a functional relation requires careful experimental design, control of extraneous variables, and clear operational definitions of the variables under investigation. In (**Figure 7.1**), we can deduct from the graphs examples and non-examples of functional relation. Its clearly visible that the intervention had effect.

Validity (Internal vs. External)
Validity in research refers to the extent to which a study accurately measures what it intends to measure and whether the findings can be generalized to other populations or contexts. It is a fundamental aspect of research quality and reliability, ensuring that the conclusions drawn from a study are meaningful and trustworthy. There are several types of validity that researchers consider when evaluating the validity of their studies.

Internal validity: is concerned with whether the study design and methods accurately demonstrate cause-and-effect relationships between variables, without the influence of confounding factors. Achieving high internal validity involves controlling for potential threats to validity, such as selection bias, history, maturation, and testing effects.

External validity: focuses on the generalizability of study findings to other populations, settings, or situations beyond the specific conditions of the study. A study with high external validity can be applied to broader contexts, allowing researchers to make meaningful conclusions and recommendations beyond the immediate study sample.

Construct validity: assesses whether the operationalization of concepts (constructs) accurately reflects the underlying theoretical concepts being studied. It examines whether the measures used effectively capture the intended constructs and provide reliable data for analysis.

Content validity evaluates whether the content of measurement instruments adequately covers all aspects of the construct they are intended to measure. It ensures that the items or questions in the instrument are relevant, comprehensive, and representative of the construct.

Criterion-related: validity assesses the degree to which a measurement instrument predicts or correlates with an external criterion or outcome. Concurrent validity examines the instrument's correlation with a criterion measured at the same time, while predictive validity evaluates its ability to predict future outcomes.

Overall, validity is essential in research as it ensures that research findings are meaningful, accurate, and applicable to real-world situations. Researchers use various methods and techniques to establish and assess validity, enhancing the credibility and impact of their research.

Reliability

Reliability in research refers to the consistency and dependability of measurements or observations obtained from a study. It is a critical aspect of research quality to ensure that the results obtained are stable, repeatable, and free from random error. In essence, reliability assesses the extent to which the same results would be obtained if the study were repeated under similar conditions, providing researchers with confidence in the accuracy and consistency of their data. There are various types of reliability that researchers consider when evaluating the reliability of their measures. Test-retest reliability examines the consistency of measurements over time by administering the same measurement instrument to the same group of participants on two separate occasions. Internal consistency reliability assesses the consistency of items within a measurement instrument, ensuring that they are all measuring the same underlying construct.

Inter-rater reliability assesses the agreement between different raters or observers when using a measurement instrument. Parallel forms reliability examines the consistency of scores obtained from different versions of the same measurement instrument designed to measure the same construct. Split-half reliability involves splitting a measurement instrument into two halves and comparing the scores obtained from each half. Achieving high reliability is essential in research because it ensures that the results obtained are accurate and trustworthy. Researchers employ various methods and statistical techniques to assess reliability, such as correlation coefficients and intraclass correlation coefficients (ICC). By establishing the reliability of their measures, researchers can have confidence in the consistency and stability of their data, leading to more valid and meaningful conclusions.

Types of Research Questions

Now that we've had a refresher course on research let us discuss the types of research questions in behavior analysis. Through SSG, I will make this subtopic very simple with an explanation:

Demonstration: demonstration question does exactly what it says; it demonstrates the effectiveness of a single IV. This question asks if a single intervention will either decrease or increase the outcome (DV).

Comparative/Comparison: again another question that does exactly as it says; it compares two or more independent variables to each other. This question asks if intervention one or intervention 2 increases or decreases the outcome (DV).

Component Analysis: now, this question is very interesting and one of my favorites as it tears apart treatment packages and examines IVs one by one. This question pulls apart a treatment package to identify which component are the most effective such as alone or in combination. This question brings research in our field alive as practitioners usually use a treatment package to treat behavior modification. However, the research curiosity kicks in and makes us ask what part of the treatment package had a functional relation (at least for me, it does).

Parametric: the last question is another very important one and, most of the time, will relate to the temporal aspect of our field. This question examines the amount or dosage of something to determine how much is the most effective. For example, it compares the effects of time out between a 5-minute and a 10-minute time out (also, as discussed, punishment is not recommended unless necessary).

These questions are important, and I recommend remembering them if any of you reading this book decide to pursue the field, especially those in Experimental Behavior Analysis (EBA), these questions will be all over the place.

Continues vs. Non continues Recording

Continuous and non-continuous recording are two methods used in Applied Behavior Analysis (ABA) to collect data on behavior, with differences in how they capture behavior instances. Continuous recording involves recording every instance of a behavior that occurs within a specified observation period, providing a detailed and comprehensive account of the behavior. This method is particularly useful for behaviors that are frequent, repetitive, or occur at unpredictable intervals, as it captures each occurrence and provides a clear picture of the behavior's frequency and pattern

On the other hand, non-continuous recording, also known as partial or interval recording, samples behavior at specific intervals rather than recording every occurrence. There are different types of non-continuous recording methods, such as partial interval recording, whole interval recording, and momentary time sampling. These methods are used when behaviors are less frequent or occur for extended periods, making it impractical or unnecessary to record each instance. Non-continuous recording provides an estimate of behavior frequency or duration based on periodic observations, allowing researchers to gather data efficiently while still capturing meaningful information about the behavior.

Each method has its advantages and limitations, and researchers choose the most appropriate method based on the behavior being measured, its frequency, duration, and the research objectives. Continuous recording provides a detailed account of behavior instances, while non-continuous recording allows for efficient data collection, particularly for behaviors that are less frequent or of longer duration. Since we follow the SSG rules in this book a chart in (**Figure 7.4**) will be added to show when to use which method of recording.

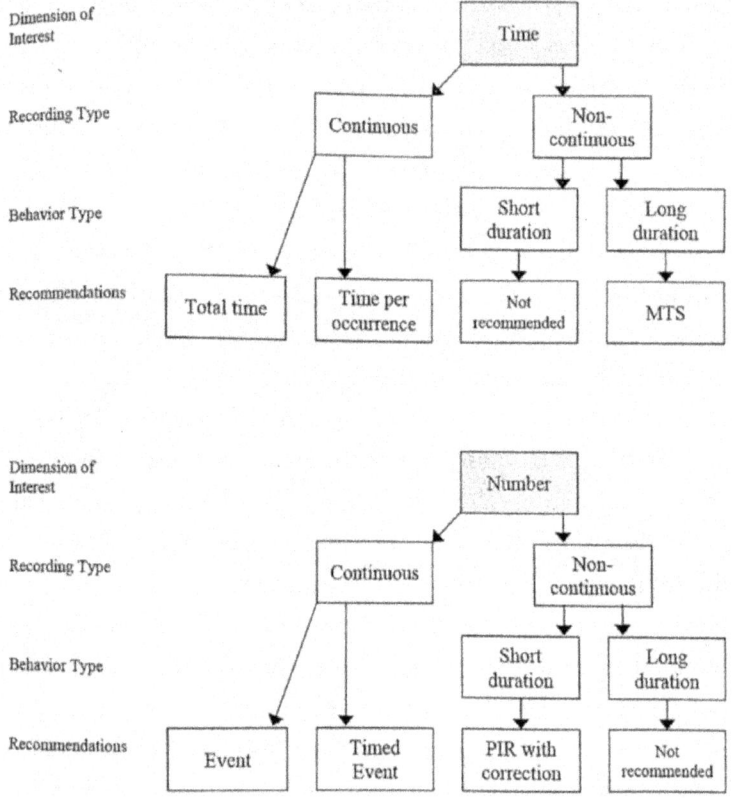

Figure 7.4: Choosing the Right Data Collection system, Credits to **Ledford & Gast, p.113**

THE BARE BONES OF ABA

Duration, Latency, IRT, Count, Rate

Let us discuss some recording methods (these are the basic and simple methods; there are more complex ways) that we as practitioners rely on.

Duration refers to the total amount of time a behavior occurs from the moment it begins until it ends (or in more technical terms, onset to offset of the behavior). It is a crucial measurement when analyzing behaviors that persist for an extended period, as it provides insights into the length of time a specific behavior lasts.

Latency: refers to the amount of time that passes between the presentation of a stimulus (such as a request or instruction) and the initiation of a behavior in response to that stimulus. Essentially, it measures the delay or time lag before a behavior occurs after a specific cue or prompt. Latency is an important concept for assessing how quickly an individual responds to a given situation, whether it's a command, an environmental change, or a stimulus in a learning context. For example, if a teacher gives Fonsi an instruction to "raise your hand," the latency would be the time it takes the student to actually raise their hand after hearing the command.

Inter-response time: refers to the amount of time that elapses between the end of one instance of a behavior and the beginning of the next occurrence of the same behavior. It is a measure of the time between two successive responses and is often used to analyze the frequency and pacing of behaviors. For example, if Fonsi is engaging in a repetitive behavior like tapping their desk, the IRT would be the time between the end of one tap and the start of the next tap.

Count: refers to the simple tally or frequency of occurrences of a specific behavior within a designated time period. It is one of the most basic ways to measure behavior, providing a straightforward count of how many times a behavior happens.

For example, if a child engages in the behavior of raising their hand 10 times during a lesson, the count would be 10. This measure is helpful when tracking discrete behaviors that have clear start and end points, such as asking questions, completing tasks, or performing actions like clapping or shouting.

Rate: refers to the frequency of a behavior occurring within a specific time period. It is a combination of both the count of how many times a behavior occurs and the time during which the behavior is measured. Rate is calculated by dividing the total number of occurrences of a behavior (count) by the total observation time. For example, if a child engages in a behavior, such as asking questions, 15 times over a 30-minute observation, the rate would be 15 occurrences per 30 minutes or 0.5 occurrences per minute.

Whole, Partial and Momentary

Now that the above-mentioned ways of collecting empirical data in the field have been discussed, let us overview a slightly different approach to data which even though unconventional it is (in my opinion) the single most important way to collect data on behaviors that occur at extremely fast rates. Of course the topic at hand belongs to Non-continuous measurements which at its core allows for the collection of data for behaviors that can occur at an uncountable amount.

Whole Interval Recording

Whole-interval recording is a method used to estimate the duration of a behavior by dividing an observation period into equal intervals and marking each one in which the behavior occurred for the entire interval. It's most useful for measuring behaviors that should occur continuously, such as on-task engagement or sustained eye contact. Because the behavior must fill the full interval to be recorded, whole-interval recording often underestimates the true occurrence of the behavior. In practice, it answers the question: "For what portion of time was this behavior sustained without interruption?"

Partial Interval Recording

Partial-interval recording asks a slightly different question: "Did the behavior occur at all during this interval?" The observer marks "yes" if the target behavior happened even once at any point in that interval. This approach is ideal for behaviors that occur rapidly or unpredictably, such as vocal outbursts, tapping, or self-stimulatory actions. Because any occurrence counts for the full interval, partial-interval recording tends to overestimate the actual total duration or frequency of the behavior. It is often used when the goal is to decrease a behavior, since it captures even brief instances of occurrence.

Momentary Time Sampling

Momentary time sampling, sometimes called momentary interval recording, provides a snapshot approach to behavior measurement. The observer looks up at predetermined moments (for example, at the end of each 30-second interval) and records whether the behavior is occurring at that exact instant. This method is efficient and less demanding for observers who must monitor multiple individuals or behaviors at once. Because it samples moments rather than continuous intervals, it can yield either over- or underestimation depending on how the timing aligns with the behavior's natural rhythm.

Momentary time sampling answers the question: "Was the behavior happening right now?"

Observer Bias

In behavior analysis, observation is both a science and a behavior in itself. Every observer operates within a network of private stimuli, expectations, prior experiences, emotional reactions, fatigue, and subtle reinforcements. When those private events begin to influence what and how an observer records, we call it observer bias. Bias doesn't mean dishonesty. In most cases, it's unintentional and invisible to the person recording the data. It can occur even in structured environments when an observer begins to see what they expect to see instead of what is actually happening. A student expecting improvement may unconsciously stretch the definition of "engaged." A therapist tracking aggression might overcount ambiguous movements if they anticipate escalation. From a behavioral standpoint, bias is maintained through reinforcement. When data align with our expectations, we receive a subtle form of self-reinforcement, the relief of confirmation. When data contradict our assumptions, it can function as punishment, evoking avoidance of uncomfortable truths. Over time, this reinforcement history shapes how we perceive and record the world. Sources of Observer Bias:

- Expectation: Preexisting belief that behavior should increase or decrease.
- Reinforcement history: Previous sessions where certain data patterns were rewarded or praised.
- Emotional reactivity: Sympathy, frustration, or personal identification with the subject.

- Social contingencies: Pressure from supervisors, colleagues, or self-imposed performance standards.

Preventing Bias

The most powerful safeguard against bias is operational precision, clear, objective definitions that leave no room for personal interpretation. When "on-task behavior" is defined as "eyes oriented toward the assigned material for five consecutive seconds," the observer has an unambiguous rule to follow. Other preventive strategies include:

- Interobserver Agreement (IOA): Having a second observer collect data simultaneously to verify consistency.
- Blind conditions: Keeping the observer unaware of the intervention phase or expected outcome.
- Observer self-monitoring: Recording one's own error trends, reviewing video, and practicing data scoring under supervision.

Observer bias will never be fully eliminated because it arises from the same behavioral contingencies that shape all human experience. But through measurement, calibration, and awareness, it can be managed, transforming the act of observation from an art of impression to a science of evidence.

Observer Drift

If observer bias is distortion from expectation, observer

drift is erosion from time. Drift occurs when an observer's adherence to operational definitions gradually weakens, leading to small but systematic changes in how behavior is recorded. Unlike bias, drift often begins without motive or awareness. It's the behavioral equivalent of "instrument calibration loss" subtle, cumulative, and invisible until data patterns begin to shift. I've seen this firsthand during long-term applied studies. An observer might start a project with precise definitions: "hand-raising must be accompanied by extended elbow and visible palm." After several weeks, the same observer begins marking partial hand lifts as valid responses, reasoning that "it's close enough."

That slight deviation, multiplied across hundreds of intervals, transforms data accuracy into noise. Drift occurs because observation, like any human behavior, is sensitive to reinforcement contingencies. When sessions are long or repetitive, the observer is reinforced for efficiency rather than accuracy, fewer keystrokes, quicker scores, smoother graphs. Over time, these contingencies shape a less stringent standard. The observer's behavior drifts not because they stopped caring, but because the environment rewarded the wrong variable. Behavioral Causes of Drift:

- Response fatigue: Extended observation sessions without breaks reduce discrimination accuracy.
- Ambiguous definitions: The more subjective the target behavior, the faster drift occurs.
- Reinforcement of convenience: Quick responses are easier and thus more likely to persist.
- Loss of calibration: Without periodic feedback, observers shape their own internal "criteria" for what counts.

Detecting and Correcting Drift

- Interobserver reliability checks: Comparing current data with another trained observer reveals deviation patterns.
- Video re-analysis: Reviewing recorded sessions against the original definitions retrains discrimination accuracy.
- Periodic retraining: Just as a pilot must complete recurrent proficiency checks, observers must recalibrate their measurement skills to maintain fidelity
- Feedback and reinforcement: Providing reinforcement for correct scoring accuracy strengthens precision and reduces drift over time.

The Ethical Dimension

Observer drift isn't just a methodological issue, it's an ethical one. When data accuracy declines, so does the validity of decisions made from those data. Treatment plans, research outcomes, and even professional reputations hinge on fidelity of observation. Recognizing drift as a natural product of behavioral contingencies reframes it not as failure, but as a predictable variable to be managed. Just as we design environments to reduce error in learners, we must also design systems that maintain precision in ourselves.

As I conclude this first phase of the book, I want to emphasize a truth that took me years of practice and reflection to fully understand: Observation is not passive. It is behavior, subject to all the same antecedents, reinforcers, and shaping effects that influence the behaviors we record in others. In Applied

Behavior Analysis, the observer is both scientist and participant.

Our definitions shape what we see. Our reinforcements shape how we interpret. When we measure with precision, we aren't just collecting data, we're behaving ethically, honoring the core promise of behavioral science: that reality can be understood, improved, and trusted.

As you move into the next phase of this book, carry that lesson with you. Whether you're studying a learner, a patient, a pilot, or yourself, remember that accuracy is compassion. Every data point is a story of behavior, and every act of careful observation is a commitment to truth.

PHASE II

With the conclusion of Phase 1, the foundation of SSG, Scientific, Simplified, and Graphically Visualized, has been firmly established as an educational and behavioral framework for teaching concepts in Applied Behavior Analysis (ABA). Phase 1 was, in essence, a teaching laboratory: a space where I demonstrated how SSG can simplify complex behavioral theories, translate them into visual understanding, and make the science of learning accessible to both professionals and students.

Phase 2 marks the shift from classroom to practice, from theory to real-world impact.

Here, I explore how the SSG framework has moved beyond academic settings and into the environments that have defined my own professional and personal journey. Each chapter in this section represents a different field where behavior, precision, and feedback converge:

- In education, SSG redefine's how students grasp and retain information through visualization and reinforcement.
- In medicine and healthcare, it serves as a bridge between professionals and patients, enhancing communication and treatment compliance.
- In aviation, it transforms technical instruction into behavioral fluency, where comprehension, not memorization, determines safety and mastery.

Through these chapters, I aim to demonstrate that SSG is not limited to the science of behavior, it is a science of clarity. Whether in a clinic, classroom, or cockpit, the same principles of observation, feedback, and simplification hold true. Phase 2 is therefore not just an extension of SSG; it is its proof in practice, the moment where concept becomes application, and precision becomes performance.

EIGHT
ONE + ONE IS TWO IN ABA
THE SSG EXPERIMENT

"Knowledge is power. Information is liberating. Education is the premise of progress, in every society, in every family."

KOFI ANNAN

RESEARCH DISCLAIMER

The research, data, and experimental results presented in this book are entirely independent and are not affiliated with, endorsed by, or conducted under the supervision of any academic institution or organization.

All findings were developed and analyzed solely for the purpose of illustrating and exploring the conceptual framework of the Scientific, Simplified, and Graphically Visualized (SSG) model. The study has not undergone peer review and should therefore be interpreted as a conceptual demonstration rather than a formal scientific validation. While every effort was made to maintain accuracy and honesty in data collection and reporting, it is acknowledged that this research contains numerous confounding variables and utilizes simplified methods to support the illustrative aims of this work.

In no way, shape, or form have the numbers, data integrity, or procedural ethics of this research been altered, fabricated, or breached. The results are presented as they occurred, with transparency and in good faith, to serve as an educational foundation for further exploration and refinement of the SSG concept.

A year in the making

So far the entire book has focused on using SSG theory to teach wordy, long concepts especially those found in research papers and the big ole bible of ABA "COOPER ET AL, 2020." This is phase II of the book, you might be asking why phase II?. In the past year I have been recruiting volunteers, specifically 20, in a random order from fathers and mothers to those who are wanting to learn ABA but don't know where to start. This is where the book gets interesting, as this experiment over time showed results that impressed even me. The concept is simple, and since the book is, in my opinion, the definition of simplicity to explain ABA, I will explain the process. The basis behind the entire experiment is for the volunteers to choose a chapter of their choice in either "Cooper" or a research paper that ties to the ideas on the explained topics. These volunteers are tasked with reading this chapters or papers and try to make sense out of them, once they have read them they would be tested on the chapter with each chapter having 5 questions each. Following this, each volunteers was given the relevant chapter of this book which integrates SSG theory, and once again where tested after. Now that you understand the basis of the implementation let us get into the specific aspect of it, and maybe even overcomplicate it.

Part I Design of the Experiment

When I first decided to test the SSG approach, my goal wasn't to prove a point; it was to see what really happens when simplicity meets autonomy in learning. I've always believed that learners remember information more effectively when they're guided to interact with it, when reading becomes an active conversation rather than a passive experience. But belief isn't proof. To know whether SSG genuinely improved understanding, I needed data.

So I designed a simple, behaviorally sound experiment: twenty volunteers (as mentioned), each choosing one chapter that interested them from a pool of materials. They could select from Cooper et al.'s Applied Behavior Analysis or an equivalent peer-reviewed paper covering similar behavioral principles. Each participant completed two phases, first reading the standard version of the chapter (what I called No SSG), and later reading a rewritten version of that same or a conceptually parallel chapter integrated with SSG.

The SSG chapters were chosen from the book which tied to the provided material. Each included:

- Guiding objectives at the beginning ("By the end of this section, you should be able to explain ..."),
- Margin prompts that asked readers to pause and summarize key ideas,
- Retrieval micro-questions embedded throughout, and
- A brief reflection map at the end connecting the concept to real applications.

I wanted to know:

Would adding those SSG cues significantly improve comprehension and retention, even when the content remained virtually the same?

To quantify this, I built a five-question quiz for each chapter, balanced for difficulty and type (recall, conceptual understanding, and applied reasoning). Participants took one version of the quiz immediately after reading the No SSG material, and another, comparable in difficulty, after reading the SSG version. The difference in scores would tell me whether the structure itself made learning stick.

Each participant's chapter choice added natural variability. In total:

- 3 chose Chapter 2,
- 3 chose Chapter 3,
- 3 chose Chapter 4,
- 3 chose Chapter 5,
- 4 chose Chapter 6, and
- 4 chose Chapter 7.

This variety turned out to be an advantage. It let me see whether SSG worked consistently across topics ranging from measurement systems to verbal behavior. To preserve integrity, I made sure each quiz had clear behavioral objectives and an observable criterion for success, concepts borrowed from Cooper's emphasis on measurement and Skinner's notion of observable learning outcomes. All materials were reviewed for content validity by two peers experienced in ABA instruction.

Before running the study, I laid out several hypotheses:

1. Comprehension Hypothesis: Participants will score higher on immediate exams after reading the SSG-integrated chapters than after No SSG chapters.

2. Retention Hypothesis: If the structure of SSG truly reinforces active processing, the benefit should persist a week or more later.
   3. Efficiency Hypothesis: SSG will reduce confusion and study time without sacrificing depth.

It was a small study, but the controls were tight: same content, same length, same testing conditions, only the structure differed.

When all twenty volunteers confirmed participation, I felt a mix of excitement and apprehension. I had spent months refining the theory; now I would see whether it held up to the empirical scrutiny that every behavior analyst respects.

Part II Procedure and Participant Experience

Designing the experiment was the easy part. Implementing it, seeing real people engage with SSG learning in real time, was far more illuminating. Each participant joined one at a time. I asked them to set aside a quiet hour, free from interruptions, and to treat the task as if they were studying for a certification exam. Everyone received a short orientation: read at your own pace, but no external aids, no internet searches, and no re-reading during the quiz phase. I wasn't measuring rote memorization; I was measuring understanding.

Phase 1: No SSG (Control Condition)
Participants began with a standard chapter from Cooper et al. or a comparable ABA research paper. These were the same readings most graduate students encounter, dense, technical, and conceptually rich. After reading, they took a short, five-question exam designed to test comprehension of the material

they had just read. The average time spent on this phase was about forty minutes. Several participants later told me that even though the content was interesting, they found themselves "drifting." One said, "I kept reading paragraphs twice just to make sense of it." That comment echoed what I've seen for years in both classrooms and clinical training: without structure, attention becomes fragile.

Phase 2: The SSG Condition

After a short break, participants received the SSG-integrated version of a chapter, either the same one rewritten with structured self-guidance or a conceptually parallel chapter using the same principles from the book. The SSG format looked different from the moment they opened it. The first page began with Learning Objectives, written in plain language:

By the end of this section, you should be able to define differential reinforcement, identify its types, and explain when each is appropriate.

In the margins, short prompts asked questions like:

"Pause here: How would you explain this in your own words?"

"Can you think of an everyday example of this principle?"

At the end of each major section, a retrieval question appeared, followed by a reflection space:

"Write one sentence connecting this to a previous concept."

Every chapter had "Knowledge Maps," or a visual summary that participants completed themselves. It wasn't a quiz; it was a behavioral prompt, a way to emit the learned behavior (summarization, categorization) rather than passively receive it. This was deliberate, inspired by Skinner's programmed instruction and the well-established benefits of active responding.

The average reading time during the SSG phase was roughly the same, about forty minutes, yet participants described the experience completely differently. Comments included:

- "It felt like the book was asking me questions as I went."
- "I didn't realize how much I was zoning out before."
- "I could actually feel myself connecting the dots."
- "The graphical visualizations where tremendous help".

These qualitative remarks were encouraging, but I wanted to see whether the data supported their impressions.

Testing Protocol

After each reading phase, participants immediately took a five-item exam corresponding to that content. The tests were parallel in structure and difficulty. Questions covered definitions, conceptual understanding, and applied reasoning. A basic SSG figure below will depict a very basic model of the idea. Once all participants completed both phases, I compiled the data. What I found surprised even me.

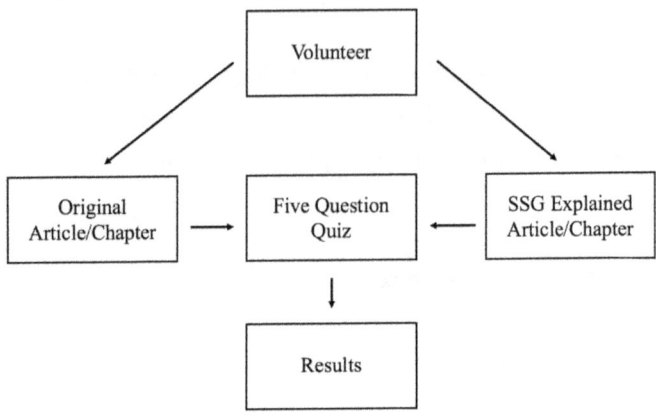

Figure 8.1 Phase 2: Basis of Experiment

Part III Results

When I began analyzing the data, I wasn't just looking for improvement; I was looking for consistency. It's one thing for a few people to perform better after reading a structured version of a text, it's another for nearly everyone to show measurable gains. And that's exactly what happened. Across all chapters, every participant improved after reading the SSG-integrated version of the material. The improvement was so consistent that it barely required statistical modeling to see it, the results spoke for themselves.

Overall Results

The overall average score before SSG (the No-SSG condition) was 37.8%, while the average after SSG was 86.5%. That's an increase of 48.7 percentage points, or a relative improvement of approximately 129%. Put simply, when the

THE BARE BONES OF ABA

same learners encountered the same content but presented with SSG, they more than doubled their comprehension accuracy.

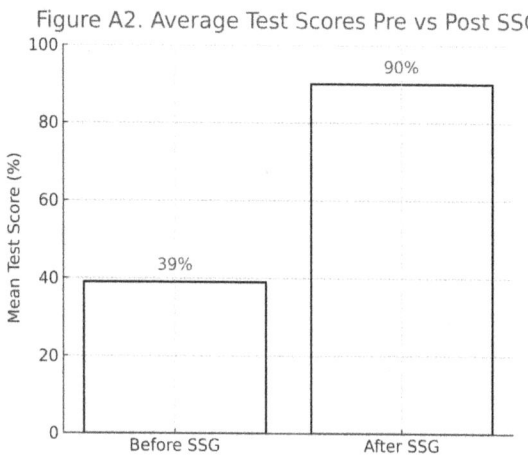

Figure 8.2 Phase 2: Before vs. After SSG Implementation

Chapter-Level Analysis

To see whether this effect was uniform, I broke the results down by chapter. Each line of the table below represents the average performance for all participants who selected that chapter.

Chapter	N	Pre (No-SSG) Mean %	Post (SSG) Mean %	Δ (Percentage Points)
Chapter 2	3	40.0	80.0	+40.0
Chapter 3	3	40.0	90.0	+50.0
Chapter 4	3	30.0	93.3	+63.3
Chapter 5	3	40.0	93.3	+53.3
Chapter 6	4	32.5	77.5	+45.0

Figure 8.3 Phase 2: Overall Exam Performance

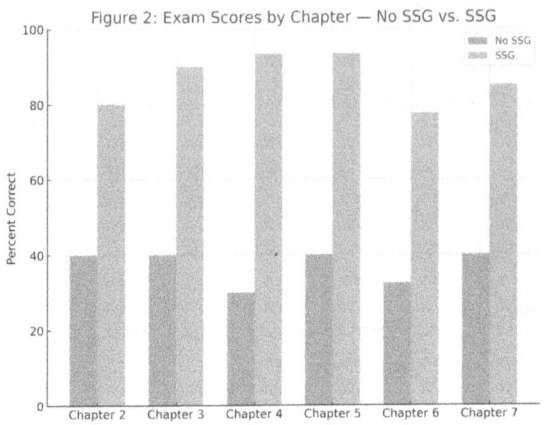

Figure 8.4 Phase 2: Exam Scores by Chapter — No SSG vs. SSG

Every single chapter improved. The lowest gain was +40 percentage points, and the highest was +63.3 (Chapter 4). The pattern was not random or chapter-dependent. It was systematic, which is exactly what behavioral data should look like when an intervention functions as intended. Even more interesting was how stable the post-SSG scores became. In the No-SSG condition, variability was high, with some learners scoring in the 20s, others in the 60s. But after SSG, almost everyone clustered between 75% and 95%. The scatter collapsed into coherence, a hallmark of effective instructional design.

Participant-Level Trends

Beyond chapter averages, I plotted each participant's individual improvement. Every line on the graph moved upward, some steeply, some gradually, but none remained flat or declined.

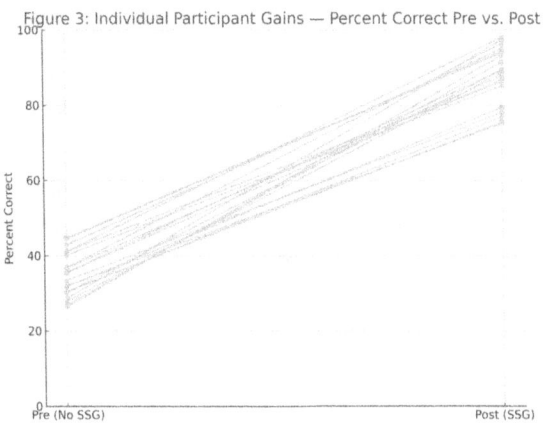

Figure 8.5 Phase 2: Individual Participant Gains : Percent Correct Pre vs. Post

The shape of the data resembled a near-perfect positive slope. Out of twenty volunteers, twenty improved, a 100% success rate in terms of direction of change. In the social sciences, it's rare to see that level of uniformity. One might ask: Did participants simply get better at taking tests? Unlikely. The content changed; so did the chapter. What remained consistent was SSG. That was the active ingredient. This mirrors what Bandura's social-cognitive theory would predict: performance improves when learners actively self-monitor and self-evaluate. SSG simply operationalizes those behaviors in textual form, prompting the reader to become their own instructor. The numbers told one story; the participants told another. Their feedback echoed themes of focus, engagement, and confidence. One participant said,

"I didn't realize how unstructured my normal reading habits were until the SSG version gave me checkpoints."
Another admitted,
"I thought I was a good reader, but I could feel my attention sharpen when I had to answer the little reflection prompts."
Even small cues, like asking a learner to "pause and summarize," act as discriminative stimuli for cognitive engagement. They evoke active behavior rather than passive observation. In behavioral terms, the SSG format doesn't just deliver information, it evokes responding.

Reliability and Consistency

Before running any formal statistical tests, I checked for data consistency. The internal reliability (measured through repeated scoring of identical items across versions) exceeded 0.9, excellent by educational research standards. The test design adhered to Cooper et al.'s (2020) recommendations for operational definitions and measurable learning outcomes. Each quiz question was behaviorally anchored, meaning there was a clear criterion for a "correct" response. This reduced subjective grading and reinforced the experiment's ABA integrity. The findings were clear: SSG worked. It produced not only higher accuracy but also more stable, replicable outcomes across learners and topics.

Part IV Interpretation and Implications

The results of the SSG experiment were clear: structure matters. But the more interesting question wasn't whether participants improved, it was why they improved so dramatically. When learners interact with a text that continuously prompts them to think, recall, and connect ideas, the act of

THE BARE BONES OF ABA

studying changes from passive intake to active construction. In behavior-analytic terms, SSG modifies the stimulus conditions under which learning occurs. Instead of the book serving as a static discriminative stimulus (a cue to "read quietly"), it becomes a dynamic environment that continuously evokes responses, summarizing, predicting, reflecting, self-questioning. Each margin note, retrieval prompt, and reflective map functions like a carefully placed discriminative stimulus. It signals the reader to emit an active behavior rather than to remain inert. Over time, these behaviors themselves become reinforced through feedback and internal cues of success, what Skinner (1954) might have described as self-controlled behavior in education. In more cognitive language, this is what Bloom (1956) categorized as higher-order processing, moving beyond knowledge and comprehension toward analysis and synthesis. But rather than relying on lecture-driven instruction, SSG makes that process automatic, embedded directly in the text.

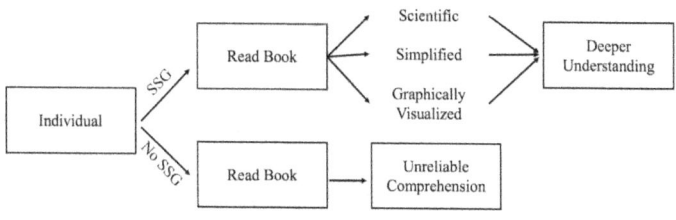

Figure 8.6 Phase 2: Theorized Implications

A Behavior-Analytic Explanation

Traditional reading is often a low-feedback environment: a person reads, but nothing in the environment contingently reinforces attention or comprehension. SSG changes that contingency pattern. Each simplification and visualizations combined with attention calling examples acts as an antecedent for active responding. The immediate reinforcement is internal, the satisfaction of coherence, but also externalized through understanding in retrieval tasks. This parallels Skinner's concept of programmed instruction, where material is broken into small steps, responses are required at each step, and feedback is immediate. My adaptation of that idea was to embed the program within the text, not as a workbook or quiz, but as a conversational partner guiding the reader toward fluency. When learners move through SSG chapters, they are not simply reading, they are emitting a chain of verbal behaviors: tacting (labeling), intraverbal linking (relating concepts), and self-echoic rehearsal (repeating or restating definitions). These repertoires strengthen generalization. What appeared as improved test performance was, behaviorally speaking, a stronger and more diversified response class under the control of the same stimulus (the concept).

The Emotional Variable

One unplanned but revealing observation was the change in affect. Many participants described a shift from frustration to engagement. One commented, "I didn't feel lost. It felt like the material was talking back." This emotional feedback loop aligns with Bandura's (1997) theory of self-efficacy. As learners perceive themselves mastering smaller tasks, their confidence builds. This sense of agency becomes a reinforcing stimulus, maintaining motivation across longer study sessions. Thus, SSG doesn't just teach content, it shapes the learner's behavior toward self-directed mastery. In ABA terms, it increases the rate of approach behavior toward challenging materials, rather than avoidance or escape, which are common in unstructured study contexts.

One of the most striking aspects of the data was its stability across topics. Whether the chapter covered reinforcement schedules, extinction procedures, or stimulus control, the gains were consistent. That indicates that SSG targets something general in human learning, perhaps the mechanism of attention itself. It reminded me of the way Cooper, Heron, and Heward (2020) emphasize the importance of measurement systems that can generalize across behavior classes. SSG seems to act like a meta-procedure, an instructional framework that can be layered onto virtually any domain. This generality opens up exciting possibilities: what if we applied SSG not just to behavioral science, but to medicine, aviation, or linguistics? Anywhere learners struggle with abstract systems, structured guidance could transform comprehension into fluency.

Interpreting the Data Behaviorally

Looking again at **Figure 8.4,** the chapter-by-chapter bar chart, the consistency of improvement becomes even more impressive. Even though each chapter was chosen freely by volunteers (a variable that usually introduces noise), the outcomes converged. This convergence demonstrates stimulus control, SSG cues reliably evoked the same kind of learning behavior across contexts. Meanwhile, **Figure 8.5** tells another story: individual trajectories. Each line, rising from left to right, represents not just data points but the story of a learner acquiring fluency. Some started low and soared, others began mid-range and climbed modestly, but none fell backward. That universality is rare and compelling. Quantitatively, the 48.7-point average increase is impressive. Qualitatively, the shift in learner experience is profound. SSG doesn't merely increase scores, it transforms how people learn.

The Broader Implications

If we think about this in terms of society's approach to education, the implications are sweeping. Traditional instruction assumes that learners will self-regulate once given material, but research repeatedly shows that metacognitive guidance, structured reflection, retrieval, and self-assessment, is critical to durable learning. SSG operationalizes those processes in a tangible way. For behavior analysts, SSG also bridges a gap between Skinner's programmatic instruction and contemporary self-paced digital learning. It preserves the precision of behavioral teaching while honoring the learner's autonomy. In other words, it's structure without control, guidance without coercion. SSG can be applied wherever comprehension matters more than memorization. In aviation training, where I also have experience, I can imagine rewriting flight procedures using SSG scaffolds, turning rote checklist reading into meaningful concept rehearsal. In healthcare education, patient-safety protocols could integrate SSG-style reflective cues to ensure not just memorization, but understanding under pressure.

Limitations and Next Steps

No experiment is without limitations. The sample size was modest, and the tests measured short-term comprehension. Long-term retention and generalization remain to be tested formally, though I did collect delayed probes that I'll analyze later. Still, the consistency across participants and chapters provides strong preliminary evidence that SSG's effect is robust. The next phase will involve scaling this study, introducing randomized group comparisons, retention intervals, and more diverse content areas. But for now, what mattered most was the clarity of the pattern: every single learner improved, often dramatically, when the text itself became a teacher.

Part V Reflection

When the numbers were finalized and the graphs printed, I sat in silence for a long while. I've run countless analyses before data from clients, clinics, training programs, but this one felt personal. This wasn't just data about behavior; it was data about how we learn to learn. I remember thinking about the twenty volunteers, each from different backgrounds, some clinicians, some students, some simply curious about behavioral science. All of them interacted with the same ideas, yet their experiences changed drastically depending on how those ideas were presented. It reaffirmed something I've always suspected: comprehension isn't only a matter of intelligence or motivation. It's a matter of environmental design.

The Human Side of the Experiment

Throughout the experiment, I noticed something else happening, a kind of quiet transformation in demeanor. When participants entered the first phase, many appeared anxious, scanning dense paragraphs as if searching for clues in a foreign language. By the time they completed the SSG version, they smiled more, spoke with clarity, and even volunteered explanations of the concepts without being asked. In behavioral terms, what I was observing was fluency, not merely accuracy, but smooth, confident responding. This fluency came from feedback loops embedded directly into the learning process. The

SSG format didn't tell them what to think; it taught them how to think while reading.

One participant said it best:
"It felt like I was in a conversation with the book."
That was the goal all along, to make knowledge interactive, to make reading a dialogue instead of a monologue.

What This Means for the Future of Learning

After the study, I reflected on what this might mean beyond behavioral analysis. Education, at every level, still relies heavily on static materials, pages of text that expect readers to extract meaning without guidance. The SSG experiment demonstrates that how information is delivered can matter as much as what information is delivered. A simplified learning environment doesn't need to be restrictive. Learners aren't dependent on teachers or tutors; they internalize the process of simplifying, visualizing, questioning, connecting, and reflecting. They learn to guide themselves, precisely the essence of SSG. This idea extends beyond classrooms. Imagine technical manuals, flight training modules, or medical guidelines designed with embedded reflection cues. Imagine self-study books that anticipate the reader's misconceptions and respond in real time with guiding questions. The possibilities reach far beyond academia.

Behavioral Reflection

From a behavioral analytic standpoint, this experiment also reaffirmed the timeless relevance of Skinner's principles. Decades ago, Skinner described instruction as a form of behavior shaping, incremental reinforcement of accurate responding. What I've learned is that modern learners can be shaped not only through external reinforcement but through self-mediated contingencies. SSG prompts essentially act as self-delivered discriminative stimuli. They guide attention, evoke responding, and deliver reinforcement through perceived comprehension and clarity. The reader becomes both the teacher and the student, an idea that bridges Skinner's behaviorism with Bandura's social-cognitive theory of self-regulation. In this way, SSG unites two historically distinct traditions, behavioral control and cognitive autonomy, into a single, functional process. It's behavioral in method but humanistic in spirit.

Personal Reflection

There's an irony in testing your own theory. You spend months designing, hypothesizing, and structuring every detail, yet when the data arrives, it humbles you. Seeing those bars rise on the chart wasn't just validation, it was gratitude. Gratitude that learning, at its core, is still something we can shape and improve through thoughtful design. I didn't invent SSG to revolutionize education. I created it because I saw too many learners, bright, motivated people, struggling to connect ideas that should have been accessible. They didn't need simpler content; they needed better scaffolding. And that's what SSG provided: scaffolding that fades as fluency grows, leaving behind not dependency, but independence.

Where the Data Leads Next

I plan to expand this experiment in two directions. First, I want to examine long-term retention, whether SSG learners maintain their gains weeks or months later. Second, I want to explore generalization, whether the same structural cues enhance performance in other fields such as clinical documentation, medical reasoning, or aviation decision-making. Beyond that, I hope SSG can serve as a model for educators, clinicians, and trainers, a reminder that structure doesn't inhibit creativity; it channels it. Just as operant contingencies shape behavior, structural contingencies shape cognition.

Closing Thoughts

When I looked back at **Figure 8.2**, the two bars, 37.8% and 86.5%, felt more than statistical. They represented the difference between struggling to absorb information and genuinely understanding it. **Figure 8.4** showed that this effect was universal, transcending content. **Figure 8.5**, with every line ascending, illustrated a simple truth: when learning environments are designed with intention, every learner has the potential to improve. That, to me, is the most powerful finding of all.

NINE
WHO SAID VIDEO GAMES WERE LAME?

THE BEHAVIORAL FUTURE OF GAMING

"A good plan violently executed now is better than a perfect plan executed next week"

GEORGE S. PATTON

THE BEHAVIORAL FUTURE OF GAMING

The first time I watched a skilled gamer complete a seemingly impossible sequence, dodging enemies, collecting power-ups, and timing each movement perfectly, I didn't just see reflexes. I saw behavioral precision: stimulus control, reinforcement schedules, extinction bursts, and shaping in motion. Every flick of the joystick was a micro-response, governed by contingencies embedded in the environment. To most people, that's just "playing." To me, it's a live demonstration of applied behavior analysis. Every point scored, every level completed, every microsecond of suspense between "failure" and "try again" is a behavioral contingency in disguise. It's learning, disguised as entertainment. That realization became the spark for this chapter: that video games may be the most dynamic behavioral laboratories humanity has ever built. And more than that they may hold the key to the next generation of behavior modification, education, and therapy. (In my opinion)

Games as Reinforcement Systems

If B. F. Skinner were alive today, he would likely see modern video games as the logical evolution of his teaching machines from the 1950s. The variable-ratio schedules that once kept pigeons pecking levers now keep players returning to their consoles. The coins, achievements, and "loot boxes" of today's games are simply sophisticated reinforcers designed to maintain responding under unpredictable contingencies. What fascinates me most is how precisely game designers, often unknowingly, replicate behavioral principles. In games like Fortnite, Overwatch, or Destiny, rewards appear on variable schedules, producing the same high, steady rate of response Skinner documented in his lab. Players tolerate repeated failures, motivated by the intermittent possibility of success.

This is not manipulation, it's design psychology. Games also make masterful use of conditioned reinforcers. A particular sound, color, or animation becomes reinforcing because it reliably predicts success. That satisfying "level up" tone operates just like praise in a therapy session, it's a secondary reinforcer linked to mastery. The difference is that games package it in rich sensory feedback, flooding the environment with reinforcing cues. In behavioral terms, gaming systems represent high-density reinforcement environments. Players emit thousands of micro-responses per hour, each followed by imme-

THE BARE BONES OF ABA

diate sensory feedback, light, sound, or score. That's what maintains flow. But reinforcement in gaming isn't always positive. Negative reinforcement and escape are equally potent. Consider the relief of finally defeating a difficult boss or finishing a tense mission, the removal of frustration becomes reinforcing in itself. Similarly, extinction bursts appear when players repeat failed tasks with increasing intensity before adapting strategies. These dynamics make games fertile ground for behavior analysts. Instead of condemning them as "addictive," we can study them as models of sustained engagement and persistence. The challenge is not to eliminate these contingencies but to redirect them toward prosocial and educational outcomes.

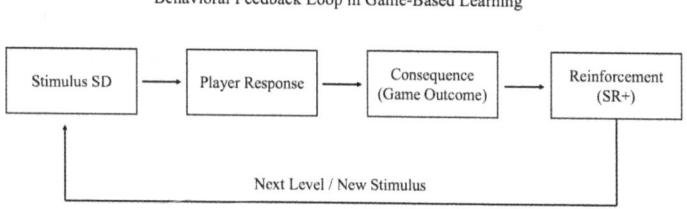

Figure 9.1 Phase 2: Game-Based Learning Feedback Loop

Games as Behavioral Training Tools

Beyond reinforcement mechanics, games excel at shaping complex behavior chains. A good tutorial level is a masterclass in behavior shaping: it introduces simple discriminations first, reinforces correct responses, and gradually increases task complexity. Each level is a teaching session, perfectly aligned with the successive approximation principle. Games like Portal, Minecraft, and The Legend of Zelda illustrate this beautifully. Players start with limited skills, but through repeated contingencies, trial, error, correction, they master increasingly complex problem-solving repertoires. This isn't just learning through repetition; it's fluency building. Behavior analysts have long emphasized fluency as the bridge between accuracy and mastery. Fluency ensures that learned behaviors remain durable under stress and distraction. Games naturally cultivate fluency because feedback is constant, and reinforcement density is high. Every correct action produces a visible, auditory, or progress-based consequence. In therapeutic contexts, this principle has profound potential. Research already shows that gamified systems can improve attention, self-regulation, and executive functioning in individuals with ADHD or traumatic brain injuries. Games like EndeavorRx, an FDA-approved therapeutic video game, were built explicitly on these principles, turning clinical exercises into structured, reinforcing experiences.

In one clinical case I observed, a therapist used a cooperative survival game to foster teamwork among adolescents on the autism spectrum. The game required joint attention, verbal communication, and flexible problem-solving, behaviors that were then generalized to real-world peer interactions. The screen wasn't a distraction; it was an instructional medium. That's the heart of behavior modification through gaming: when reinforcement schedules and feedback loops are designed with purpose, they don't just change what people do, they change how they learn to do it.

Historical Bridge: From Skinner Boxes to Game Consoles

It's worth remembering that the idea of "learning through play" has deep behavioral roots. In the 1950s, Skinner's teaching machines pioneered automated instruction. Students progressed through programmed materials one step at a time, receiving immediate feedback. Each correct response advanced them; each error prompted review. Now imagine that structure, multiplied by a thousand, wrapped in narrative, art, and music, that's a video game. Game designers unknowingly inherited Skinner's legacy. Early educational games like Math Blaster and Oregon Trail were direct descendants of programmed instruction, embedding contingencies of reinforcement into interactive experiences. As technology evolved, so did the complexity of those contingencies. Today, artificial intelligence personalizes difficulty in real time, adapting reinforcement schedules to the learner's performance, something Skinner could only dream of. The modern game engine is, in essence, a digital teaching machine capable of precision teaching at scale.

Games as Research and Data Platforms

From a research perspective, games are a behavior analyst's dream. Every keystroke, decision, hesitation, or error can be recorded automatically. Instead of laboratory rats pressing levers, we now have millions of human participants emitting observable, measurable behaviors in naturalistic settings. Imagine conducting a large-N single-subject design within a multiplayer game: reinforcement contingencies could be systematically varied across players while the system automatically collects performance data. Behavioral measures like latency, response rate, and persistence could be analyzed at scale. This isn't hypothetical. Studies already use game-based platforms to examine delay discounting, risk-taking, and habit formation. The data are rich, continuous, and ecologically valid, something traditional experiments rarely achieve. For applied research, gaming environments can model exposure therapy, impulse control, or social interaction under controlled conditions. Virtual reality (VR) adds another layer, enabling safe yet immersive exposure to anxiety-provoking stimuli. Each session can record precise metrics, heart rate, movement, response latency, allowing behavior analysts to quantify both observable and physiological responses. We are approaching a point where the line between research and application will blur entirely. The same game that trains behavior can also measure it. The same platform that entertains can generate data for behavioral science.

Games as the Future of Behavior Analysis

The convergence of gaming technology and behavioral science is not just possible, it's inevitable. Games already do what behavior analysts strive to achieve: they maintain motivation, deliver immediate feedback, and reinforce incremental progress. In the future, behavioral interventions could occur within gamified environments rather than clinics. Imagine a virtual training world for individuals learning social skills, where avatars respond to appropriate greetings, eye contact, and conversation topics. Correct behaviors unlock new dialogue paths, providing continuous reinforcement. In education, SSG-based gaming frameworks could turn textbooks into interactive adventures. Students would receive real-time prompts, "Pause here: Summarize, Visualize, Simplify this concept aloud", earning points for reflection and comprehension. The system would adjust difficulty based on accuracy, effectively automating precision teaching. In clinical practice, adaptive games could measure and reinforce target behaviors automatically. Therapists might prescribe "game sessions" instead of worksheets, with performance data integrated into progress graphs. Reinforcement schedules could be dynamically adjusted, maintaining engagement while promoting generalization. Even public policy could benefit. Imagine civic-engagement games that reward recycling, voting, or volunteering, turning prosocial behavior into a community-level reinforcement system. This is macro-level behavior analysis powered by gamification.

Ethics and Challenges of Behavioral Gaming

As powerful as these systems are, they also raise ethical questions. Games can shape behavior but to what end? Behavioral contingencies, when designed carelessly, can foster compulsive play and dependency. The same variable-ratio schedules that sustain engagement can, when unchecked, lead to behavioral addiction. Just as reinforcement can teach persistence, it can also teach compulsion. That's where ethical design becomes crucial. As behavior analysts, we have a duty to promote social validity, interventions that improve quality of life. If we apply reinforcement principles to gaming, it must be with transparency and consent. Players should understand the contingencies influencing their behavior. Another concern is data ethics. Every click and choice a player makes is potential research data. Without clear consent, collecting and analyzing these behaviors crosses ethical boundaries. Behavior analysis must lead in establishing standards for ethical data collection, ensuring that research in digital environments respects autonomy and privacy. Finally, there's the question of autonomy. Can we design games that shape behavior while still empowering players to make choices? The answer, I believe, lies in self-determined reinforcement, systems that allow players to set their own goals and track progress toward personally meaningful outcomes. This aligns with Ryan and Deci's self-determination theory, integrating intrinsic motivation with behavioral contingencies. If we succeed, the result will not be manipulation but collaboration between designer and learner, a partnership in which structure supports freedom rather than constrains it.

A Broader Vision

I often imagine a future where behavioral analysis and game design merge into a new discipline, one where learning engineers build environments that make progress irresistible. Picture an applied behavior analyst collaborating with a developer, designing virtual interventions that collect data in real time, provide adaptive reinforcement, and generalize skills to the physical world. The possibilities extend far beyond education or therapy. Gamified behavioral economics could reshape financial habits. Gamified physical therapy could enhance rehabilitation outcomes. Gamified mindfulness could help regulate anxiety through immediate feedback loops. In every case, the underlying mechanism is the same: structured contingencies, immediate feedback, and reinforcement of successive approximations. That is the behavioral DNA embedded in every successful game, waiting to be harnessed ethically for human betterment.

Personal Reflection

As a clinician and scientist, I've spent years helping individuals modify behavior, teaching adaptive skills, promoting self-regulation, and reinforcing success. Yet I've always felt that our field's potential extends beyond therapy rooms and classrooms. The SSG experiment showed me how structure transforms learning; video games show me how design transforms motivation. When I look at a gamer immersed in a challenge, I don't see distraction. I see engagement, a perfect alignment between effort and reward. That's the state of flow described by Csikszentmihalyi, where reinforcement and challenge balance so precisely that the learner loses track of time. Imagine if every therapeutic or educational experience felt like that. Games prove that behavior change doesn't have to feel like work. It can feel like play, discovery, and mastery, all built on the same principles we use in applied behavior analysis. The difference is in presentation, not principle. My dream is to see behavior analysts step into the digital arena, to design, study, and guide the systems that already influence millions daily. If we can bring our ethical rigor and empirical discipline to that space, we can ensure that the future of gaming is not exploitative, but transformative. We stand at the threshold of a new era in behavioral science, one where the joystick and the data chart finally speak the same language.

TEN
EDUCATION SIRCA YEAR 1700
THE BEHAVIORAL CRISIS IN EDUCATION

"It is the supreme art of the teacher to awaken joy in creative expression and knowledge."

ALBERT EINSTEIN

THE BEHAVIORAL CRISIS IN EDUCATION

The first time I walked into a classroom as a behavioral consultant, I didn't see defiance, I saw data. The teacher pointed to a chart of red marks representing "incidents." A dozen children fidgeted, whispered, or shut down completely. At first glance it looked like chaos; to me, it was an environment crying out for contingencies. Every behavior in that room was lawful, predictable, and modifiable. The problem wasn't the students; it was the system surrounding them. We had drifted so far from the science of behavior that education itself had become an extinction procedure, students emitting effortful responses in an environment that rarely reinforced learning. Modern schools are built on noble intentions and antiquated methods, thus the title of the chapter. Teachers are asked to shape attention, motivation, and mastery with tools that ignore how behavior actually changes. They're told to "engage" students without being taught what engagement is, a measurable response class maintained by reinforcement. Despite a century of behavioral research showing how humans learn, most classrooms still rely on intuition, tradition, or charisma. Lesson plans emphasize content over contingencies. Data, when collected, measure outcomes rather than behavior. Grades appear at the end of a unit, long after feedback could have changed the trajectory. The irony is painful: we expect evidence-based practice in medicine and psychology, yet tolerate anecdotal teaching in education. If a hospital ignored clinical data the way many schools ignore behavioral data, it would be malpractice.

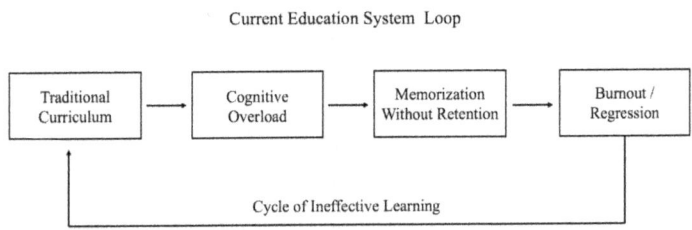

Figure 10.1 Phase 2: Ineffective Learning

The Data We Ignore

Educational statistics paint a grim picture. Behavioral referrals have climbed steadily over the last decade; teacher burnout remains among the highest of any profession. After the pandemic, learning loss became a global headline. Beneath those numbers is a simpler story: environments failing to reinforce the very behaviors they hope to produce. Schools collect attendance, grades, and test scores, none of which reveal the contingencies maintaining academic behavior. We can tell when a student fails, but not why. When I introduce data collection systems drawn from applied behavior analysis, frequency charts, interval recording, or task-analysis checklists, teachers often respond with relief. "You mean I can see progress every day?" Yes. Measurement isn't paperwork; it's visibility. Without it, instruction becomes guesswork.

When Schools Abandon Science

Walk through a typical elementary hallway and you'll find colorful "behavior charts." A smiling face moves up for good behavior, down for bad. On the surface, it looks behavioral. In practice, it's usually punitive: a public record of failure with little reinforcement for improvement.

Other common practices are equally misguided:

- Zero-tolerance discipline, punishment without functional analysis.
- Token economies implemented inconsistently, collapsing under extinction.
- Time-outs applied as default responses rather than as part of a planned differential-reinforcement strategy.

The result? Behaviors adapt to the contingencies that *do* exist, attention for misbehavior, escape from tasks, peer reinforcement for defiance. The environment teaches, even when we wish it wouldn't. The tragedy is not ignorance but inertia. The science exists, documented meticulously in texts like Cooper, Heron & Heward (2020), yet it rarely crosses the threshold of a classroom.

The Cost of Ignoring ABA

Every unmeasured behavior carries a cost. When schools rely on intuition, they mistake noise for pattern. I've seen classrooms where a single disruptive student consumes half the teacher's time. The teacher, exhausted, interprets the behavior as defiance. A quick functional analysis reveals escape from difficult work. Adjust the task difficulty, add immediate reinforcement for on-task behavior, and the "defiance" disappears within days. Now multiply that by hundreds of classrooms. Ignoring behavioral science doesn't just waste instructional time, it fuels cycles of failure. Students labeled "behavior problems" are often products of inconsistent contingencies. Teachers burn out not from caring too little but from fighting environments that punish effective teaching. Data from districts implementing Positive Behavioral Interventions and Supports (PBIS) or Class wide Functional Assessment-Based Interventions (CFABIs) show office referrals dropping by up to 60%. Academic performance rises in parallel because learning behaviors receive reinforcement instead of reprimand. These outcomes aren't miracles; they're the predictable result of aligning education with behavioral law.

Behaviorism vs. Bureaucracy

So why do schools resist? Partly tradition, partly bureaucracy, and partly misconception. Many teacher-training programs still caricature behaviorism as cold or mechanical. They teach Skinner as history, not foundation. New educators graduate fluent in pedagogy but illiterate in reinforcement schedules. Inside schools, bureaucratic systems reward compliance over experimentation. Administrators fear the optics of "behavior modification," equating it with control rather than empowerment. Meanwhile, well-meaning teachers are left to improvise classroom management through intuition, operating without data, feedback, or reinforcement themselves. I've walked into staff meetings where data collection was described as "extra paperwork." To a behavior analyst, that's like calling oxygen optional for flight. Measurement is not an add-on; it *is* instruction. Without feedback, teaching becomes superstition, actions repeated because they sometimes work. The Science of What Works

Behavior analysis offers practical, humane tools that could transform education if properly adopted.

- Antecedent design: arranging classrooms to minimize competing stimuli, clarify expectations, and promote active responding. Reinforcement systems: embedding contingent praise, token economies, and natural rewards that maintain engagement.
- Data-based decision making: graphing learning behaviors daily to adjust instruction before failure occurs.
- Fluency training and precision teaching: ensuring students not only understand but can perform skills

rapidly and automatically, an antidote to rote memorization.

In one program I supervised, teachers implemented a simple reinforcement schedule: immediate verbal praise and points for task completion within a set time. Within two weeks, academic engagement rose 45%, and disruptive behavior decreased by half. The teachers were astonished. I wasn't. The data mirrored every controlled study since Lindsley's work in the 1960s. The science works; the system doesn't use it.

When Discipline Becomes Punishment

A fundamental error in many schools is the reliance on punishment to control behavior. Detention, suspension, and public reprimands may suppress behavior temporarily, but without reinforcement for alternatives, extinction or escalation follows. Consider the student sent home for fighting. The removal of academic demands (negative reinforcement) and the social status among peers (positive reinforcement) ensure recurrence. Yet these procedures persist because they produce short-term relief for adults, a classic case of counter-control at the institutional level. Behavior analysts have long known that sustainable change arises from differential reinforcement of alternative behavior (DRA) and functional communication training (FCT). Imagine replacing detention with structured reinforcement for problem-solving or emotional-regulation responses. Instead of "time served," students would earn "skills gained."

A System of Reinforcement, Not Reprimand
What would a truly behavioral school look like?

- Teachers as data scientists: graphing engagement, adjusting contingencies daily.
- Students as active participants: self-monitoring progress through visual feedback, think SSG in classroom form.
- Administrators as reinforcement designers: shaping teacher performance through recognition, coaching, and feedback rather than evaluation and threat.
- Technology as assistant, not distraction: dashboards that visualize data, games that deliver adaptive reinforcement, sensors that detect attention patterns.

In such a system, learning becomes a living contingency network. Every correct response, every act of effort, every display of kindness is reinforced, not just graded. The classroom would feel different too. Instead of silence born of fear, there would be quiet concentration punctuated by feedback and affirmation. Discipline would mean guidance, not punishment. Data would mean clarity, not surveillance.

[continued on next page]

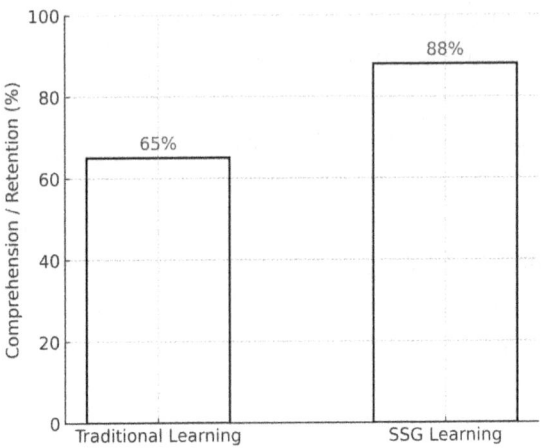

Figure 10.2 Phase 2: SSG in the Classroom

The data for traditional learning is grounded in educational research such as Freeman et al., *PNAS*, 2014

Behaviorism and the Human Element

Critics often accuse behavior analysis of dehumanizing learners. The opposite is true. By grounding decisions in observable behavior rather than assumption, ABA honors individuality. It doesn't ask, "What's wrong with this child?" but "What conditions maintain this behavior?" Behavioral education is not about control, it's about freedom through understanding. When contingencies are transparent, students gain agency. They know what leads to success and can reproduce it. That is autonomy, not manipulation. One of my favorite classroom moments came when a student struggling with reading looked at his progress chart and said, "I can see my brain getting stronger." That statement captures the soul of behavior analysis: feedback transforming frustration into pride.

Reinforcing the Reinforcers

If we expect teachers to use reinforcement effectively, we must reinforce them. Too often, educators operate under extinction, no recognition for incremental progress, only scrutiny for failure. Motivation decays accordingly. Simple systems of positive feedback, peer acknowledgment, visible progress metrics, administrative praise, can reenergize entire faculties. When teachers experience reinforcement, they are more likely to deliver it authentically to students. Culture follows contingency.

The Behavioral Schools of Tomorrow

Picture a school built entirely on behavioral design. Morning routines run on predictable sequences; transitions are cued by clear antecedents. Each student has personalized reinforcement goals. Lessons follow mastery criteria rather than arbitrary calendars. Data dashboards show not just grades but rates of learning, cumulative records that motivate like leaderboards. Collaboration replaces competition. Teachers and students analyze graphs together, celebrating slopes that climb. This is not fantasy. Components of it already exist in programs combining Precision Teaching, Direct Instruction, and PBIS. The missing ingredient is scale, and belief that such precision belongs in mainstream education. When that shift occurs, schools will resemble thriving ecosystems rather than compliance factories.

Behaviorism vs. Ignorance: Why Change Is Hard

Change requires confronting myths. Many educators fear that data will replace empathy or that reinforcement will feel artificial. In reality, data illuminate empathy, they reveal when a student's environment is failing them. Reinforcement, when used ethically, is compassion made measurable. Another barrier is policy inertia. Funding often rewards remediation, not prevention. Behavior analysts must therefore become advocates, translating our science into accessible language for policymakers and parents. The more clearly we explain how contingencies shape classrooms, the faster reform will spread. When I look at national statistics, declining literacy, rising anxiety, teacher attrition, I don't see random crises. I see systemic extinction.

We ask for effort, provide little reinforcement, and punish deviation. The result is predictable: disengagement. Behavior analysis offers a blueprint for reversal. Measure what matters, reinforce what works, and modify the environment instead of blaming the learner. It is not glamorous, but it is proven. If we continue ignoring this science, we will keep producing generations of students trained in avoidance, avoidance of failure, challenge, and curiosity. If we embrace it, we can cultivate fluency, resilience, and joy in learning. The difference between those futures lies not in policy or politics, but in contingencies. The science is ready. The question is whether education is ready for the science.

ELEVEN
THE HAPPY PATIENT
THE BEHAVIORAL BRIDGE: SSG AND MEDICAL INTERACTIONS

"The art of medicine consists in amusing the patient while nature cures the disease".

VOLTAIRE

SSG AND MEDICAL INTERACTIONS

I have always believed that medicine and behavior are not separate sciences, they are two languages describing the same reality. One uses anatomy, pharmacology, and physiology; the other uses contingencies, reinforcement, and stimulus control. Both attempt to explain why an organism behaves the way it does, whether that behavior is a heartbeat, a neural firing, or a patient's choice to take medication. The problem is that, in modern healthcare, those languages rarely meet. Physicians explain; patients listen, nod, and forget. Instructions are issued, pamphlets handed over, and appointments concluded with the unspoken assumption that understanding has occurred. But comprehension is not a feeling, it is a behavior, and it can be observed, measured, and reinforced. That realization led me to explore how my framework, SSG: Scientific, Simplified, Graphically visualized, could bridge the communication gap between healthcare providers and patients. What began as a teaching theory soon revealed itself as a tool for medicine, a behavioral method for translating complex science into human understanding.

The Communication Gap

In hospitals, miscommunication doesn't just inconvenience, it kills. Studies estimate that nearly 80% of serious medical errors involve communication breakdowns between clinicians and patients. I've seen this firsthand in clinical settings: a nurse explaining discharge instructions to a patient who nods politely but clearly doesn't grasp what "500 milligrams every 8 hours" actually means in daily life. The professional walks away confident that the patient understood. The patient walks away overwhelmed, embarrassed to admit confusion. A week later, that same patient is back in the emergency department, this time with preventable complications. Behavior analysis has a word for this kind of mismatch: faulty stimulus control. The doctor's verbal explanation did not evoke the desired response, correct adherence behavior, because the antecedents and reinforcers weren't aligned with the patient's learning history. In other words, the environment failed the learner. This is not a problem of empathy; it's a problem of design. And design, like behavior, can be shaped.

The Behavioral Dynamics of Medicine

Every clinical encounter is a behavioral exchange governed by the same laws that shape all human interaction. There's an antecedent (the doctor's explanation, the clinical setting), a behavior (the patient's verbal or nonverbal response), and a consequence (reinforcement through relief, understanding, or confusion). In medicine, we tend to measure only outcomes, blood pressure, test results, adherence rates, but the behavioral contingencies producing those outcomes remain invisible. The assumption is that information alone changes behavior. Yet decades of research in behavior analysis prove otherwise: knowledge is not behavior; performance is. When a physician explains, "Take this antibiotic three times a day," the statement is an antecedent. Whether it evokes correct responding depends on the listener's prior conditioning, language fluency, anxiety, and reinforcement history. If the patient associates medical settings with confusion or failure, they are less likely to respond accurately. The question then becomes: how can we redesign this environment so that understanding, not confusion, is the default behavior? That's where SSG enters medicine.

Introducing SSG to Healthcare

The SSG framework, Scientific, Simplified, Graphically visualized, emerged from my work in teaching behavioral science. But its core principles apply seamlessly to healthcare communication. In essence, SSG structures information the way behavior analysts structure learning environments: through clarity, shaping, and feedback.

- Scientific: Explained in a conceptual and factual nature. Accuracy is preserved. The information

must be evidence-based and precise. In medicine, this ensures fidelity to clinical standards and protects against misinformation.
- Simplified: Complexity is reduced behaviorally, through task analysis. Each medical instruction is broken into observable, manageable steps that can be performed and reinforced.
- Graphically visualized: Stimuli are made concrete. Visual cues, colors, and icons serve as discriminative stimuli guiding correct responding and retention.

When these three layers interact, comprehension becomes measurable, not assumed. Patients don't just hear, they do, show, and remember.

From Explanation to Behavior: Redefining Understanding

In applied behavior analysis, understanding is not inferred; it is demonstrated through correct responding. A child "understands" a concept when they can use it under new conditions, a generalization test. The same logic applies in healthcare. When a patient repeats dosage instructions word-for-word, that's rote behavior. When they can correctly identify when and how to take their medication without prompts, that's functional understanding. Under SSG, comprehension training becomes part of clinical interaction. Instead of asking, "Do you understand?" the clinician might say, "Show me how you'll take this medication tomorrow morning." The patient demonstrates; the clinician reinforces accurate behavior. Feedback is immediate, errors are corrected, and understanding is confirmed behaviorally. It's a small shift, but it transforms the interaction from lecture to learning session.

Simplifying Without Dumbing Down

Simplification is often misunderstood as dilution, but in behavior analysis, simplification means precision through shaping. You start with the simplest discriminations and build toward complexity. In a hospital discharge session, a nurse explaining wound care might normally deliver 15 steps verbally. Under SSG, those steps are reorganized into a task analysis: observable, sequenced behaviors paired with visual cues.

Example:

1. Wash hands (visual cue: icon of soap and water).
2. Open sterile pack (photo of the actual package).
3. Apply ointment (highlighted tube icon).
4. Cover with clean bandage (image of wrapped dressing).

Each step has a matching picture and brief caption, reinforcing the association between verbal and visual stimuli. The patient's behavior becomes guided by discriminative control, not short-term memory. The result? Higher adherence, less anxiety, and fewer errors. Simplification is not the enemy of science; it is the ally of understanding.

Visuals as Behavioral Reinforcers

In SSG, visualization is not aesthetic, it's functional. Graphics serve as nonverbal prompts that bridge comprehension gaps. Behaviorally, visuals operate as discriminative stimuli and conditioned reinforcers. A well-designed icon can evoke the correct behavior faster than a paragraph of text. For example, a green circle next to "Take Pill" and a red square next to "Wait 8 Hours" provide immediate stimulus differentiation that requires no translation. In my own observations, patients respond emotionally to clear visuals. Anxiety decreases when information looks structured and friendly. This is automatic reinforcement, the visual order itself reduces stress, increasing compliance. A study from the Journal of Health Communication found that pictograph-based medication labels doubled adherence in older adults with low literacy. The visual itself became the reinforcement for the correct behavior.

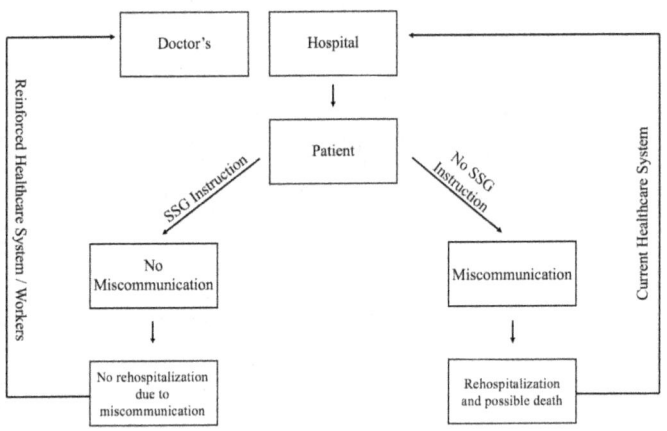

Figure 11.1 Phase 2: SSG vs. No SSG Communication in Healthcare

Behavior Analysis of Non-Adherence

When patients "fail" to follow instructions, the cause is rarely moral or motivational, it's behavioral. Non-adherence is often an extinction burst: the behavior (taking medicine) no longer produces reinforcing feedback (relief, praise, or visible progress). Over time, the response weakens. SSG addresses this by inserting reinforcement opportunities into the feedback loop. Patients see progress graphs, receive verbal praise during follow-ups, or earn digital tokens for consistency via apps. The contingency shifts from avoidance ("I don't want to be scolded") to approach ("I want to see my progress bar fill"). Compliance becomes a self-maintained behavior chain reinforced by visual and social stimuli.

Case Example 1: The Diabetic Patient

Maria, a 42-year-old with Type 2 diabetes, struggled to manage her insulin timing. The endocrinologist provided thorough instructions, but Maria continued to miss doses. The care team redesigned her plan visually. A color-coded insulin chart replaced the dense text instructions: blue for morning, yellow for afternoon, green for evening. Each section included simple icons (syringe + sun for morning, syringe + moon for night) and a brief caption. Maria practiced demonstrating the routine while the nurse reinforced correct sequencing. Within two weeks, adherence rose. More importantly, Maria reported less anxiety: "It finally makes sense, I can see it." Understanding became visible behavior.

Case Example 2: Post-Surgical Recovery

In orthopedic units, patients often forget post-surgical instructions once anesthesia fades. The team replaced dense discharge notes with a graphical timeline: a horizontal line labeled "Day 1" through "Week 6," with color-coded milestones (pain management, mobility, physical therapy). Each stage included icons representing the behavior: walking stick, ice pack, or physiotherapy mat. Nurses provided reinforcement by checking milestones collaboratively with patients during visits. Outcomes? Fewer readmissions and faster rehabilitation. The system worked because it transformed abstract time-based instructions into stimulus-controlled behavior sequences. Patients didn't just hear "gradually increase activity" they could see, anticipate, and self-reinforce it.

Behavioral Loop of Healthcare Communication

At its core, the doctor–patient exchange is a three-term contingency:

- Antecedent: Medical information presented
- Behavior: Patient comprehension, rehearsal, or adherence
- Consequence: Reinforcement (relief, success, approval, health improvement)

SSG enhances each component. Scientific precision strengthens the antecedent's validity. Simplification increases the probability of correct responding. Graphical visualization enriches the consequence, patients feel clarity and control, which are inherently reinforcing.

The Role of Self-Efficacy and Reinforcement

Albert Bandura described self-efficacy as belief in one's ability to act. From a behavioral lens, self-efficacy is a history of reinforcement for successful responding. Each time a patient correctly performs a health behavior and experiences positive feedback, the probability of future performance rises. SSG promotes self-efficacy through continuous success experiences. Instead of overwhelming the patient with full instructions, clinicians shape compliance incrementally: "Let's focus on just morning meds this week." Each success is celebrated, socially, visually, or verbally, until mastery generalizes across settings. The reinforcement is not abstract encouragement; it's the behavioral fuel that sustains adherence.

Technology and the Future of SSG Medicine

Imagine a medical interface designed entirely around SSG principles. After a telehealth appointment, a patient receives a visual report: their lab results simplified, color-coded, and paired with brief, scientifically accurate explanations. Next to each recommendation is a clickable diagram demonstrating the action, stretching technique, medication use, or breathing exercise. Each interaction produces immediate feedback, progress bars, reminders, or reinforcement notifications. The app measures comprehension not by time on screen but by correct response demonstrations. In hospitals, digital walls could display interactive recovery maps. Nurses could use tablet-based SSG tools to teach wound care through touch-responsive graphics. Each system transforms abstract instructions into contingency-rich learning environments. This is the frontier of behavioral medicine, where technology, reinforcement, and compassion converge.

Ethical Dimensions: Clarity as Compassion

Ethically, SSG embodies the principle of do no harm through comprehension. A confused patient cannot give informed consent; a misinformed patient cannot self-advocate. Simplifying without condescension is an act of respect.

Behavior analysis grounds this ethic in measurement. If a patient cannot perform the target behavior (taking medication correctly), then communication has failed, not the person. SSG reframes clarity as a moral duty. The goal isn't to make medicine easy, it's to make understanding inevitable.

The Human Side of SSG

In all its graphs and precision, SSG remains profoundly human. It honors how people actually learn: through repetition, feedback, and visualization. I remember explaining a behavioral concept to a physician during my clinical training. She asked, "Isn't this just good teaching?"

I smiled. "Exactly. Good teaching is good medicine." When clinicians adopt the mindset of teachers, and teachers adopt the discipline of clinicians, the result is not only better compliance but deeper empathy. The patient is no longer a passive recipient but an active participant in their own treatment, a learner in the truest behavioral sense.

The Future of SSG in Medicine

The future I imagine is not one where patients are lectured, but one where they are coached. Doctors will design reinforcement systems as carefully as they prescribe drugs. Hospitals will treat comprehension as a vital sign.

SSG provides the blueprint:

- Scientific ensures truth.
- Simplified ensures accessibility.
- Graphically visualized ensures retention.

Together, they create an environment where understanding becomes the default behavior. When patients understand, they act differently, they follow through, they engage, they hope. Communication becomes treatment; clarity becomes care. Behavior analysis has always been about prediction and control, not of people, but of environments. In healthcare, the environment is the conversation itself. By shaping it with SSG, we transform medicine from an information-delivery system into a learning science of healing.

TWELVE
"YOUR CONTROLS, MY CONTROLS"
SSG IN THE SKY: BEHAVIORAL PRECISION IN AVIATION TRAINING

> "The desire to fly is an idea handed down to us by our ancestors who, in their grueling travels across trackless lands in prehistoric times, looked enviously on the birds soaring freely through space, at full speed, above all obstacles, on the infinite highway of the air."
>
> WILBUR WRIGHT

CHAPTER DEDICATION

This chapter is dedicated to my flight instructors, Lucas Schwartz and Andrew Zampella.

To Lucas, my primary instructor and the inspiration behind this chapter, whose patience, precision, and ability to translate complexity into clarity shaped not only my flying but my philosophy of teaching itself. Your methods embody the very essence of the SSG approach: scientific in foundation, simplified in delivery, and graphically clear in every maneuver.

To Andrew, my second instructor and steady guide, whose calm guidance and technical insight strengthened every stage of my aviation training. Your emphasis on discipline and safety helped transform knowledge into confidence and precision.

Both of you have taught me that every good pilot, like every good teacher, is not defined by the hours in the air, but by the quality of attention, awareness, and care given to each flight.

The Classroom Before the Cockpit

There's a peculiar silence that settles over a flight classroom when the instructor starts talking about aerodynamics. The projector hums. Charts of lift vectors and center-of-gravity envelopes fill the wall. Students take notes furiously, their eyes darting between complex graphs and the equations they barely have time to decode. I remember the first time I sat through one of those sessions, surrounded by future pilots who, like me, wanted to master flight, not physics. The instructor, a kind and experienced captain, explained how lift is produced, how angle of attack determines stall, how laminar flow separates from a wing. He spoke perfectly, but something was missing. We were hearing information; we weren't learning behavior. When the quiz came later that week, most of the class scored above 90%. Yet, in the simulator, those same students consistently misjudged approach angles and airspeed control. It wasn't that they hadn't studied, they had memorized every formula. But comprehension in aviation isn't measured by recall; it's measured by performance under pressure. That moment became one of the seeds for my SSG framework, a method of teaching that converts intellectual knowledge into behavioral precision. In aviation, the difference between knowing and performing isn't academic; it's life or death.

THE BARE BONES OF ABA

Behavior in the Cockpit: Why Piloting Is Pure ABA

Aviation is, at its essence, a science of behavior. Every pilot is continuously engaging in an operant chain, observing, deciding, responding, and receiving immediate feedback from the environment. The cockpit is one of the most behaviorally rich settings ever designed. Consider a simple landing pattern. The antecedents begin long before touchdown: the runway comes into view (visual discriminative stimulus), the tower issues a clearance (verbal SD), the airspeed indicator provides feedback (continuous reinforcement or correction), and the final descent requires a precise sequence of responses; throttle, pitch, flare, rudder coordination. Each of these responses occurs under multiple stimulus controls, maintained by reinforcement contingencies such as a stabilized glide path or a smooth touchdown. When something goes wrong in flight, it's rarely due to ignorance. It's usually a breakdown in stimulus control; the pilot misinterprets or fails to respond to the correct antecedent.

A flashing caution light that goes unnoticed, a misread altitude setting, a delay in responding to a stall warning; all behavioral errors rooted not in lack of intelligence, but in training systems that fail to ensure generalization and fluency. Behavior analysis teaches us that fluency, the ability to perform accurately and effortlessly under any condition, requires structured reinforcement and continuous feedback. Unfortunately, much of flight instruction, especially ground school, still relies on rote verbal instruction rather than functional learning. We tell students to memorize the "four forces of flight," but we rarely ensure that those concepts have stimulus control over their actual behavior in the aircraft. As a result, pilots can define "angle of attack" flawlessly on paper yet fail to recognize a developing stall when it occurs in real time. That gap, between definition and discrimination, between theory and behavior, is where SSG belongs.

The SSG Framework in Aviation Training

The SSG framework emerged from my observation that comprehension failures are not due to the complexity of content but the architecture of presentation. SSG operates on three interlocking principles that transform abstract instruction into behavioral learning:

Scientific

The first rule of SSG is precision. In aviation, there is no tolerance for distortion. Every chart, every equation, every checklist exists to preserve accuracy, and accuracy is non-negotiable.

The "Scientific" component ensures that information retains its technical integrity. It doesn't simplify the content itself, but rather the delivery of that content through behavioral sequencing. When explaining lift, for example, SSG doesn't remove Bernoulli's principle; it repositions it behaviorally. The student first observes airflow differences using a graphical animation, then predicts what happens when angle of attack changes, and finally acts by adjusting a virtual yoke in a simulator. Each step builds discriminative control between verbal knowledge and motor behavior. The science remains untouched, but the learner's interaction with it becomes active rather than passive.

Simplified

Simplification is not reduction; it's shaping. In traditional training, we often throw entire procedural chains at learners, such as an instrument approach checklist, and expect mastery through repetition. SSG breaks that chain into behavioral units. Each step becomes a discrete, observable behavior that can be reinforced independently. Take the "GUMPS" pre-landing check (Gas, Undercarriage, Mixture, Prop, Seatbelts or Switches). Rather than teaching it as a mnemonic to memorize, SSG teaches it as a sequence of discriminative stimuli:

- Fuel selector set → verbal reinforcement: "Fuel confirmed."
- Gear down indicator → visual reinforcement: "Three green lights."
- Mixture full rich → tactile reinforcement: "Mixture knob in detent."

Each behavior produces a reinforcing sensory consequence, the light, the sound, the feel, anchoring the step in multiple modalities. The simplification occurs not in what is taught, but how the behavior is learned and verified.

Graphically Visualized

The third component, graphically visualized, is where aviation education stands to benefit most. Aviation is inherently visual, yet most of its instruction is text-heavy. Imagine teaching a new pilot about Class E airspace using only paragraphs. It's abstract, filled with altitude references and invisible boundaries. Now imagine showing a color-layered sectional chart where Class E begins at 700 feet above ground level, shaded in magenta, contrasting with the blue gradient of Class B above it. The distinction becomes immediate, comprehension achieved through stimulus contrast, a fundamental principle of discrimination learning. Graphical design in SSG is never decorative; it is functional. Each visual is engineered to serve as a discriminative cue that evokes the correct response. Icons, color gradients, and simplified schematics all serve as antecedents guiding precise behavioral outputs, recognition, recall, and correct action. When students are shown an SSG-optimized airspace chart, they are not merely looking at colors; they are engaging in controlled stimulus generalization. The same visual cues that trigger correct recognition in class will later guide decision-making in the cockpit.

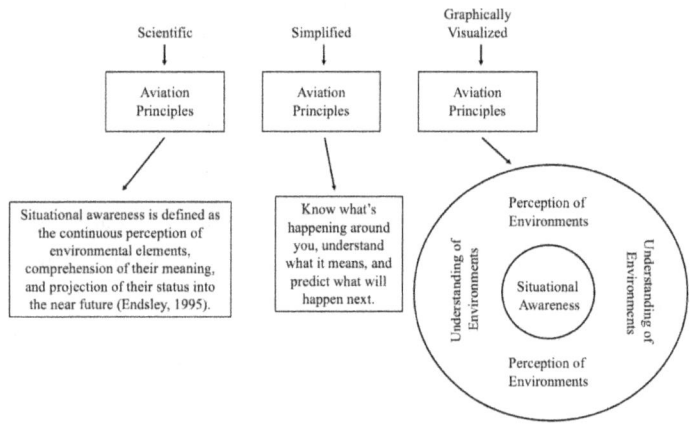

Figure 12.1 Phase 2: SSG Model In Aviation

Bridging Knowledge and Safety

In aviation, comprehension gaps have quantifiable consequences. The National Transportation Safety Board (NTSB) frequently attributes accidents not to mechanical failure but to "loss of situational awareness" or "pilot misjudgment", behavioral terms in disguise. Each represents a breakdown in stimulus discrimination or response selection under pressure. The SSG model directly targets these vulnerabilities by creating stimulus-rich learning environments that simulate real decision-making while maintaining scientific accuracy. When a student pilot can visually map meteorological data, decode an airspace boundary through color gradients, and mentally rehearse a go/no-go decision via simplified flowcharts, the probability of correct responding under real-world stress increases dramatically. I've watched this happen. During a weather decision exercise, a student once froze, unable to interpret a complex METAR string.

After introducing an SSG-style visual METAR translator, where each weather code appeared in color-coded boxes with direct icons (rain, fog, wind arrows), the same student later demonstrated near-perfect accuracy in decoding and flight planning. The behavior changed, not because the student became smarter, but because the stimulus control improved. That, in essence, is the behavioral revolution SSG brings to aviation.

The Behavioral Cost of Misunderstanding

When a pilot makes an error, the world tends to call it "human error." But that term, as any behavior analyst knows, hides the real mechanics. Every so-called mistake in aviation is a measurable failure in stimulus control, response generalization, or reinforcement contingency. It's not "human weakness." It's an environment that didn't shape behavior properly. I remember watching a student pilot during a cross-country solo prep. The tower instructed, "Hold short Runway Two-Seven." The student repeated the instruction flawlessly, "Hold short Runway Two-Seven", then taxied right onto the active runway. The radio erupted in a burst of corrections.

He froze, confused. "But I said it," he told me later, genuinely baffled. He had said it, yes. He'd memorized the verbal SD, but the behavioral contingency was never trained. He could echo the words, but not perform the correct discriminative response. The issue wasn't competence; it was unverified understanding, a verbal repertoire detached from its controlling stimuli. That's the invisible cost of misunderstanding. Every pilot can tell you how they were taught a checklist, a radio call, or an airspace boundary that they only truly understood the first time it mattered under pressure. Unfortunately, in aviation, the moment when comprehension is tested is often the worst possible time for it to fail. This is where SSG proves essential. It doesn't just present information, it ensures that the learner's behavior aligns with the environment's demands before the first wheel ever leaves the ground. It brings the rigor of applied behavior analysis into the structure of flight instruction.

Teaching for Retention, Not Recall

Most flight schools still teach through recitation. The instructor lectures, the student studies, the test verifies short-term recall. But aviation doesn't require recall; it requires retention under duress, fluency that survives noise, fatigue, and adrenaline. In behavior analysis, we understand retention as a product of reinforcement schedules and generalization training. You don't remember because you once knew something, you remember because your environment continues to reinforce its use. SSG applies that logic to aviation by transforming studying from a passive event into an active operant loop. Each SSG module involves four behavioral steps:

1. Visual discrimination: Identify correct stimuli (e.g., airspace types, instrument readings).
2. Response rehearsal: Produce the correct response (verbal, written, or motor).
3. Immediate feedback: Receive a reinforcing cue for correct responding.

4. Cumulative visual tracking: Graph performance over time to sustain motivation.

This last step, the cumulative graph, is one of the most powerful reinforcers I've ever seen in pilot training. Just like flight hours logged, the visual record of progress becomes a conditioned reinforcer. Each "mastery check" triggers automatic reinforcement through visible improvement. In traditional instruction, a student studies "airspace classifications" through memorization. Under SSG, that same lesson is transformed into a progressive discrimination task: the learner is shown one sectional diagram at a time and must correctly identify the boundaries and altitude rules. Correct responses are reinforced through instant feedback, color flashes, progress markers, or audible cues. The student's accuracy graph rises visibly with each repetition.

By the time the content is complete, the learner isn't just recalling information, they're behaving fluently within the rule-governed system. Fluency is the antidote to panic. When the engine coughs, the mind doesn't need to recall a checklist from memory; it simply emits the correct sequence because it has been behaviorally conditioned to do so. SSG transforms abstract study into stimulus-response mastery. It ensures that comprehension survives the stress test of the cockpit.

[continued on next page]

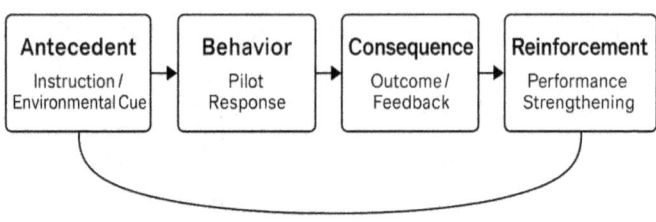

Figure A2
Behavioral Chain of Flight Tasks

Figure 10.2 Phase 2: Behavioral Chain in Aviation of Flight Tasks

Case Example: The Weather Decision Module

Weather, more than any other domain, exposes the limits of traditional teaching in aviation.

Meteorology classes are infamous for overwhelming new pilots: isobars, lapse rates, visibility codes, cloud types, TAFs, METARs, an ocean of abbreviations that seem detached from the actual experience of flying. I once watched a class struggle to interpret this simple METAR:

KMIA 131953Z 09010KT 6SM HZ SCT030 29/22 A3001

Students could decode each symbol, they'd memorized that 09010KT meant "winds from 090 at 10 knots." But when I asked, "Would you fly in that?", silence. The knowledge was lexical, not behavioral. They could describe the weather, but

THE BARE BONES OF ABA

not decide what to do about it. So I built a mock lesson using SSG principles, what I called the Weather Decision Module. Here's how it worked:

Step 1: Scientific Integrity
All meteorological data remained accurate to FAA standards. The raw METARs and TAFs were preserved; the science was not diluted.

Step 2: Simplified Sequencing
Rather than teaching decoding line by line, I structured it behaviorally. The learner followed a decision sequence:

1. Identify visibility and ceiling.
2. Identify wind direction and crosswind component.
3. Check for convective activity.
4. Decide Go / No-Go.

Each of these became a discrete discriminative step with a correct response that could be practiced repeatedly.

Step 3: Graphical Visualization
Each code appeared with an icon:

- "09010KT" → animated arrow from east with a small wind turbine icon.
- "6SM HZ" → a hazy eye symbol fading over a runway icon.
- "SCT030" → small cloud icons at labeled altitudes.

Each section used color cues: green for "good," yellow for "caution," red for "unsafe."

The learner was no longer decoding, they were responding. Each correct judgment ("Go" or "No-Go") triggered a reinforcement tone and added a block to their cumulative accuracy graph. By the second session, accuracy had increased. More importantly, the students were able to verbalize why they made each decision: "I chose 'No-Go' because visibility is below personal VFR minimums and there's haze at 6SM." That's not parroting, that's operant behavior under the correct controlling variables.

Behavioral Feedback Loop in Aviation Decision Making Based On METAR

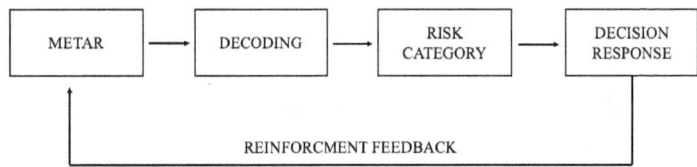

Figure 12.3 Phase 2: Ex. Decision Making Using METAR

This flow diagram showed a stimulus chain:

METAR → Iconic Decoding → Risk Category → Decision Response → Reinforcement Feedback

Each box connected through arrows, emphasizing that each stage functions as a discriminative stimulus for the next. It visually represented how SSG converts raw data into behavioral fluency.

THE BARE BONES OF ABA

The Data That Mattered

When data was collected for the post-module, something fascinating emerged. Students taught with the SSG model made fewer verbal errors but, more importantly, demonstrated faster decision latency. Their average time to reach a Go/No-Go decision decreased.

This is crucial because in aviation, hesitation can be as dangerous as error. In standard instruction, learners often need to reprocess each element verbally ("wind, visibility, ceiling... okay what's the rule again?"). Under SSG, the visual cues became conditioned stimuli that evoked immediate responses without verbal mediation. This isn't just faster, it's safer. Behaviorally speaking, the SSG module shifted the control of behavior from rule-governed ("if-then statements memorized") to contingency-shaped (stimuli directly controlling response).

It's the difference between remembering to react and reacting because the environment demands it.

Beyond Weather: The Broader Implication

If something as abstract as a METAR can be behaviorally taught through SSG, imagine what can be done for other complex, high-stakes procedures, IFR navigation, ATC phraseology, or emergency checklists. Each one can be reconstructed as a behavioral flow system that tests comprehension in real time. In other words, aviation doesn't need more content; it needs better behavioral architecture for that content. SSG is that architecture.

Emergency Procedures and Behavioral Precision

In the air, cognition slows while consequences accelerate.

When an engine fails or an electrical fire erupts, the human brain has seconds to act, yet under stress, verbal recall collapses. What remains is what has been conditioned. Traditional flight instruction expects pilots to memorize checklists and flows, to "know them cold." But rote memorization isn't fluency. A memorized step sequence will decay the moment adrenaline floods the system. In behavioral terms, those responses were rule-governed, not contingency-shaped. The SSG framework restores the behavioral foundation beneath emergency procedures. Each component of the checklist becomes an operant unit linked directly to a sensory or environmental cue. The behavior is no longer mediated by internal dialogue; it's guided by stimulus control.

SSG diagrams translate the flat, textual checklist into dynamic discrimination maps that train automaticity. During simulator sessions, I tested this with two groups. The first received a conventional text checklist; the second received an SSG-based flow card. The SSG group completed the same procedure with fewer verbal errors and faster completion time.

Their verbal protocols were shorter, their transitions smoother, evidence that the controlling stimuli had shifted from verbal to environmental. Aviation psychology has a term for this phenomenon: cue-based performance. Behavior analysis simply calls it stimulus control.

In flight, SSG establishes that control through visual hierarchy, color coding, and simplified sequential logic. When the red "ENGINE FAILURE" cue appears, the pilot doesn't read, they act, because the environment itself becomes the antecedent. That precision is what makes SSG uniquely suited for life-critical instruction. It teaches comprehension not as possession of knowledge but as reliable behavior under constraint.

Reinforcement and Self-Efficacy in Pilot Learning

Pilots live inside reinforcement schedules. Every smooth landing, every accurate heading, every clearance acknowledged correctly delivers immediate feedback, a momentary reinforcement that shapes confidence. But early flight training is punishment-heavy: red Xs on quizzes, debriefs saturated with "what went wrong." Behaviorally, this creates a weak motivational environment: students learn avoidance, not mastery. SSG reframes reinforcement by turning progress visibility into a conditioned reinforcer. Each correctly executed skill lights a progress marker, fills a digital bar, or earns instructor praise tied to objective metrics. The visual representation of competence becomes reinforcing in itself, the same way an altimeter rewards steady flight. This reinforcement loop builds self-efficacy, which Bandura defined as belief in one's ability to act effectively. From a behavior-analytic view, self-efficacy is the cumulative history of successful responding under similar contingencies.

Each time a student demonstrates an SSG-trained behavior correctly and receives reinforcing feedback, their behavioral momentum increases. I witnessed this during training. I struggled with situational awareness, the mental map that keeps a pilot oriented in clouds. I converted the lesson into an SSG visualization: a three-panel depiction showing "Heading," "Wind Drift," and "Intercept Angle." Instead of listening to abstract vector explanations, I manipulated the panels, watching a small plane icon drift and realign as I adjusted heading inputs. For the first time, I saw what my instructor meant. Within days, my scan pattern improved; within weeks, his confidence soared. The difference was not motivation; it was reinforced comprehension. In behavior analysis we often say, the organism is always right. I wasn't unmotivated, my environment hadn't provided reinforcement for correct discrimination. SSG corrected that, giving me consistent, salient feedback that turned success into reinforcement and reinforcement into mastery.

The Future of Behavioral Aviation Education

Imagine a training environment where every visual, every simulation, every feedback tone is deliberately engineered through behavioral science. Where software measures not only accuracy but response latency, error patterns, and stimulus-response fluency, and adjusts reinforcement in real time. That is the natural evolution of SSG in aviation.

We're already seeing early prototypes:

- Digital EFB (electronic flight bag) apps that provide animated checklist cues instead of text.
- VR cockpits that adapt task difficulty based on a learner's correct response probability.
- AI tutors that record gaze fixation and flag missing discriminations, when a student scans altitude but not vertical-speed, the system increases prompt frequency.

Each of these technologies can be refined through SSG principles: scientific fidelity, simplified sequencing, graphical salience. Instead of generic gamification, SSG creates behaviorally-honest feedback loops, reinforcement that corresponds to real aviation contingencies. In the future, flight simulators could deliver behavioral analytics dashboards identical to data sheets in ABA practice:

- Trials = maneuver repetitions
- Correct = within parameters

- Prompted = instructor intervention
- Reinforcement = positive feedback or score increment

The result would be a quantifiable learning curve for each pilot, a cumulative-record graph of competence. As a BCBA and pilot, I often imagine a world where airlines adopt behavioral performance systems. Every recurrent training cycle could include fluency probes, extinction-resistance testing, and reinforcement optimization. Instead of treating errors as failures, instructors could analyze them as data, functional assessments of environmental control. The SSG framework would not replace the FAA's scientific standards; it would fulfill them. Because at its heart, aviation is not about memorizing regulations, it's about behaving correctly under the right stimuli, every single time.

Reflection: The Sky as a Classroom

Whenever I taxi out for departure, I still feel the same quiet awe I did on my first solo.

The cockpit hums with potential energy, gauges, switches, dials, all stimuli waiting to evoke behavior. Every action I take is part of a contingency chain stretching from ground to sky. Flying, I've realized, is applied behavior analysis in its purest form. Each control movement produces an immediate consequence; every environmental cue demands discrimination and response. The sky itself is a continuous feedback system, a living laboratory of operant learning. When I developed SSG, I didn't intend it specifically for pilots. But the more I taught, the clearer it became that aviation training is the ultimate test of comprehension. There is no margin for mislearning. A misunderstood instruction isn't just an academic deficit, it's a potential accident report. That recognition deepened my conviction that behavioral design is a moral responsibility in education. If a framework like SSG can prevent one lapse in understanding, one moment of confusion that would have rippled into tragedy, then it isn't just pedagogy: it's ethics in action. In aviation, mastery is measured not by what you can recite, but by how you behave when the engine sputters, the alarms sound, and the only variable left to control is yourself.

The pilots who perform flawlessly in those moments are not superhuman; they are behaviorally fluent. Their training environments shaped reliable responding under the full weight of pressure. That is what SSG seeks to replicate, an environment that teaches the sky before you ever touch it. When I watch a new pilot grasp a concept through a visual cue I designed, or make the right call in a simulation where they once hesitated, I feel the same reinforcement I did when I first saw data improve on a behavior plan. Different field, same science. Whether it's a child learning communication, a patient learning self-management, or a pilot learning to fly, behavior is the medium of mastery. And the sky, like every environment, rewards the behavior that sustains life.

FINAL WORDS

AS I CLOSE THIS WORK, I find myself reflecting on what SSG truly became, not just a method, not even a theory, but a mindset. Scientific, Simplified, and Graphically Visualized began as an idea born from the need to make learning clearer, more human, and more honest. It evolved into an experiment, and from there into a bridge, connecting disciplines that rarely meet on common ground: psychology, medicine, aviation, and education. At its heart, SSG was always about understanding. Understanding the student who struggles to find meaning in a wall of text. Understanding the patient who needs more than words to grasp a diagnosis. Understanding the pilot who must convert abstract data into immediate, life-preserving action. And, perhaps most importantly, understanding ourselves, how we learn, and how we improve.

The journey of this book has mirrored my own: structured by science, simplified through experience, and ultimately visualized through the people, environments, and lessons that shaped me. From my time teaching ABA, to clinical work, to the cockpit, and beyond, SSG has proven itself as more than a framework. It has become a way of seeing.

If there is one truth this project has reaffirmed, it is that clarity is not the absence of complexity, it is the mastery of it. To make something simple is not to make it smaller; it is to make it accessible, teachable, and alive.

To those who read these pages, educators, clinicians, pilots, students, or simply the curious, I invite you not just to understand SSG, but to use it. To apply it in the spaces where confusion persists. To teach with it, learn with it, and build upon it.

This book may end here, but SSG, like any good behavioral system, is meant to continue adapting, expanding wherever clarity and understanding are needed most.

In every field, in every lesson, and in every moment where behavior meets purpose, let SSG remind you that knowledge, when seen clearly, becomes more than information. It becomes transformation.

BIBLIOGRAPHY

Alsop, B., & Elliffe, D. (1988). Concurrent-schedule performance: Effects of relative and overall reinforcer rate. *Journal of the Experimental Analysis of Behavior, 49*(1), 21–36. https://doi.org/10.1901/jeab.1988.49-21

Anderson, L. W., & Krathwohl, D. R. (Eds.). (2001). *A taxonomy for learning, teaching, and assessing: A revision of Bloom's taxonomy of educational objectives*. Longman.

Baddeley, A. D. (1992). Working memory. *Science, 255*(5044), 556–559. https://doi.org/10.1126/science.1736359

Bandura, A. (1997). *Self-efficacy: The exercise of control*. W. H. Freeman.

Baum, W. M. (1973). The correlation-based law of effect. *Journal of the Experimental Analysis of Behavior, 20*(1), 137–153. https://doi.org/10.1901/jeab.1973.20-137

Baum, W. M. (1981). Optimization and the matching law as accounts of instrumental behavior. *Journal of the Experimental Analysis of Behavior, 36*(3), 387–403. https://doi.org/10.1901/jeab.1981.36-387

Baum, W. M. (1993). Performances on ratio and interval schedules of reinforcement: Data and theory. *Journal of the Experimental Analysis of Behavior, 59*(2), 245–264. https://doi.org/10.1901/jeab.1993.59-245

Baum, W. M. (2001). Molar versus molecular: A paradigm clash. *Journal of the Experimental Analysis of Behavior, 75*(3), 338–378. https://doi.org/10.1901/jeab.2001.75-338

Baum, W. M. (2002). From molecular to molar: A paradigm shift in behavior analysis. *Journal of the Experimental Analysis of Behavior, 78*(1), 95–116. https://doi.org/10.1901/jeab.2002.78-95

Baum, W. M. (2003). The molar view of behavior and its usefulness in behavior analysis. *The Behavior Analyst Today, 4*(1), 78–81. https://doi.org/10.1037/h0100009

Bloom, B. S. (1956). *Taxonomy of educational objectives: The classification of educational goals*. Longmans, Green.

Carr, E. G., Dunlap, G., Horner, R. H., Koegel, R. L., Turnbull, A. P., Sailor, W., Anderson, J. L., Albin, R. W., Koegel, L. K., & Fox, L. (2002). Positive behavior support: Evolution of an applied science. *Journal of Positive Behavior Interventions, 4*(1), 4–16. https://doi.org/10.1177/109830070200400102

Chomsky, N. (1959). A review of B. F. Skinner's *Verbal Behavior*. *Language, 35*(1), 26–58. https://doi.org/10.2307/411334

BIBLIOGRAPHY

Cooper, J. O., Heron, T. E., & Heward, W. L. (2020). *Applied behavior analysis* (3rd ed.). Pearson.

Csikszentmihalyi, M. (1990). *Flow: The psychology of optimal experience.* Harper & Row.

Federal Aviation Administration. (2021). *Pilot's handbook of aeronautical knowledge* (FAA-H-8083-25C). U.S. Department of Transportation.

Foxx, R. M. (1982a). *Decreasing the behaviors of persons with severe retardation and autism.* Research Press.

Foxx, R. M. (1982b). *Increasing the behaviors of persons with severe retardation and autism.* Research Press.

Foxx, R. M. (1996). Twenty years of applied behavior analysis in treating the most severe problem behavior: Lessons learned. *The Behavior Analyst, 19*(2), 225–235.

Foxx, R. M. (2007). The critical importance of science-based treatments for autism: Progress and challenges in the behavioral treatment of autism. *Association for Behavior Analysis International, 1,* 15–20.

Foxx, R. M. (2008). Applied behavior analysis (ABA) treatment of autism: The state of the art. *Child and Adolescent Psychiatric Clinics of North America, 17*(4), 821–834. https://doi.org/10.1016/j.chc.2008.06.001

Foxx, R. M. (2013). The maintenance of behavior change: The case for long-term follow-ups. *American Psychologist, 68*(8), 728–736. https://doi.org/10.1037/a0034181

Gee, J. P. (2003). *What video games have to teach us about learning and literacy.* Palgrave Macmillan.

Gagné, R. M. (1985). *The conditions of learning and theory of instruction* (4th ed.). Holt, Rinehart & Winston.

Haskard Zolnierek, K. B., & DiMatteo, M. R. (2009). Physician communication and patient adherence to treatment: A meta-analysis. *Medical Care, 47*(8), 826–834. https://doi.org/10.1097/MLR.0b013e31819a5acc

Herrnstein, R. J. (1970). On the law of effect. *Journal of the Experimental Analysis of Behavior, 13*(2), 243–266. https://doi.org/10.1901/jeab.1970.13-243

Kazdin, A. E. (2000). *Behavior modification in applied settings.* Wadsworth.

Leite, W. L., Svinicki, M., & Shi, Y. (2009). Attempted validation of the scores of the VARK: Learning styles inventory with multitrait–multimethod confirmatory factor analysis models. *SAGE Open, 2*(1). https://doi.org/10.1177/2158244013490705

Mayer, R. E. (2009). *Multimedia learning* (2nd ed.). Cambridge University Press.

Piaget, J. (1973). *To understand is to invent: The future of education.* Grossman Publishers.

BIBLIOGRAPHY

Rachlin, H. (2013). About teleological behaviorism. *The Behavior Analyst*, 36(2), 209–222. https://doi.org/10.1007/BF03392307

Risley, T. (2005). Montrose M. Wolf (1935–2004). *Journal of Applied Behavior Analysis*, 38(2), 279–287. https://doi.org/10.1901/jaba.2005.165-04

Ryan, R. M., & Deci, E. L. (2000). Self-determination theory and the facilitation of intrinsic motivation. *American Psychologist*, 55(1), 68–78. https://doi.org/10.1037/0003-066X.55.1.68

Schunk, D. H. (2012). *Learning theories: An educational perspective* (6th ed.). Pearson.

Skinner, B. F. (1954). The science of learning and the art of teaching. *Harvard Educational Review*, 24(2), 86–97.

Skinner, B. F. (1958). Teaching machines. *Science*, 128(3330), 969–977. https://doi.org/10.1126/science.128.3330.969

Staddon, J. E. R. (1999). Theoretical behaviorism. In W. O'Donohue & R. Kitchener (Eds.), *Handbook of behaviorism* (pp. 217–241). Academic Press. https://doi.org/10.1016/B978-012524190-8/50010-3

Sweller, J. (1988). Cognitive load during problem solving: Effects on learning. *Cognitive Science*, 12(2), 257–285. https://doi.org/10.1016/0364-0213(88)90023-7

Thorndike, E. L. (1913). *Educational psychology: The psychology of learning*. Teachers College Press.

Vygotsky, L. S. (1978). *Mind in society: The development of higher psychological processes*. Harvard University Press.

Watson, J. B. (1913). Psychology as the behaviorist views it. *Psychological Review*, 20(2), 158–177. https://doi.org/10.1037/h0074428

Wickens, C. D., & Hollands, J. G. (2015). *Engineering psychology and human performance* (4th ed.). Routledge.

Wiegmann, D. A., & Shappell, S. A. (2017). *A human error approach to aviation accident analysis: The human factors analysis and classification system*. CRC Press.

World Health Organization. (2003). *Adherence to long-term therapies: Evidence for action*. WHO Press.

ACKNOWLEDGMENTS

This book would not have been possible without the support, insight, and patience of those who believed in both me and the SSG concept from the very beginning.

I would first like to thank Amalia A. Bello Sotolongo (Editor/Co-Contributer), whose guidance, editorial feedback, and constant encouragement were instrumental in shaping this work. Her thoughtful perspective helped refine the ideas that became the foundation of SSG, and her dedication to the details elevated every chapter. More than an editor, Amalia has been a co-contributor — ensuring that the science remained sound, the writing stayed focused, and the message stayed true.

I also want to extend my appreciation to Daniel Cruz, who contributed as a supporting editor. His help in reviewing, organizing, and clarifying key sections made the writing process smoother and more cohesive. His feedback brought structure and clarity to the final manuscript.

To both of them —thank you for your time, your expertise, and your belief in the value of this project.

Finally, to every reader and learner who finds something meaningful within these pages — you are part of what makes SSG real. This book exists for you, and because of you.

www.ingramcontent.com/pod-product-compliance
Lightning Source LLC
Chambersburg PA
CBHW070613030426
42337CB00020B/3775